GO NORTH, YOUNG MAN

Modern Homesteading in Alaska

By
GORDON STODDARD

BINFORDS & MORT, *Publishers,* Portland, Oregon

Go North, Young Man: Modern Homesteading in Alaska was originally published in 1957 by Binfords & Mort, Portland Oregon.

A PATHFINDER BOOK REPRINT EDITION
Printed in the United States of America
ISBN: 978-1951682644

Go North, Young Man

Chapter I
Don't Come Home

"DON'T COME HOME until you've made good," said my father.

I gulped and stepped on my starter. My last bridge was burning.

"But," continued Dad, leaning through the car window and laying an affectionate hand on my shoulder, "if you get into trouble or run short of cash — drop me a line." Good old Dad.

We shook hands — hard. I raced the motor, pulled away from the curb. Dad was still standing there on the sidewalk beside the tall, gray apartment house, his blue suit rumpled in the way it always was, his curly white hair lifting slightly in the stiff morning breeze, when I took my last, long look at him in my rear view mirror.

As I wove my way through the traffic of Van Ness Avenue, I wondered what kind of a sendoff my father's father had given him in 1910, when he had headed for the frozen north. Had it been a case of "Don't come home" then? But he had come home, he had made good. And now I was traveling the same old path. But there was a difference: while my father had ended up in northern British Columbia, I was trying to go him one better by aiming farther north — at Alaska.

And there were other differences. My father had left San Francisco with only $58 in his purse; I was starting out with $1200. He had trekked by steamer, on horseback and by dogsled; I was driving an almost-new business coupe which would, I hoped, take me all the way. He was a has-been; I was a 1950 Model Pioneer. Make good? I couldn't help making good!

*

When I was discharged from the Navy in 1946 I had been like thousands of other ex-G. I.'s: restless, switching jobs at a moment's notice, starting college and then quitting to try something else, having no definite goal in mind but searching, searching, searching for I didn't know what. I was in a rut. I didn't like cities, I didn't like the pace of post-war life, I was a guy whose greatest joy had always been to get away from it all — preferably with a fishing pole as my only companion beside a high mountain stream. Was I doomed forever to the drab existence of the unhappy commuters I saw rushing past me on the streets?

One day in San Francisco I met a fellow who talked to me about Alaska. Alaska — the last frontier, a place where a veteran could homestead 160 acres and own them in seven months; where a man had to work only six months out of a year to make a good living; where the fish jumped onto your hook without formal invitation and the moose stood still to be shot.

"I'm a horticulturist," I said. "Do you suppose there's any growing land up there?"

"Well, the Matanuska Valley's the agricultural center of the Territory, but that's all taken up. But have you ever heard of the Kenai Peninsula? It's almost as big as California. I hear tell there's a lot of good farming ground there, and it's open to homesteaders now."

"That's for me!" I shouted. And sending away for pamphlets, books and government bulletins, I had started laying plans.

For two years I had made my preparations. I had gathered all the available information on homesteading, collected maps on the Alcan Highway and Alaska itself, stayed on my job as a plant propagator for a big wholesale-retail nursery, saved my money, bought a new car for the trip, collected equipment I thought I would need — a war surplus parka, a crab net, a Coleman stove, and some new fishing gear.

And I had listened to my father. As far back as I could remember he had told me yarns about his conquest of northern British Columbia, of how, as a "cheechako," he had created a town, founded a newspaper in a wilderness where he had had to "make" the news in order to have something to set up in type. I had asked him to tell the stories again, and when I told him of my dream of going to Alaska his enthusiasm had risen to fever pitch. "I always knew one of my sons would want to see the north country some day, too," he had chortled. "Go to it, boy! You have my blessing!"

*

I stepped on the gas and all 90 horses at my command leaped to obey — 90, to my father's one. And as I drove I sang. The tune was an old one — every California kid sings it from the time he can open his mouth — but the words were my own: "Alcan Highway, here I come, right past where Dad started from . . ."

Somewhere around midnight of that day — the date was May 1 — I hit my first planned stop, Twin Falls, Idaho. I had rushed through California, ignored Nevada: I was a man in a hurry to get to my goal.

Since sleeping in my car as often as possible was a necessity if I didn't want to spend too much money along the way — and I didn't — I pulled off onto a side road and curled up in my sleeping bag, using the luggage compartment as my bed and the driver's seat, with the back laid flat, as my pillow. In the morning I awoke to find a flat tire on my right rear wheel. After unloading the sleeping bag, extra blankets, Coleman stove, well-stocked grub box, ten gallons of extra gas, five gallons of water, assorted fishing tackle, assorted clothing and my crab net, I managed to reach the spare tire and bumper jack. Then I knew what my father had meant when he said, "Better leave all that junk behind, son. When I went north all I took was a bearskin coat and a cocker spaniel pup."

"Maybe so," I had replied, grinning. "But what was the fur coat for?" That's me: the kidder of the family.

During the next week, in spite of my original haste, I acted like a tourist. When I found a spot I liked, and where the fishing was good, I lingered for awhile. Yellowstone Park was the site of one long stopover, Glacier National Park another. At the latter park it was a couple with a pretty daughter that held me, and the only thing that saved me from lingering longer, and from forgetting all about Alaska and the frozen north, was their sudden departure for the same destination. They promised, as they left, to meet me in the Yukon Territory "for some more fishing," but I followed them as far as Calgary, lost them in the traffic and never saw them again. Another roadside romance had gone with the gas — but it *had* served the purpose of advancing me a few steps closer to my goal.

At Edmonton, Alberta, I was forced to turn all my attention to my driving. The road very rapidly became a morass of dirt, mud, ruts and potholes, sometimes disintegrating into nothing more navigable than a couple of wheel tracks zigzagging haphazardly across somebody's hay field. Gas stations almost entirely disappeared. Flat tires occurred with increasing frequency, and when I stopped to cook a meal on the Coleman stove and grab a few hours of rest, battalions of vicious mosquitoes and clouds of flying bugs fought me for every bite of food, every wink of sleep.

The start of the Alaska Highway—or the Alcan, as it is more often called—is at Dawson Creek, British Columbia, a thriving little city where the prices, I felt, were unreasonably high. I found everything I thought I would need for the trip ahead in the stores of the town but parted with considerable cash in the process. Then I loaded up with gasoline, squared my shoulders and took off for the wilderness. This, I knew, was the point of no return.

The road, after the dry stream bed I had been traveling for so many miles, was a pleasant surprise—two full lanes, and nicely graveled. Nevertheless, the tales I had heard about the Alcan echoed hollowly in my head. "You can't travel it in the spring—only in the winter, when it's frozen, or in the summer, when it's dry," I had been told. "And if your car breaks down, look out. There are only a few service stations along the way, and no real garages. Take all the car parts you think you'll need and plenty of extra gas and water. Take plenty of gas PERIOD: the prices are prohibitive. Better take lots of food, too: it might be days before another traveler came along and found you stranded. And as for tires—you can wear out twenty of them without half trying."

Five days and 600 miles later, after nosing through acres of unbroken forest—part of which was burning, unattended—and after passing only one real settlement—Fort Nelson—and changing at least ten of the twenty tires I had been warned about, I arrived at Watson Lake, just over the border from British Columbia in the Yukon Territory.

Watson Lake was marked in red on the map. It should have been: it represented red-letter food prepared by somebody else, a red-letter hotel room and a red-letter bath.

The Watson Lake Hotel, a big log, two-story building, was almost full up—so much so that it looked like a Shriners' Convention at Atlantic City, except that the guests, far from being fat, jolly and obnoxious, looked lean, hungry and discouraged. I talked to some of them and found out why: most of them were Americans heading back to the States because "there ain't no work in Alaska." The carpenters and plumbers, they told me, were on strike in Anchorage; the jails were full of broke construction men, and the gutters of Alaska—when there were gutters—were full to overflowing. "We're gettin' out while the gettin's good," they said. "You'd better turn around right now, sonny, and hightail it back for home."

I listened to more tales of woe. A great many of the men—some of them around my age (25)—were selling everything they owned to raise enough cash to buy airplane tickets to the States. One enterprising ex-pioneer had held an open-air auction the day before I arrived and sold his entire stock of canned goods, clothing and camping equipment to the Indians. He had been a homesteader, he told me.

"But what happened? What went wrong?" I asked him.

He looked at me in a funny way. "Homesteading's

fine, but you can't keep it up without holding down a summer job too," he said.

I felt for my wallet in the hip pocket of my jeans. Still there. "I'm rich," I told myself. "I can live for a long time without getting a job." But just the same I made up my mind to get out of Watson Lake after a couple of days' rest and head—fast—for Anchorage. No more tourist stuff for me. I had lingered too long on the road.

Once the word got around that I had "plenty of the green stuff" in my possession—and those things do get around—a concerted campaign began. I was invited to several impromptu parties in the various rooms of the hotel and usually found myself buying all the drinks. Even the proprietor of the hotel got into the act: he tried to sell me some mangy wolf pelts and a couple of silver fox furs "cheap." Reasoning that he probably had in mind skinning me in Canada before I could be fleeced in United States territory, I bargained with him, using a system I had learned—the hard way—in the Philippines during the war. When I got him down to a fair price, I walked away.

This probably accounted for the trouble I had with the proprietor on the following morning, when I paid my bill with a hundred-dollar traveler's check. The exchange was ten percent in favor of Americans at that time, but there was a rumor that it would go back to par within a few days, and he seemed to think those few days had already passed. We haggled back and forth until I was glad to take five percent, just to keep the peace and be on my way. I wasn't to realize my mistake in accepting Canadian currency at all until my arrival in Anchorage three days later.

Chapter II
Flat Broke

THERE I WAS in Alaska—flat broke.

As I sat on the steps of the United States Post Office watching the people of Anchorage hurrying through the swinging doors, I fingered, for the hundredth time, the contents of my wallet. There was a cashier's check for $600. There were three hundred-dollar traveler's checks. There was $84 in Canadian currency. I knew them by heart.

I shifted my position, dug into my pockets, came up with fifty cents in American silver coin.

Yet I was as good as broke. It was late Saturday afternoon, and no one would take a chance on cashing one of my checks. I had tried bar after bar, store after store. "No, no, no," they had said. And they had laughed when I proffered the Canadian bills. Did I think Canadian money was legal tender in Alaska? On your way, brother.

As for the quarter, two dimes and a nickel—well, I wasn't sure they would buy me even a full cup of coffee in this boom town of 1950.

Getting up to start walking aimlessly down the main street of "the biggest city in the Territory," I gazed disconsolately around. Except for the snow-capped mountains towering behind and the immense inlet—Cook Inlet—at its feet, Anchorage was like any small city in the States. There were the same stores with the same "modern" fronts, the same busy people hurrying to catch the last bus home, the same hundreds of unfamiliar faces rushing past me without a glance in my direction, all bent on their own problems and errands. As I passed a bar a shabbily-dressed, unshaven character clutched my arm. "How about lending me a buck, mate?" he rasped. "I haven't eaten since yesterday." Spreading my hands to show that I was in the same condition as he, I shook him off. "It's the same everywhere you go," I thought. What had ever made me think Alaska would be different?

Rummaging through my pockets again in an effort to find a stray dollar bill, I found instead a crumpled slip of paper inscribed in my father's fine, bold hand. The name I read was that of a lawyer, a former mayor of Anchorage, a fraternity brother of Dad's. I bit my lip, stared off into space. "Contacts" was my father's favorite word, and the gospel he preached to his sons. "You can't get along in this world without contacts," he had always said. I had never agreed with him. "Ability," I had insisted stubbornly. "Ability's what counts." But now I was in a spot in which any straw was to be grabbed at. By gosh, I'd see this contact!

It didn't take me long to find the address written on the slip of paper. It was a big, modern office building, and as I entered its marble halls I became acutely conscious of my three-days' growth of beard, of the ragged condition of my dirty shirt and jeans. Prosperous-looking men in well-pressed business suits went in and out while I studied the bronze plaque listing the building's tenants, and I imagined—or maybe I didn't—that they were calling me "bum" under their well-bred breaths.

On the third floor I reached my objective, a heavy glass door with the legend, "John Manders, Attorney-at-Law," engraved in impressive gold leaf. With a slightly shaking hand I opened the door to be confronted by the cold, unfriendly eyes of two women seated behind desks.

"Yes? What is it?" said one of them, looking me up and down.

I turned halfway around with the idea of escaping before someone called a policeman, but thinking better of it, I stared boldly back at the woman who had spoken and said, "I'd like to see Mr. Manders."

"And just what would you like to see him about?"

Ignoring her tone of voice, I decided to make a clean breast of my situation. And as I told my story the two secretaries visibly thawed, and one of them asked me to sit down and wait until Mr. Manders had finished with a client.

Flat Broke

After fifteen minutes—during which I consumed one cigarette after another in my nervousness—the door to the inner sanctum opened and a well-dressed woman walked out. In the doorway stood a man of about my father's age, short and heavy-set, with a few scattered white hairs on an almost bald head. "What can I do for you, young man?" he said.

"You can do a lot for me, sir," I answered. "My father, Harry Stoddard, gave me your name and address and said to look you up when I got here. Well, here I am." Now we'd see how well contacts worked!

Suddenly I wasn't a bum any more: I was the younger son of a beloved friend. "Well, well, well!" cried the lawyer. "Come in, my boy! Come in! I've been expecting you!"

Seated in a large, comfortable chair and feeling considerably more at ease than I had since entering Anchorage that morning, I basked in the warmth of Mr. Manders' broad, cordial smile. "Here's a letter from your father," he said, sliding it across his desk. "Received it just a couple of days ago. He asked me to do anything I could to help you out. So: what can I do? You short of cash?"

I explained about not having any money I could spend, and he solved that problem immediately by cashing one of my hundred-dollar traveler's checks, advising me to leave the rest of my checks in his office safe until Monday morning, when I could deposit them in a local bank. Then we talked for an hour, he asking me, with flattering interest, about my plans, I asking him a series of questions about Alaska. When we parted with a firm handshake, Mr. Manders said, "If you need any further advice or help, I'll feel insulted if you don't come straight to me. The best of luck!"

A short time later, surveying the remains of a large, juicy steak in a clean, well-lighted restaurant, I felt fine. Anchorage, I told myself, wasn't such a bad place, after all. My wallet was again full of negotiable bills and I had at least one good friend. "Waiter!" I called with new bravado. "My check, please!"

Out on the neon-lit streets again, I saw a new picture of the city. The businessmen and other white-collar workers had gone home for the day and a different type of citizen had taken their place: the surly, growling panhandlers whom I later heard described as "construction stiffs"—construction workers out of a job. I could see, as I passed hundreds of dirty, bearded men lounging against the buildings, that it was unfashionable not to be flat broke in Anchorage. I had the feeling that all eyes were glued to the wallet on my hip, that all minds were estimating, by its fatness, its total in dollars and cents. I knew then why John Manders had advised me not to carry my entire bankroll on my person, and I was as glad as I had been sorry a few hours before that I hadn't shaved in three days. "I'm safe," I told myself. "No one would cut the throat of a fellow bum."

Selecting a cheap, $2-a-night boarding house on an unpretentious side street for lodgings, I found myself sharing a room with four other men. From then on I spent most of my time pumping my fellow boarders for information about jobs, homestead possibilities, etc., and as I pumped and learned that there was lots of land open for homesteading on the Kenai Peninsula and possible work in the fish canneries near a town called Kenai, a beautiful picture began to form in my mind. I saw myself—hard, tanned and bearded—standing beside a trim little log cabin in a clearing in the woods. Right back of the cabin was a stream in which 50-pound salmon pushed each other around like the crowds on Market Street on New Year's Eve. A pretty tourist had stopped her shiny red convertible at my gate. She was saying, "And is this yours, all yours? How much land does your property include?" And I was answering, with a sweep of my arm, "One hundred and sixty acres, ma'am. As far as the eye can see. It's mine. All mine."

I also found out that there was no possible way to drive a car down to the Kenai Peninsula: the highway which was then under construction between Anchorage and the Sterling Highway, which began at Moose Pass, wouldn't be finished for a year. What I would have to do was ship my car to Moose Pass on the Alaska Railroad and follow it a day later on a passenger train. Arranging for all this would take until the end of the week—a fact which, when I learned it, made me restless and itchy: I couldn't afford to stay in Anchorage very long. With the simplest restaurant meal with no trimmings costing $2.50, the cheapest room in which you could cook your own meals at least $100 a month, eggs $1.15 a dozen, milk 40 cents a quart and hamburger $1.00 pound, I would be joining the "stiffs" on the streets in no time.

But the arrangements went through without a hitch, and at 3 o'clock on Sunday morning I got off the train at Moose Pass—"The Gateway to the Kenai Peninsula"— to find myself without a car. A few other passengers had disembarked with me, and none of their cars were there, either. There wasn't even a station, unless you counted the old railroad car sitting, wheelless, beside the tracks. There was also no hotel, no restaurant and no station master to tell us what to do. I couldn't remember ever having seen a lonelier spot in my life.

After huddling around a pot-bellied stove in the abandoned railroad car for awhile, the other passengers and I—four adults and four children—decided on a practical course of action. We were all hungry, and our first consideration was food. Accordingly, while we men rigged up trout lines out of odd pieces of string and bent nails and went out to see what we could catch from the railroad trestle crossing a glacial stream next to the "station," the women built a roaring fire on the beach. We caught a good mess of lake trout, cooked them on sharpened sticks over the fire and tore them—half raw— to bits, using our fingers shamelessly like hungry savages. A few hours later one of the group located a grocery store about a half mile up a lonely road, and we filled up the gaps with crackers and canned peaches. Our automobiles, which had, through some mistake, followed us rather than preceded us, showed up that afternoon, and we parted to go our separate ways—some to Seward, the port town, the rest of us over the mountains to the little fishing village of Kenai.

The land I drove through, after the scenery I had seen in the Yukon Territory after leaving Watson Lake, was depressing. In the Yukon, every turn in the road had revealed a 35-mm. composition in full color. Everywhere there had been water—huge, blue-green lakes, icy rushing streams, their sources undoubtedly the glaciers I could sometimes glimpse so far above. Everywhere there had been mountains, and as I had driven through them, watching the peaks rising higher and higher on either side of the road, I had had a feeling of complete—though not unpleasant—isolation. But this—this Alaska—was desolation: nothing but flat, brown, burned-over ground bristling with thousands of upright corpses—bare, dead spruce trees that told me that even here, in the unpioneered wilderness, the careless tourist had left his mark. Where was the Alaska I had read about?

Suddenly the vista changed, became a forest of green, living trees. My heart lifted, and 20 miles later I saw the first sign of civilization: a board nailed to a tree with the word "Kenai" scrawled across it. I rounded a curve and there it was—a handful of tumbledown shacks by the water, a few false-front stores, a Russian church, its brightly-painted dome the only spot of color in the entire drab, dull scene. I drove slowly down the muddy street.

Chapter III
The Wrong Pew

"How Much Experience have you had?"

"None," I replied.

"Good," said the superintendent. "You're hired."

That was how I got my first job in Alaska. I didn't really need a job—my money would hold out for awhile—but on my arrival in Kenai I had learned that the road to Homer and the homestead country hadn't been completed yet and wouldn't be open to traffic for at least another two months; in the meantime, I had to do something, and working in a salmon cannery, I figured, could be interesting.

The next morning I was knee-deep in interest and fish. The first job they gave me was called "pewing." A pew, I discovered, was a stick with a long, metal, needle-sharp point on one end, and when you stuck the point into a salmon and tossed it somewhere, you were "pewing."

Pewing, to the amateur, could be something like playing with a boomerang. You were supposed to pew the fish through a two-foot-square hole in a bin as fast as you could without looking, but if your aim wasn't entirely accurate the fish would bounce off the wall and slap you in the face. And if you could avoid that, there was always the chance of pewing the wrong kind of salmon into the wrong kind of bin. There were four different bins for four different varieties: the idea was to select the right kind of salmon from a huge Duke's Mixture and hit the right bin every time. After pewing humpies into the red salmon bin and silvers into the dog salmon bin and failing to find a place to pew the king salmon at all, I was demoted to pewing on the tender.

The cannery tender was a large boat with a very small, dark hold in which two pewers with pews pewed salmon into a barrel. After the barrel was filled it was winched up and dumped into a hopper, and a conveyor belt took the fish into the cannery. I was pewing with a will and thought that I was doing quite well until the superintendent yelled down from the wharf, "Pew them in the head, you ———, you!"

My partner, an Eskimo with an expressionless face, turned to stare at me in the darkness of the hold. I stared back. We were waist-deep in fish, and it was almost impossible to tell the heads from the tails without minute examination. But we followed directions, and it wasn't long before the operation slowed down to a standstill.

Soon we heard a new voice—that of the owner of the cannery. "Pew the ——— fish anyplace!" he hollered from above. "I want that barrel filled up NOW!"

Fish flew in all directions as we bent to our task, my partner pewing with really admirable zeal. With a powerful thrust he drove his pew into a pile of salmon, gave a mighty heave and sent two fish, my left leg and me spinning smartly toward the barrel. "See what I mean?" called the owner.

Two days later, when I was able to walk again, I was given an "easy" job on the "sliming" table. It was to the sliming table that the salmon came on moving belts from the "iron chink," an ingenious machine which cut off their heads, sliced off their tails and fins and very neatly disemboweled them in one swift, simultaneous operation. Using sharp knives, a dozen workers received what remained and scraped off any clots of blood left inside. This was a job which took fingers of steel to hold the slippery salmon steady and the sure hand of a surgeon to wield the knife, and, probably because they're supposed to be impassive, most of the workers were Indians. They were also women, and working with a bunch of mothers and grandmothers made me feel like a little boy helping with the dishes. It took some doing to keep up with them, too, but gradually I got my speed up to where I could hold my own with the slowest.

At this point I was informed that I was to be transferred to the cutting machine. I was so overjoyed at the news—I hadn't liked the sliming job—that when I went into the sliming room to hang up my rubber apron on my last night I failed to notice that a plank had been removed from the floor for the purpose of washing the gurry through to the tide flats ten feet below. Digging my way out of an immense, stinking pile of rotting fish heads and entrails, I surprised two dining seagulls, who flew away screaming in terror. Then I looked around for a way out. Where I was it was dark, but far off in the distance was a point of light which I knew must be the midnight sun shining at the end of the cannery wharf. Slipping, sliding and falling, I crawled toward it. When I finally emerged, it took me two hours to clean salmon guts from my clothes and body.

On reporting for work on the following morning, I was led to the cutting machine, which was to be my constant companion for the next four days. As operator, I was supposed to grab the salmon as they came from the sliming room and toss them onto the cutting machine belt on their backs. The machine would then chop them into slices and send them on to the canning machine. The job looked simple enough, but even at this I wasn't successful. The canning machine operator, who controlled both his machine and mine, would speed up the cutting machine to such a peak that it was impossible for me to place the salmon in the proper position. I got my revenge one day when I sent a few choice fish heads, a pair of gloves and my shirt through to him on the belt. The next day he and I were ordered to switch jobs.

Now I found out what real work was. There were three levers to work, the most important being the one which controlled the canning line: this started the entire canning process and stopped it when there was a "jam-up." The other two levers controlled the stopping and starting of the cutting machine and speeded it up or slowed it down. In addition to working these levers, I had to keep an eye on the salt hopper to see that the salt flowed at the correct rate of speed, manipulate the valve which controlled the salt flow, keep a steady hand pressure on the chunk fish moving into a trough and going down a chute, and watch the empty tin cans which came down a chute from upstairs to see that they never stopped coming. With my left hand on the speed lever, my right hand pressing salmon, my left eye on the cans and my right eye checking the salt flow, my feet felt ashamed.

One thing I couldn't control was the speed of the can line: this was done by the superintendent, somewhere up above. He gave me a week to get the feel of the machine and then pulled out all the stops. The empty cans came clunk, clunk, clunk down the chute like bullets shot from a gun, and the noise they made reminded me of target practice in the Navy. I speeded up the cutting machine to match the pace but it went berserk, splattering pieces of salmon all over the cannery floor, ceiling and me. I tried to shut off the machine but the lever was stuck. Then the salt hopper shook as though in anger, the salt stopped flowing and all hell broke loose. It was as though the machine was a person and the person had gone mad. "Shut down the line!" somebody bawled. And somebody did.

And then there were the times when a defective can entered the chute. All would be well until it was filled with salmon and sent with its brothers to the end of the line where, when it entered the lidding machine, it would be squashed flat. This would precipitate the other cans violently in all directions, sprinkling the walls and workers with hot cooked fish. And it always took a mechanic an hour or more to pull the mangled tin bodies from the machine with a pair of pliers.

But all the thorns in my side didn't come from the mechanical department. Two women sat on either side of the canning line clipping the bones and meat off the tops of the too-full cans with scissors and filling in the cans that weren't full enough with extra chunks. And they were always complaining. Either the line was too fast or it was too slow. Theirs was the roughest, toughest job in the plant. And whose fault was it? Mine.

One day I became sick of their constantly-repeated tale of woe. When I started the line after lunch I purposely put a little less pressure on the fish in the chute. A second later the two women jumped to their feet, dropped their scissors and started to yank half-empty cans from the line. For every can they filled they had to snatch three more from the conveyor belt, and in five minutes cans were stacked so high around them that they were completely lost from sight. After awhile I relented and put the pressure back on, and everything returned to normal in a very short time. But yes, they did have the roughest, toughest job in the plant that day. And after that there was no more complaining—not in my hearing, at least.

Life in a cannery could be dangerous. One day when I was pressing fish down into the canning machine an especially bony piece of salmon caught my right hand and gradually pulled it down with it. I had visions of my fingers turning up on assorted crackers at a fashionable cocktail party and was so fascinated with the thought that I made no move to stop the inexorable process. But when my arm had disappeared and my shoulder began to follow suit, I managed to reach up with my left hand and pull the lever to stop the line. Then I sat down and shook for awhile.

The superintendent of the cannery had an annoying habit of coming into the canning department and destroying the peace and calm of the place. Sputtering and fuming in his muddy Norse dialect, he upset the workers so much that they weren't much good for anything for the rest of the day. He bothered me, too, and once, when he was passing my machine, I pushed down hard on the fish in the trough. A great spurt of gurry cascaded up, splattering him from head to booted toes like an enormous custard pie. I apologized, he smiled weakly and turned and walked out. I expected to receive my walking papers that night, but I didn't. From then on, when the superintendent wanted to supervise, he did it from the safety of the doorway.

Once when the line had been going along steadily for two hours without a breakdown, I felt in need of a rest and stopped the entire proceedings. The silence attracted the super to the door. "What's wrong?" he inquired.

"Nothing," I said.

"What for you stop the line?"

"I felt like it," I said. "We all need a rest." I looked at him with what I hoped was a leer and dared him, silently, to do something about it. In laboring circles—I later learned—this attitude is known as being "stake-happy." All Alaska workers and construction men catch the disease when their pockets are full of greenbacks toward the end of a season. My pockets weren't full of greenbacks—you didn't get paid as you went along, on this job—but they were likely to be, very soon, and I, apparently, was as stake-happy as they come.

The superintendent probably couldn't see my glaring eyes for the gurry on my glasses, but he was intimidated, just the same. "Ya, sure," he said nervously. "You take a rest for a few minutes. You've earned one." Then he made a hurried exit.

We were working fourteen hours a day, now, and the strain was beginning to tell. My domestic worries weren't helping my disposition any, either. While working in the cannery I was sleeping in my car in a cow pasture nearby, and though I was the interloper—not the cows—it had begun to seem as though one of us would have to go. To keep them away from my improvised fireplace and grub box, I had built a rough enclosure of spruce branches. One morning I awoke to find a group of Elsies trying to knock it down. I drove them off before they could do much damage, but the next morning they came back again with some new recruits, and I opened my eyes to the sight of my fence knocked flat and about ten ruminating cows standing around. One of them had an emptied ten-pound flour sack between her teeth and another was worrying what was left of a bag of sugar. Leaping out of the car with blood in my eye, I courageously dispersed the mob with a stick I picked up off the ground. Then I surveyed the damage. The grub box was open and half cow-licked jars of jam and peanut butter lay broken in the ruins. The camp was a wreck. And most crowning insult of all: my frying pan was filled to overflowing with fresh cow pie—all ready for the frying.

One day I heard that someone had driven to Homer and back again. The road was still officially closed but not, apparently, impassable. The flow of salmon into the cannery had almost stopped by then, and I figured that the cannery could do without me. But when I approached the cannery owner with my resignation and a request for pay, I learned something new about the fish industry in Alaska. "Why don't you wait until the run is over?" said the owner. "Then I will know what to pay you."

"What's that got to do with it?"

He very patiently explained to me why the rate of pay depended upon the profit made in an entire season. The first 10,000 cases of salmon, he told me, paid the expenses of the operation. After that it was all pure profit, and if, at the end of the season, that profit was high, the hourly rate paid the workers was high. "So if you'll stay on for a couple of weeks more," he concluded, "I can probably pay you more per hour. Anyway, we never pay off until the end of the season."

But I was anxious to get going, to find my homestead in the woods. I convinced him that, with all my mistakes, I had been worth $2 an hour, pocketed a month's salary, said goodbye to the rest of the slaves and drove south along the Sterling Highway.

Chapter IV
The Search

AT THE LITTLE TOWN of Soldotna the road forked. The left road led north, toward Anchorage. I took the right turning—toward Homer.

As soon as it had crossed the Kenai River, the highway wound up into the hills, and for the next ten miles it dipped and curved, dipped and curved, leaving forests of birch and spruce to drop to the lowlands of muskegs and lakes and then climbing again. After over twenty miles of tedious driving, I drove across a big bridge spanning another river—the Kasilof River, according to my map, and like all the rivers I had seen so far, the color of chalk from the glacier silt it carried. A sign pointed down a dirt side road to indicate that there was a town named after the river somewhere in the area, but I didn't think it worth investigating at that time.

I drove on. There was no evidence of habitation along the highway—not even a sign advertising gasoline. If this was the homestead country, where were the homesteaders? I asked myself.

About ten miles south of the Kasilof River my question was answered. Rounding a big turn in the highway, I could see a log cabin here and there, and finally a sign: "Clam Gulch Store." The store was only the living room of a homesteader's cabin and the groceries were few, but the man and wife in charge made up for the lack of goods in friendliness. "What can we do for you?" they inquired with real sincerity. "How can we help you?" I asked them how far it was to the next town. "Twelve miles," said the man. "It's called Ninilchik. But you can't get through. The road's closed."

"There's no possible chance of my making it?"

The storekeeper eyed my car. "We-ll," he drawled. "Looks like your Plymouth's in pretty good shape."

Leaving Clam Gulch with two candy bars and the good wishes of the store people, I drove on. Within a couple of miles I came to a large sign blocking the road.

"ROAD CLOSED" it stated in letters fully a foot high. "DO NOT PROCEED FURTHER."

I worked carefully around the road block and drove on. Rocks hammered the underside of the car as it lurched through deep ruts and potholes. Loose dirt and gravel showered the body. The tires spun madly in puddles of black, sticky mud, and every moment of activity, I feared, would be my last. Both the car and I took a terrific beating: we were sweating out every foot, every yard, every mile.

Suddenly I rounded a curve and nearly collided with three gravel dump trucks which were spreading their loads. As I passed them I could hear the angry yells of their drivers, but I didn't stop to listen to the epithets they undoubtedly shouted: I knew I had no right to be on the road they were building, but it was too late to turn back now.

After a couple miles more I passed another road block sign and I was in the clear. Then, coasting down a long hill, I crossed a small river and drove onto a short side road into the fishing village of Ninilchik. The town consisted of a jumble of rotting shacks, a few natives lounging about on what passed for streets and a swarm of ferocious malemute dogs which ran out from every direction to snarl at me and look longingly at my tires. I waited for someone to call the dogs off so that I could get out of the car. When nobody did, I honked my horn to clear a path through the dogs and drove on.

From Ninilchik to Homer I saw cabins and shacks at frequent intervals along the highway. At the top of a long hill that led down to the town and—according to my map—Kachemak Bay—I stopped the car and got out to stretch my legs. The view was spectacular. Off to the right was the wide stretch of water that was Cook Inlet, reaching for at least fifty miles toward the jagged mountains of the Alaska Range. To the left rose a series of grassy hills splotched with patches of lavender—fireweed, I was later to learn. In front of me the road disappeared into a grove of spruce trees where I knew the town of Homer lay hidden, and extending out from the town and bisecting a large, blue bay was a narrow spit of land. Across the bay the mountains reached up to the sky, and in two of the mountain valleys I could see an expanse of white which I knew was a glacier flowing to the inlet. This was the Alaska I had dreamed of, seen pictures of.

But when I drove into Homer I was in for a shock. There was no grandeur here. Only a few frame buildings with false fronts not unlike those in a California ghost town. Only mud streets and no sidewalks. Just another town.

In looking Homer over and doing a little inquiring around, I found out that it boasted one drugstore, one hardware store, two hotels, two general stores, one laundry, two churches, two restaurants, two lumber yards and five bars, and that the proprietors of these establishments made their living from farmers, homesteaders, fishermen and tourists. So far, I was a tourist.

I walked into the drugstore to buy a pack of cigarettes. The man who waited on me introduced himself as Vern Mutch, Sole Owner. He was in his forties, of slight build, wore glasses and had a receding forehead. He reminded me of a thin Scattergood Baines. His friendliness—were all these wilderness people friendly?—soon had me talking about myself, my plans for homesteading, etc., and he listened attentively, dropping a piece of advice now and then.

Finally, seeing that another customer had entered the store, I turned to leave. As I did so I said, "Oh, by the way. Where can I get a cheap room in this town?"

Vern Mutch, Sole Owner, studied me for a moment through his glasses. Then he said, "Why don't you come back later and go home with me? You can stay at my place until you get located."

I had been in the drugstore exactly ten minutes, and already I had made a friend and received an invitation. I didn't know it at the time, but I had been treated to a prime example of Alaskan hospitality.

The Search

Six weeks later I was still in Homer, still a house guest of Vern Mutch. In an effort to repay him for his kindness—he wouldn't hear of accepting cash for room and board—I had volunteered my services at the store, fished for salmon at the nearby Anchor River so that he would have plenty for canning, dug pails of razor clams and picked bucketsful of high bush blueberries to replenish his larder. I had learned that everyone around Homer lived off the wild products of the country and I felt that it was the least I could do. Besides, I enjoyed fishing, clamming and berrypicking.

The Mutch drugstore was like no other drugstore I had ever seen. Besides being stocked with alarm clocks, toys, perfumes, film, projectors, cameras, bicycles, antifreeze, Jeep trucks, chain saws, tires, Jeep parts, fishing tackle, souvenirs and pressure cookers, it had a full stock of drugs. Vern was the nearest thing to a doctor for miles around, and he also acted, on occasion, as the town veterinarian. He had been a druggist in the States, too, but tiring of life in a Michigan city as I had tired of life in any city, he had sold his store and brought his wife and young son to Alaska to "retire." Now he was busier than ever before. In addition to running his store, he was in the process of starting up a cement block plant, owned an interest in a bus line and was one of the directors of a bank that hadn't opened its doors yet. He was growing with a growing town and getting, he said, a big kick out of it.

During my six weeks in Homer I was always on the lookout for a homestead. I asked thousands of questions of the homesteaders I met and was told that all the best land around Homer had been taken up. But I wasn't discouraged. Every day or so I drove north on the Sterling Highway to see what I could see. "There must be *some* land left," I told myself.

One day I stopped at a farmhouse a few miles north of the Anchor River with the idea of asking the people about the available land around them. Knocking, I waited. Suddenly the door swung open and several assorted dogs, cats, chickens and people rushed out. A rather pretty young woman standing in the doorway said, cordially, "Come on in. The dogs won't bite."

I wasn't so sure: the malemute on my left was eyeing my left leg with obvious appetite and the malemute on my right was licking his chops. I moved my legs one at a time. When nothing happened, I walked into the cabin. The next thing I knew I was sitting at a table eating a huge piece of blueberry pie and drinking a very good cup of coffee. More Alaskan hospitality.

I explained my business, and obligingly my hostess brought out a large map of the district and proceeded to show me the land she thought might be available. When I picked out a plot adjoining her homestead she said, "You're married, aren't you?"

"No," I said. "I'm a bachelor."

"Oh. Well, you wouldn't be interested in this land, then." Her voice was decidedly hostile. "We'd much rather have a family living next to us. Why don't you go up and see the Doners? They have the next homestead up the road."

Climbing into my car, I looked back at the house. The door was already closed and the malemutes stood on guard. Apparently it was a capital crime to be single in Alaska.

I drove up a hill and stopped in front of the next house—a nicely-painted, friendly-looking house this time, and I hoped its inhabitants were more of the same. As I left my car I was nearly knocked flat by a little brown bundle of fur which leaped on my chest and managed to lick me twice before falling to the ground. "Don't worry," said the man who appeared around the corner of the house. "He won't bite."

I believed him. I introduced myself, told him what I was looking for and waited for the question. It came. "Are you married?" he asked.

I backed toward the car. "No, I'm not," I said, somewhat defiantly.

"That's too bad. A wife could be a great help to you

in homesteading. The winters up here are pretty long, you know, and most bachelors don't last until spring. Then the homesteads are abandoned and the land goes to waste. We need people who will build the country up—families!"

"Well, thanks for talking to me, Mr. Doner. I guess I'll move along." I opened the car door and started to climb in.

"Hey! Hold on! Don't you want to see some land?" Mr. Doner was waving me back.

"Well, sure," I said, feeling better. "Where is it?"

During the rest of the afternoon Mr. Doner showed me the plot of ground lying next to his property. It consisted of 33 acres running between the highway and the bluff overlooking Cook Inlet, and it pleased me very much. There was a wonderful view of the inlet, and across it, Mt. Iliamna of the magnificent Alaska Range. There was half a mile of road frontage and enough good timber to build a cabin. This was for me.

I jumped into the car and drove like a madman back to Homer and its airport. There was an Alaska Airlines plane just leaving for Anchorage: I took it. The landing wheels had hardly stopped spinning when I leaped out, hurried to the Land Office, barged through a door, demanded to see a map on the Homer area and requested the necessary filing papers. Running a finger across the map, I found the Doner homestead and—right next to it— "my" land. "There it is," I told the clerk in attendance. "That's what I want!"

The clerk leaned over my shoulder and put his own index finger on the map. "Read what it says," he directed.

"WITHDRAWN FROM PUBLIC ENTRY," I read. "But—but—"

"Happened just yesterday," said the clerk. "Government took the land for fishing sites. No homesteading there, any more."

Two weeks later, having recovered from my so-near-and-yet-so-far blow, I resumed my hunt for land, determined to buy some if I couldn't get it any other way. This time I drove past the Doner homestead and stopped at a little creek that crossed the road. The land beside it looked like a fine place to build a cabin, and my hopes began to rise. There was a crude road nearby and I drove down it to see where it went. Presently I came to a large, two-story, round-log house. The door didn't open at my knock, but a loud, gruff voice produced practically the same effect. "COME IN!" it roared.

I entered the house to find myself confronted by a veritable giant of a man. He stood at least six feet four inches in his stocking feet—and he was wearing his stockings at the time. His shoulders were as broad as a bookcase, his hands were like hams of the type L'il Abner carts around, and I almost expected to hear him say, "Fe, fi, fo, fum. I smell the blood of an Englishman."

But he didn't say that. He just said, "Sit down. You're just in time for dinner," and handed me a plate and fork.

"But—but—but—" I stammered, thinking he had mistaken me for somebody else.

"You're hungry, aren't you?" he boomed.

"Yes, but —"

"Well, sit down and shut up!" And when I didn't move to obey him, he pushed me down on a bench in front of the table. It took only a forefinger to do it.

This was my meeting with "Greasy" Grogan, the overlord of Stariski Creek—a meeting that was to play a big part in the shaping of my life in Alaska. But I didn't know it at the time. After eating a large meal of fried salmon steaks, pie and coffee, I managed to whisper to mine host that I was looking for land and ask him if he knew who owned the plot down by the bridge.

"*I* own it; that's who," said Greasy. "Whadaya wanta know for?"

"Well, I thought I might be interested in buying some of it. Would you be interested in selling?"

He screwed his surprisingly babyish face into a very adult frown and scratched his head. "Could be," he said.

"How much per acre?"

He considered for a moment. Then he said, "One hundred dollars."

The price was much too high for unimproved wilderness land, I knew, but I was afraid to tell him so: he was bigger than I. But during the next week I thought the matter over and decided to meet his terms on at least five acres. "Five acres at five hundred dollars. Right, Mr. Grogan?" I said when I went to see him.

"Five acres at a thousand dollars, you mean," he said. "Where'dya get the idea I'd let you have it for $100 an acre?" It was no deal.

While drowning my sorrows in vodka at the Kachemak Bar in Homer a few days later, I got to talking to a man who seemed to be interested in my dilemma. He told me that a Mr. Jones who lived in Anchorage had filed on a homestead up Stariski Creek from Greasy Grogan's land and had never proved up on it. "He might be interested in relinquishing the land to you," he said. "Why don't you write him?"

"Sure, why not?" I said listlessly. "What can I lose?"

I wrote the letter that night, and a few days later I received an answer from Mr. Jones. He would be glad to relinquish the land to me, he said. All I had to do was send the necessary papers to him and he'd sign them. I hadn't seen the land, of course, but I figured that out of 160 acres—the maximum homestead acreage—there should be enough good land for what I wanted to do. I got the papers from a surveyor in Homer and sent them to Mr. Jones immediately, along with $100 to make sure that he wouldn't change his mind. They came back signed by return mail.

But I wasn't a homesteader yet: by relinquishing his claim to the land, Mr. Jones had simply given it back to the government, and I, at that point, had no legal right to it. My next step was to make out filing papers and send them, together with the relinquishment papers, to the Land Office in Anchorage. Having done that, and having been assured by the government surveyor in Homer that everything would go through without a hitch and that I could take possession any time, I made preparations to move to my new home.

But this, in some ways, wasn't as easy as I had supposed. My druggist friend, Vern Mutch, was opposed to the whole idea. "Why do you want to go homesteading?" he said. "Why don't you stay here with us this winter and help me in the store? Why don't you come in with me and buy forty acres near town? Why don't you come in with me on the block plant? Why do you want to make trouble for yourself?"

But all his arguments, entreaties and offers had no effect on me. My answer was always: "Because I want to go homesteading. That's what I came up here for."

He finally threw in the towel. Lending me some tools, loading up my car with food and making me a present of a malemute puppy, he said, "Good luck. I'll see you soon."

I headed north on September 15.

Chapter V

The Homestead

"Where Is It, Ski?" I said to my malemute pup. "It must be around here somewhere."

Trying to find a homestead you have never seen and survey lines made forty years before and long since overgrown was a job for a prospector or a water-hunter with a divining rod, I decided. I had pitched my pup tent in a grove of spruce trees near the highway, but I didn't know whether I was trespassing on somebody else's land or camping on my own domain. Then I had spent half a day tramping through the woods looking for the survey lines on the roughly-sketched map the Land Office had given me. But it was hopeless. Every time I found a line of stumps that could have been boundaries there was a spruce tree among them that looked to be over forty years old, and I knew I was on the wrong track again. (The stumps, I later found out, had been left by trap pole cutters and had, as I had suspected, no relation to boundaries.)

It looked as though I would have to call on Greasy Grogan for help. I hated to do it—that business of raising the price on the land hadn't made me like him very well, or trust him either, for that matter—but a cold gust of wind at my back made me think of winter, and winter made me think of getting some sort of shelter erected before the first snow came drifting down. But how could I build if I didn't know where my land was? I had visions of myself in a snowstorm, crawling on my hands and knees through the drifts, still holding my tattered map, still hunting for boundaries. No, there was nothing else to do but call on Greasy Grogan.

Greasy was in a help-the-poor-dope mood that day. He took me directly to a half-mile survey stake which was, he told me, at one of my corners. We then walked north along a faint blazed line until he stopped and said, "This is your other corner. All the rest of this land is mine." Then he disappeared into the woods.

29

Standing where he had left me in a kind of daze, I gazed with something like rapture at the wilderness of trees and brush which in time I would call my own. Excitedly, I searched through the forest until I found what looked like an ideal building site. It was close to the highway and not far from a spring. It had only one drawback: it wasn't, as far as I could tell, on my land—it was on Greasy's.

But just to make sure, I paced off 1320 feet from the corner stake. According to my map, this distance formed the front of my homestead. No! Greasy was wrong! The building site I had selected *was* on my land. Delighted, I moved my tent to the new location.

The patch of ground I had chosen was large enough to contain a cabin: no clearing away of trees or stumps would have to be done. But as it was, it took me two days of digging up two feet of tangled moss and tree roots to get to bare dirt. Then I decided that it would be a good idea to dig a small cellar before going any farther. Fighting clouds of mosquitoes with every shovelful of dirt, I didn't make too much headway on the first day. On the second day I built a small smudge fire to drive the pests away, only to discover that I had attracted an even worse pest—whitesox. These were tiny gnats with white markings on their legs, and no amount of smoke or bug repellent would keep them from biting me. They would cluster around my eyes and forehead when my hands were occupied with the shovel and depart with sizeable chunks of raw meat before I could slap at them. By the time my cellar was six feet deep and six feet square, I called it quits; my eyes were almost swollen shut and I no longer felt like digging and fighting bugs at the same time.

Trading my shovel for an axe, I went into the woods and managed to dodge the bugs long enough to cut down two fair-sized spruce trees, trim them, saw them into eighteen-foot lengths and drag them to the cabin site to use as sill logs, or foundations. Now I was ready for my lumber. I drove up the highway to a sawmill I had noticed in my travels, expecting to return the same day with the 2000 board feet of lumber I had figured I would need for building a simple shack. Instead, the owner of the one-man mill told me I would have to wait two weeks for my boards. Forlornly I returned to my camp to do battle with the whitesox, and with a new bug I recognized immediately—my father had had his troubles with it in British Columbia—as a "no-see-um." The latest arrival raised welts as big as silver dollars on the most tender portions of my body and, being almost invisible as its name suggested, was impossible to fight. What a country!

Greasy Grogan made an enraged appearance on the fourth day. Charging through the woods like a bull after a toreador, he shouted, "Get the —— off my land, you —— squatter! I showed you where to build!"

When he had calmed down I explained the situation to him. Sputtering, he left, but in a short time he was back with a 50-foot tape. Together, we spent two hours measuring the survey line again, and when we finished we discovered that I had ten feet more of land than when I had paced it off. Greasy grumbled and fumed, but finally—by way of apology, I guess—he invited me over to his cabin for dinner.

That night Greasy was the perfect host, and just as I was about to leave he made me what sounded like a very reasonable offer. If I would help him and his 18-year-old son, Tommy, pour a cellar for his home, he said, he would haul my lumber from the sawmill in his truck and stack it at my site. "That's the way we do it up here," he explained. "When we're short of cash, we exchange labor."

On the following day we began a backbreaking three-day task. I hauled cement, sifted gravel, pumped water, carried rocks and, in general, worked like a Roman slave, stopping only for meals and laboring far into the night by the light of a Coleman lantern. Each night Greasy tried to persuade me to remain as his guest so that I could get an early start in the morning, but I always had to return to my camp to feed my dog and he didn't get away with that. At the end of the third night, I staggered back to my little tent and slept the clock around.

When my lumber was ready Greasy kept his part of the bargain. At least, he provided the truck and hauled the lumber from the sawmill. But when it came to unloading the lumber, Greasy demurred, lounging lazily in the truck cab while Tommy and I did all the work. He seemed to feel that he had paid off his work debt in full. I didn't agree, but I was so glad to be able to start construction on my cabin that I failed to point to him that, by the standards of the "labor exchange" system he had so carefully explained to me, he owed me at least a couple of days' work.

With a lot of guesswork, several clumsy mistakes, some fool luck and a small pamphlet entitled, "How To Build a Cabin," I finished the framework and covered a roof with boards within three days. My shack was to be a story-and-a-half affair with a living room downstairs and a bedroom upstairs—pretty elaborate, really—and it was well on its way to completion.

Then the rainy season began. Hurriedly, with the steady downpour threatening to ruin everything it hit, I moved all my gear into the unfinished cabin, stacking it on some loose boards laid across the floor joists upstairs. At night I had a miserable time trying to keep dry under the leaking roof, trying to keep from rolling off the temporary platform onto the floor below, and trying to keep Ski, the malemute pup, from crawling into my sleeping bag when she was soaking wet.

Whenever the rain let up, I would slap as many boards on the side of the shack as I could before it started again. Within a week the cabin—except for the windows—was enclosed, and there was 90-pound roofing on the roof. The lumber yard in Homer to which I had gone to purchase five windows had informed me that they would arrive "some time in the future," so I would simply have to do without that little luxury for awhile. But I was stubborn: I talked Greasy out of some plastic glass to cover some of the holes and tacked tarpaper over the rest.

The heating problem was solved when I found a 50-gallon gasoline drum, cut a hole for a door in one end and a hole for a smokestack on the top. Every homesteader in the area, I was told, had a stove like that: it was called a "barrel" stove. It wasn't the most efficient stove in the world—sometimes it would roar and grow so red that it looked as though it might melt and set the house on fire, and sometimes no amount of poking or kerosene would start it burning—but it was the best I could make at the time.

For cooking, I decided to use the two-burner Coleman stove I had brought with me from the States, and I was to use it continuously during my entire stay in Alaska. Later on I intended to order a wood and coal-burning cookstove from Montgomery Ward's—mainly for baking pies, and to have an oven to keep my feet warm on cold winter nights.

The furniture in my dream house—such as it was—was constructed of odds and ends left over from the building lumber. I made a "homesteader" table big enough to hold everything from cigarette papers to my total supply of foodstuffs. I made a bed of rough lumber —just the right size to contain my thin cotton mattress and my sleeping bag but only a few degrees better than sleeping on the cold, wet ground. I figured I wouldn't need any chairs because I wasn't expecting any company just then.

But my cabin still wasn't complete: I was told I would have to insulate it in some way. Accordingly, I collected a large number of cardboard cartons in Homer, flattened them out and tacked them over the studs on the inside walls. Then I built a fancy bookcase with five boards against the day when I might own some books. My mansion was done.

It was pointed out to me by Greasy a few days later, however, that I still lacked one important item: an outhouse. This seemed to me to be an unnecessary luxury: hadn't I 160 acres of forest? But on the other hand, who was I to flaunt convention? I dug a hole 100 feet behind the cabin and built a fancy one-seater with an excellent view of a muskeg (a mossy, wet piece of ground—they were everywhere) and stocked it with a generous supply of mail order catalogs. Now, let them sneer!

By that time—the middle of October—the weather had begun to change. There were frosts every morning and many windy days. I began to realize that, like the squirrel, I would have to be storing up some food for the winter. Just as I conceived this thought I ran into Vern Mutch in Homer. "Want to help me harvest my vegetable garden and dig my potatoes?" he said. "I'll give you a share of the produce if you will." Two days later I left Homer with my car groaning under the weight of 300 pounds of potatoes, a sack of carrots, a sack of turnips, a dozen large heads of cabbage and numerous boxes of radishes, green onions, peas, lettuce and Swiss chard. These were in the luggage compartment. Up front with me were some cans of salmon, some cans of clams and several pounds of smoked salmon Vern had given to me in return for the help I had given him in catching the fish and digging the clams. I could hardly wait to get home with my loot, and when I did, I immediately started construction on some shelves and bins in my cellar to hold it all. When everything was stored away in its proper place I was a proud and happy man.

Then I began to think over the matter of canning. It was woman's work, but what a wonderful way to preserve game and the fruits of the field! On my next trip to Homer I bought a medium-sized pressure cooker, a half dozen cases of pint jars and a book on the art of canning. I also bought a cheap .22 rifle and a couple of boxes of ammunition. Throughout the last two weeks of October I hunted spruce chickens (a kind of grouse) and put them up in jars, and in my travels I found wild cranberries and mossberries and cooked them up into a mess resembling jam. So pleased was I with my project that if my dog had been a little fatter and a little bigger at the time I'm afraid she, too, would have ended up in a jar.

My cast-iron cook stove arrived from Portland, Oregon, at about that time. It was the second smallest in the catalog and cost only $29, but it looked mighty beautiful to me. But now I was faced with the problem of finding fuel. The beaches from Homer for 38 miles up the coast past my place to Ninilchik, I had heard, were literally littered with big and little chunks of coal. They came from submerged reefs in Cook Inlet and dropped from seams that lined the bluff encircling it, and anybody who wanted them could take them. But how could I? Only a four-wheel-drive Jeep or a Dodge power wagon could drive out on the beaches and return with a heavy load, and I possessed neither.

But I was in luck. I found out that Mr. Doner, just down the road, owned a Dodge power wagon, and that he would be agreeable to picking up a load of coal for me for $20. I went along with him to help and to find out more about this coal business. We drove six miles up the highway and turned down a road leading to the beach at Happy Valley Creek. Sure enough: big chunks of coal were everywhere! As Mr. Doner drove slowly along the hard sand, his boys and I tossed the shiny black stuff into the back of the truck. Once I picked up a brown piece and was aggrieved when everybody laughed. "You don't ever want to take that brown stuff," Mr. Doner explained. "One bucket of that'll make two buckets of ashes. Always take the shiny black kind. It makes a much better fire, and it's only about twenty percent ash."

My load, when delivered, proved to be about two and a half tons. I carried it piece by piece from the highway and stacked it carefully against the cabin. That pile was to last me through the winter and part of the spring.

I was getting to the stage, now, where I would have to watch my money: I was down to less than a hundred dollars, and there was certainly no more coming in. But

I had an asset: my car. It was still new and in fairly good shape, and I made up my mind to trade it in on a cheap, second-hand Jeep and pocket the difference. I told Vern Mutch what I was planning to do. "Good," he said. "I'll go along with you to Seward. You can pick up an old Jeep there, and I can pick up a new Jeep that's just arrived by boat for my store."

There isn't much traffic in Alaska. You can drive for miles and miles without ever meeting another car, especially during the fall, when the roads are slippery with ice. Nevertheless, just 25 miles from Seward I rounded a curve in the Plymouth and CR-ASH!

Finding myself in a five-foot ditch against a spruce tree, I climbed out from behind my bent steering wheel and surveyed the scene. The other car stood in the center of the road where we had met. Silently, I helped its driver, an old man, pick up his headlights and what was left of his grillwork. Then the cursing began. Seeing that I was liable get the worst of it, I muttered, "See you later," and went back to my car to see how Vern was feeling. I found him with his head in his hands and nursing a growing bump. Apart from that, neither of us was more than slightly shaken up.

Our efforts to back the car up onto the highway proved futile: the reverse gear wasn't working. When this became apparent, Vern hitchhiked to Moose Pass and brought back a wrecker which pulled us out in short order. In the meantime, the old man in the other car had disappeared.

In Seward I heard the bad news: only my second and third gears were working, the whole front of the car was a twisted mass of steel and chrome, and the repair job, with parts being ordered from Seattle, would probably take several months. Worse still: cost on the job was estimated at over $400, and I had cancelled my insurance policy only the week before, planning to buy new insurance with an Alaskan company when I bought a Jeep.

Back at the homestead I examined my plight: I was starting out my first winter in Alaska with no transportation, a large debt hanging over my head and only about ten dollars in cash to see me through to spring. Don't come home? I could *never* go home!

Then I remembered my family in California and sent out a series of airmail calls for help. I wrote my parents, my brother, my sister. I even considered asking my father for the loan of enough money to enable me to crawl home with my tail between my legs like the beaten cur I was. But luckily that was one letter I didn't write. In the following days, while waiting for answers to my letters, I began to see the light. First, I told myself that I had only six months to go out of the seven required for a veteran to prove up on a homestead. Second, I had a warm little shack to live in rent-free with no fuel, light or water bills to pay. Third, the cellar was stocked with enough food to last at least a couple of months and I could charge whatever else I needed in a Homer store. If I could just figure out some means of raising enough money to pay the repair bill on my car so that I could sell it for a decent sum instead of letting it go for junk, I could turn into a hermit for the winter and live, in a measure, like a king.

A week passed before my break came in the form of the Farm Training Program for veterans. Six miles south of my homestead, Greasy told me, classes were held once a week in the Anchor Point schoolhouse, and any veteran who took them was entitled to $67.50 a month for subsistence. I could go with Greasy in his truck: he had been taking the classes for a year.

In my circumstances, $67.50 looked like a veritable fortune. I signed up at once. In the meantime, checks had started to arrive from the States. Though I wouldn't be able to get my car out of hock for some time to come, it looked as though I would be able to survive the winter after all.

Chapter VI
Greasy Grogan

ONE MORNING IN NOVEMBER I awoke with the feeling that something was wrong. Something was missing, some sound that I was used to hearing. I remembered a pocket book story I had been reading in which the character awakes to find himself the last man alive in the world. It was something like that.

Springing out of bed, I hurried to the front window to look out. Wrong? Nothing was wrong! Everything was right! It was snowing, by golly, and it was the first time I had seen it fall in my life!

Dressing quickly, I rushed outside to feel and taste the miracle. Great big doughy flakes were pelting softly down, and they were already piled several inches deep on the ground and flouring the trees. Even Ski, the malemute pup, was powdered with them, and when I released her from her chain she dashed madly around, as happy as I to see the new clean white world. Together we rolled in it, played in it, ate it. "Our first snow, Ski!" I shouted. "It's our first snow!"

After awhile I felt the cold seeping through my thin summer clothes. I returned to the shack and found my winter gear—long woolen underwear, heavy wool socks, clumsy shoepacks, a wool shirt, my parka. I gobbled a quick breakfast and then went out in my new outfit to walk through the woods.

Everything was quiet, everything was hushed. It was as though a blanket of silence had been dropped over the countryside. I felt for the first time that I was completely alone in the world, shut off from all other human beings. And I didn't mind the feeling: I liked being alone.

But I hadn't counted on Greasy Grogan. With that first snowfall my giant enemy-friend came out of his den and began his favorite winter sport of paying unexpected calls on all his neighbors—a neighbor being anyone within 50 miles who would open his door to him. And because I was his closest neighbor, my shack always seemed to be the last stop on his way home from Homer, where he went frequently to take on a full load of booze. At these times he would hang around, roaring and cursing and knocking things down, until he had driven me to the verge of insanity. But there was nothing I could do: Greasy was much too big to throw out.

Some of the other homesteaders I had met at Greasy's called him "Obnoxious" Grogan behind his back. I had no difficulty in understanding the reason for that, but I wondered about the origin of the nickname "Greasy" until the night he invited me and some of the other neighbors over for a pinochle session. Then I knew.

Greasy had planned to serve refreshments both before and after the card game, and I went over to his place early in the day to see if I could be of any help. I found him busily mixing up a batch of doughnut dough. He was using a large washtub for a bowl, and into it he was throwing large handsful of flour and indiscriminate amounts of lard, using a gallon can for a lard scoop.

"Are you measuring your ingredients?" I asked him.

"Naw," he replied. "Never use a recipe. When I make doughnuts I make 'em big, though, hey?" He added another gallon of lard to prove his point.

That evening six of us waded through about ten gallons of spaghetti and moose meatballs—Greasy's specialty—and then proceeded to play cards while our host made doughnuts. The doughnuts started to arrive on the table and Greasy, shoving huge platesful of them at us, boomed out, "Don't be afraid to eat 'em all! There's plenty more!"

The first doughnut I bit into was so full of grease that most of it dribbled down my chin and cascaded onto my shirt. Gazing around the table, I could see the pained expressions on the faces of the other guests as they, too, tried unsuccessfully to stop the flow of oozing fat. Said Greasy: "Good, huh? Have some more!"

Being well aware of what could happen to the man who crossed Greasy in his own house, we all pitched in valiantly to get rid of the sinkers. I tried to feed some of mine to Greasy's dog but he only looked sick and backed as far away from me as the walls would permit. This went on until Greasy was tired of making doughnuts, it was 3 o'clock in the morning and we were all permitted to leave.

I spent the next two days sitting in my outhouse reading catalogs. On the third day, Greasy caught me and invited me to lunch. It was more of a royal command than an invitation, and I forced my trembling legs to carry me to his house. I was relieved to see that there were no doughnuts in sight; apparently Greasy had been baking pies instead. But when I bit into the pumpkin pie he offered me, I discovered, to my horror, that it tasted just like his doughnuts. "Greasy," I said, shakily. "What did you make this pie crust of?"

" Made it out of the doughnut dough, of course. Made some pancakes from it for breakfast, too. You ought to stay for dinner. I'm baking a cake."

Another of Greasy's favorite indoor sports was pinochle. I had never played the game before arriving in Alaska, but soon after meeting Greasy I became an expert: he forced me to learn it, I think, so that he could keep in practice by beating me. Three or four nights a week he would come by my shack and yell, "Let's go pinochling!" It was useless to refuse: I would climb into his truck and away we'd go. There were only two other families that played the game in the area at that time, so one night we'd drop in on the Baileys, three miles away, the next on the Keelers, two miles away. And since neither family ever received any advance notice of our coming, it was always something of a shock.

It was the Baileys we shocked most often. After practically splitting their front door with his earthshaking knocks, Greasy would stride in—with me diffidently trailing behind—and start issuing orders. "Get out the cards!" he'd yell. "I'm gonna beat you tonight!" It didn't matter if the Baileys had already started to bed or made any other plans for the evening: we were guests, and the only way guests could be entertained, as far as Greasy was concerned, was with pinochle. The sessions would last until late in the morning, with Mrs. Bailey keeping us all awake with pots of strong coffee and food. Poor Mrs. Bailey. She was usually Greasy's partner in the four-handed game, and she hated it. After she had gotten a bid and played a hand out, Greasy would spend the next five minutes telling her what she had done wrong. She *had* to be Greasy's partner: none of the rest of us would have touched him with a ten-foot pew.

Greasy's outdoor passion was hunting, especially moose hunting. In the wintertime it was illegal to kill moose, but that didn't bother him in the least. He was a retired policeman, he told me, and the law didn't apply to him. After an all-night pinochle session, when he had lost and I had won, he would delight in routing me out of bed just as I had gotten into it and taking me out hunting. Lugging heavy 30-0-6's, we would snowshoe countless miles through the woods and over the frozen muskegs without seeing so much as a rabbit. But my eyes were better than Greasy's, and once in awhile I would spot a moose just disappearing behind a tree. "There's one over there," I would whisper.

"Where? Where?" he'd whisper back, loudly enough to have startled a moose wearing a hearing aid. "I don't see anything."

"Over there." When we would arrive at the tree I had pointed out and there'd be no moose there, Greasy would turn, glare at me and shout, "Stoddard, you're a —— —— liar!"

"No, I'm not, Greasy. Look. There's the fresh tracks."

"Fresh tracks? Why you ——! Those're *old* tracks! Stoddard, I'm never gonna take you moose hunting again. You're such a —— liar!"

But I never could count on that. If I didn't hide out in the woods or in the outhouse, I knew I'd be dragged moose-hunting any time Greasy got the idea.

One day in early winter the overlord of Stariski Creek

showed up at my cabin to say he had just shot a moose and wanted my help in packing it out. This was good news: I was about out of canned fish and clams and had a strong urge for fresh meat, and the rule of the country said that anyone who helped butcher an illegal moose and pack it out was entitled to his share—up to half—as "hush money." My mouth watering with the thought of the good steaks I would eat within the next few days, I said, "Sure."

That evening we went over to the Baileys' to play pinochle until about midnight and then excused ourselves without giving a reason: you can't trust even your best friends with the news of the shooting of an illegal moose, Greasy had told me.

We drove up the highway to a point about a mile past my place and parked the truck. Walking back down the road, we entered the woods a half mile away and Greasy led me through a network of trees to where a mammoth bull moose was lying dead in the snow. Using flashlights—but sparingly—we proceeded to the messy job of removing the heavy hide, cleaning the moose and cutting it into quarters. This consumed an hour. Our next task was to carry the meat to the highway. Tying a leg apiece on our packboards, we snowshoed to the birm (a pile of snow-covered dirt and brush left by the roadbuilders), where we hid the meat and returned for another load. We used our lights as little as possible during our comings and goings so as not to attract the attention of a wandering game warden or anyone else who might happen to come along. This led to frequent fallings and stumblings over stumps and logs, but we didn't even dare curse out loud. When the meat was all piled near the road Greasy went and got his truck while I stood guard. Presently the truck appeared with no lights showing. Then, while Greasy idled the motor for a quick getaway, I threw the meat in the back of the truck as quickly as possible. We drove like madmen to Greasy's house, buried the meat under the snow just outside his door and relaxed.

After a cup of coffee I expressed myself as anxious to get home with my share of the meat.

"Sure," said Greasy, magnanimously. "Take a front quarter."

I pawed through the already frozen meat until I found what I thought should be a front quarter, tied it to my packboard and walked the half mile back to my shack. Greasy woke me up early the next morning. "You made a mistake, you ---!" he roared. "You took a *hind* quarter!"

Hind quarter, front quarter, what difference did it make? Nevertheless, to keep the peace, I waited until after dark and took the quarter back to Greasy's. As I started to tie another quarter to my packboard Greasy stopped me. "Tell you what," he said, wheedlingly. "To save you lugging that quarter back half a mile, I'll can up your share when I can up mine. Then I'll bring you the cans."

I thought it over. Probably, when Greasy brought the cans, he'd bring me some fresh steaks, too. "Okay," I said.

Three days later Greasy presented me with ten cans of meat. Ten pounds of meat from a moose that dressed out at 800. "Phooey!" I shouted after Greasy's retreating form—though not so loudly that he could hear me. "That's the last time I help *you* bring in an illegal moose!"

But 790 pounds of meat, apparently, wasn't enough for Greasy. About a month later I heard two rifle shots in back of my cabin, and an hour after that Greasy snowshoed in to announce, proudly, that he had just shot two bulls, and did I want to help him pack them out? "Hell, no!" was what I should have said. But I didn't. Greasy was too big.

That night Greasy led his son, two neighbor boys and me to his kill. One dead moose, it seems, had gotten up and walked away, because there was only one to be seen. Greasy was furious. So was I—but for different reasons: the moose had only been wounded, I reasoned, and it had undoubtedly dragged itself over the snow to die miles away. What a cruelty—and what a waste!

It was about midnight when the five of us began the tedious job of skinning. The temperature was about 20 degrees below zero and our cold-stiffened hands were clumsy implements for wielding skinning knives and peeling the heavy hide off an already-frozen carcass. Suddenly I stopped work and stood up. "Listen," I whispered. The others fell silent.

From the direction of Stariski Creek, just a short distance away, came a weird, high-pitched moan. Above the moan was a grunting noise, halfway between a cough and a growl. A green light showed above the trees—a shimmering light that filled the whole northern sky, dancing up and down in rolls and waves. Then it seemed as though rifles were cracking all around us. Dropping my knife, I croaked, "Hey, l-let's get out of here."

My companions laughed, Greasy loudest of all. "What a cheechako you are, Stoddard!" he boomed, slapping me so hard on the back that I almost lost my balance. "Don't you know anything? That moaning you hear is the ice cracking on the creek. It always does that, when it gets this cold. The cold makes the birch trees split, too: that's what sounds like shots. Don't worry: there aren't any game wardens after you!"

"What about that grunt?"

"Hell, that's probably just some old bull moose trying to get this dead one to come out and fight like a man. If I'd brought my gun along I'd go and shoot him now."

"But the light. What was that?"

"Haven't you ever seen the aurora borealis before?" cut in one of the boys. "Help me with this hind leg."

I still didn't feel easy in my mind. The noises and the ghostly light made the woods an ideal setting, I felt, for a murder. But only a moose had been murdered, and soon, with Greasy barking gruff commands, we had it cut into quarters and ready to pack on our backs to the shack. At this point Greasy returned to the cabin with the butchering tools and no load of meat, leaving the rest of us to do the heavy work.

I was wearing my skis that night; there weren't enough snowshoes to go around. I started out with the first piece of meat to beat a trail over the half mile back to my shack, but with a ski pole in each hand I was unable to carry a flashlight and had to move blindly. Arriving at the edge of a gully, I tried to ski slowly down the slope. I ended up flat on my face, with the 100 pounds of meat on my back pressing me deeper into three feet of soft snow.

I lay there, floundering, until one of the boys found me and helped me to my feet. Then I started to climb the opposite slope. Halfway up I slipped, and there I was on my back at the bottom of the gully again, helpless as a butterfly pinned to a board. After being found by the boys on their return trip from the cabin and propped into an upright position, I removed the treacherous skis. "Hell," I said. "I'll never get anywhere this way. I'll use my own two feet." But even my feet were traitors. I started to cross a section of muskeg, but with first one foot and then the other breaking through the crust, I managed to make only a hundred feet before giving up and unloading my pack. Leaving the meat behind, I covered the rest of the distance to my shack partly on my hands and knees, partly by leaping lightly from snowshoe track to snowshoe track like a barefoot boy on a stove.

I found Greasy straining the strength of my one and only chair by giving it the full benefit of his brawny bulk. He looked like a general mapping a campaign as he drank my coffee, ate a huge hunk of my apple pie and issued orders to the boys to pile the meat next to the highway in front of my shack. While I commandeered a pair of snowshoes and went back for the meat I had dropped and another load at the kill, Greasy went over to his house for his truck. After everyone but Greasy had participated in loading the meat—except for my share, a front quarter—the great moose-killer disappeared down the highway with his helpers. And not bothering to clean up the blood on the floor, I climbed into my bag and was instantly asleep.

The next morning I awoke in the grip of a horrible thought. Rushing outdoors, I found my worst fear an awful actuality. Sure enough, the highway in front of the shack, the snowbank where the meat had been piled and the snowshoe trails from cabin to kill were covered with bright, red blood. And the "camp robbers"—second cousins to the blue jays of the state of my birth—were already gathering for the feast—a sure giveaway to a flying game warden that a moose was dead. It was a cinch that it would be I, not Greasy, who spent the next six months in the Territorial hoosegow in Anchorage.

Working faster than I had ever worked in my life, I covered the evidence with snow, and for the rest of the day I used the snowshoes Greasy had left behind to make hundreds of false trails leading from my house to nowhere. And until the next snowfall—which would remove any little clues I might have forgotten—I sat in my cabin listening for the sound of planes and the heavyhanded knock of the law. The front quarter I had received for my participation in the crime was left untouched until the danger was over, though I had been dying for a bite of fresh meat. "Never again," I swore. "Never again."

Greasy gave me no more illegal moose trouble that winter, mainly because I wouldn't have anything to do with him. He tried to entice me over to his place with promises of batches of doughnuts and six-handed games of pinochle, but I refused every offer he made: I had had enough. As far as I was concerned, Greasy was a thorn on the side of the country, and the less I saw of him the less the pain would be.

Besides, I had new problems to worry about.

Chapter VII

The Actor

CHRISTMAS HAD COME and gone. It had been a lonely time, but my family in California had come through with a lot of useful presents. My parents and sister had sent me three crates of assorted canned vegetables, canned fruit and pocket books, and my brother had expressed me a radio battery which I didn't know what to do with until the radio to go with it turned up a couple of weeks later. With plenty of food, reading material and a radio with which to hear what was going on in the outside world—and I could hear *everything* in the outside world, from China to Scandinavia—I was as snug as a hibernating bear.

I looked like one, too. One morning after the New Year I examined my face in the broken piece of glass by which, if I had been shaving, I would have shaved. I was a hairy success. My growth of reddish, coarse beard, tangled with hairballs and sticky with egg yolks, was long enough and bushy enough to qualify me for service as an emaciated Man Mountain Dean.

I was pleased. Not since my Navy days had I achieved such a beard. But alas, this beard was to enmesh me in trouble.

One night late in January a group of people I had seen in the area but didn't know by name stampeded into my shack and shoved a sheaf of typewritten pages into my hands. "This is your part in our play!" they yelled. "Read it!"

Protesting that I couldn't act, I had lots of work to do and that I wouldn't, under any circumstances, take a part in a play, I was dragged out of my comfortable chair and held unmoving while they read the play to me. Then they handed me "my" part again and begged me to "read it with us—just for the fun of it." I gazed around the overcrowded room. People in parkas were everywhere, leaning against the walls, sitting on the floor. They looked like nice people; they were my neighbors—

homesteaders and their wives. And they were waiting. I obliged.

The reaction, as I read, was out of all proportion. Every time my cue came up and I spoke a line, cries of "You're wonderful!" "Great!" and "Bravo!" filled the air. I had never thought of myself as an actor—never wanted to act—but if they thought I was good, well, maybe. . . .

I was a gone goose. Half unaware of what I was saying, I gave my promise to memorize the 149 speeches of my part in time for a rehearsal at the Anchor Point school on the following night. And as my guests, triumphant, trooped out of the door, one of them, a fifteen-year-old girl who was the only female in the group who wasn't somebody's wife, delivered a parting shot: "Don't you dare shave off your beard. We need that wonderful beard in the play." The door closed, then opened again. "We need you, too, of course." said the girl.

When all was quiet again, I settled down to study my part. Looking over the pages, I found that I was to be the star of a three-act opus called "Henry Gubbins' Mail Order Wife." As Henry Gubbins, I was to play the role of a homesteader—*that* wouldn't be too difficult—and in general to act the fool, which I had already done by accepting the part. A Mrs. Tucker, "a widder woman" stamped, I gathered, with the imprints of a long, hard life, was to come in answer to my mailed proposal. But there would be obstacles to our achievement of wedded bliss, and a mixup would occur in which I would marry —not Mrs. Tucker, but a male neighbor disguised as same. In the end, everything would be straightened out to the audience's satisfaction, with two miserable people condemned to living unhappily ever after. Great drama? Well, hardly. But the play, I told myself, was to be put on in a good cause: to raise money to finish construction on the Anchor Point school. And participating in it would be a good way to get to know my neighbors. So I would do it if it killed me—though I would live, I suspected, to regret it.

The Actor

At the first rehearsal in the schoolhouse my legs were shaking so continuously that I had to hold onto a desk for support. And though everyone but me was wearing a parka and shoepacks—the temperature, that night, was below freezing—I burned and sweated and removed every piece of clothing I could decently take off. I tried several times to bolt out the door, but they would always drag me back. "No!" I shouted. "I've changed my mind! I can't do it!"

"Yes!" they shouted back. "You've got to!"

Finally came the time for my first cue. Everyone looked at me expectantly, but I opened my mouth and gasped. I had forgotten my lines, every one. I had memorized them so well that I had been able to reel them off to my dog like a woman telling the dirt on a neighbor, but I couldn't recall a one of them now.

The cue came again, and with it a clue from the prompter. Suddenly my lines reentered my memory, and I managed to fumble through the first scene of the play. Then I collapsed into a chair.

On my call for the second scene, I found that I could actually walk, and, getting up from my chair, I took my place on the stage without assistance. I stumbled through the first few lines without mistake, but when a particularly long line came my way I said five words and stopped. The cast waited. I waited. There was hardly a sound but that of my heavy breathing. Finally I spoke. But the words I spoke were not the words of the playwright: they were my own. And to give them emphasis, I rolled my eyes and assumed the accent of an Ozark hillbilly.

"By God, Stoddard's lines are better than the lines in the play," said the director when the laughter had died down. "Keep up that ad-libbing, Stoddard. It's wonderful!"

From then on, I gradually threw away the script until my part was pure corn, pure invention and had very little relation to the original play. Bill Rabick, the other lead, changed his part, too, and pretty soon the play was twice as long as the original, and twice—we thought —as good. All that was left of the first "Henry Gubbins' Mail Order Wife" was the skeleton, and not very much of that.

Two months later we put on a public performance at the schoolhouse in which we had done all our rehearsing. We played to a capacity crowd of 86, ad-libbing throughout, even to the extent of bringing in, in what we thought was a most natural and artistic way, the names of a few of the people in the audience. We were a hit! "Hot damn!" said the actor standing next to me while we took curtain call after curtain call. "We could run this thing for a year if everyone in the area weren't here tonight."

"A *year!*" I whispered back. "All I can think about is how glad I'll be to get back to my fire and chair."

And I was. Returning to my homestead that night, I was greeted by my faithful retainer, Ski, the malemute dog, like a successful knight returning from the wars to spend his declining days in peace. "Boy!" I said as I picked myself up from the snow where Ski, a bit overenthusiastic, had planted me with her paws. "Am I glad *that's* over!"

A violent pounding on my door the next morning catapulted me just as violently from my bed. The cast of "Henry Gubbins" was waiting for me outside with a gleam in its collective eye. "We're going on tour!" one of them shouted. "We're putting on the play at Ninilchik next Saturday night!" said someone else. "We're going to Homer and Kenai, too!"

"I'm going back to bed," I whispered. "I'm sick."

Oh, you poor, misguided fools, I thought, when they had driven away. We'll be butchered in Ninilchik, slaughtered in Homer, hanged in Kenai. It's all very well to put on a play for a bunch of your indulgent friends, but performing before strangers—rough, tough fishermen who will cut us to shreds with their webbing knives if we don't amuse them—well, that's something else again. Oh, you fools!

The Ninilchik performace was to be staged in an old school house on top of a hill above the town. It was a good spot, we figured, for a quick getaway—and by that time there were several of the cast members who, having gotten my idea about the folly of performing before strangers, were interested in a quick getaway. Hiding three toboggans at the rear entrance to the school so that we could be sure of making a mad dash to our waiting cars below—where special drivers had been bribed to keep the motors running throughout the duration of the play—we decided all was in readiness: the play could begin.

The audience was composed of about a hundred grim-looking people, the men wearing their moose-skinning knives at their belts and the women, I imagined, holding frozen salmon heads on their laps ready to throw at the first bad joke. The patchwork quilt we were using for a curtain was pulled aside and the show was on.

The play was a bigger hit than at Anchor Point. After the final curtain, the townspeople of Ninilchik poured onto the stage to congratulate the cast. Then the chairs were pushed back, a small orchestra tuned up and we all began to dance. "You'll just have to do a repeat performance tomorrow night," we were told. "We want to see it again."

But we didn't feel like tempting fate a second time. Nevertheless, our reception in Ninilchik had put heart, blood and bones into all of us, and we talked about nothing else on our return trip to our homesteads but "how we'll knock 'em dead in Homer Friday night."

Backstage in the Homer Theater—a moving picture theater, with 250 seats—we bubbled over with exhuberance. We were actors tried and true, and though the audience was bigger than any we had faced before, we were absolutely confident of success. We were feeling so good, in fact, that we assured each other that we would surpass, that night, our previous performances.

To our horror, none of the audience laughed in the proper spots. They sat like statues, and hardly a person cracked a smile. I tried my corniest lines. No response. I wove the name of a local merchant into every scene. No one laughed. The only time they reacted was when, while stumbling off the stage in my role of Henry Gubbins, I accidently tripped and fell against the fake interior of our homesteader's cabin and almost knocked it down. They laughed—but at me, not with me.

In discussing our failure later, we could see no reason for it except that the audience in Homer was too sophisticated for our play. "They've seen too many movies," someone said. "That means they've got something to compare with our brand of entertainment."

"Naw," said someone else. "I think it's because there was a high school play here two nights ago. Maybe they've had enough 'dramy' for awhile."

There was a glum silence. "Well, maybe Kenai'll like us," said someone finally—without, however, much hope in his voice.

It took us two long hours to get to Kenai, 50 miles from Anchor Point, and on the night we traveled in that direction the thermometer had dropped to 30 degrees below zero. To the cast of "Henry Gubbins," huddled in parkas in the back of a truck, it seemed like an endless ride. We sang to keep warm and to keep our spirits up, and I passed around a gallon of dried prunes I had brought along.

Arriving in Kenai, we found we had plenty of time in which to move our simple props into the modern school building which was to serve as our theatre, hang up our curtain and set up the stage. Since Kenai was a fair-sized town, with a population numbering around 1000, we had planned our most elaborate performance. "Henry Gubbins" was to be stretched far beyond its usual limits and a couple of piano solos and another skit had been added to the program. And besides that, I had dug up some dirt on the local townspeople and was prepared to slip it into the action.

The play went along smoothly—but a little too fast. To extend a scene in which I was supposed to be writing a letter to a lovelorn column, I sat there eating prunes and spitting the pits in all directions. The audience seemed to appreciate this piece of business so I kept it up until the entire stage was spotted. They howled when another member of the cast made his entrance on one side of the stage, slipped on a prune pit and slid clear across the stage and out of sight.

While waiting for him to make his entrance again, I decided to do a little extra ad-libbing. Lifting a whisky bottle filled with the traditional stage tea to my mouth, I was prevented from drinking it by a large "clunk!" The tea had frozen solid on its trip in the truck. Shaking the bottle up and down, I remarked, "Well, goldang. What kind of anti-freeze is Kenai Joe putting in his booze these days?"

That line brought down the house: Kenai Joe was a well-known local bar owner.

In another scene I mentioned the name of a man who had just been picked up by the game warden for shooting a moose out of season. The audience roared, but I didn't learn why they found the line so hilarious until afterwards: it seems the wife of the unfortunate hunter had been there that night, accompanied by the game warden's wife.

Yes, our final performance was an unconditional success. Following the last curtain, we were fed by a local women's club, after which we all retired to a nearby bar and dance hall to celebrate a successful run and danced and drank until morning. And as the star of the play, I was the most popular guy in town. I, who had been a stranger, a cheechako, a man to be looked upon with suspicion by the old-timers in the area, was a celebrity for the first time in my life. Everybody from Homer to Kenai knew me now, everybody wanted to congratulate me, and everybody's wife and not a few half-Indian girls fought for the privilege of being my partner in the dance. Acting had been a strain, but if popularity was the result, it had been worth it, I decided.

*

A week later I turned up at a square dance in Anchor Point and was snubbed by one and all. I had shaved off my beard, and there wasn't a soul who recognized me in the role of plain old, unassuming, unglamorous Gordon Stoddard.

Chapter VIII
Ski and the Crazy Cat

SKI, MY MALEMUTE DOG, was only six weeks old when Vern Mutch gave her to me as a parting gift in Homer. At that time, with the thick, heavy coat that gave her the appearance of being square in shape, the upright, pointed ears and the bushy tail arched over her back, she looked like a chow. But her coloring was all her own: she was mostly black, with white stockings on her legs, white on the tip of her tail and on her face. I was grateful to Vern: this friendly, wriggling bundle of fur would be the perfect distraction from my troubles and worries when I started life as a homesteader.

I christened her "Ski" for Stariski Creek, and for whisky, for no reason at all. However, anyone who heard me yell "Damitski!" as often as I did would probably have interpreted the name as being totally of Russian origin and deemed it quite proper in this land the Russians had settled so long before.

During our first couple of weeks together, growing like an expanding balloon and twice as lively, Ski slept at the foot of my sleeping bag in the pup tent I used for shelter while building my shack. One night, hoping for a good long sleep uninterrupted by her scratchings and snufflings, I put her outside. That she didn't like. Ignoring the flap as a means of re-entry, she charged through the side of the tent like a bull through the brush, ripping a great, dog-sized hole and collapsing the tent poles so that both of us were engulfed, enfolded and surrounded by yards of musty, dusty canvas. In a matter of moments the tent was in shreds and a frightened puppy and an enraged homesteader were out in the cold. "Damitski!" I shouted. "Dammit!"

Whenever I left the homestead for a day, I was in the habit of tying Ski to a tree that leaned at a 40-degree angle over the entrance to my tent. Before I departed, I usually fed her from a bucket of clam guts Greasy Grogan had given me after taking me clamming (he kept the clams), then hung the bucket about six feet off the ground on a branch of the tree. Returning at nightfall after a trip to Homer one day, I saw no signs of my dog. Suddenly I heard an almost human belch. I looked up at the hanging bucket. Peering over its side was the puppy's head, a miserable, cross-eyed head, lolling on its neck like a broken toy. Ski had eaten her way through almost four gallons of clam guts and was so bloated she would have to be pried from the bucket. How she had climbed the tree has always been a mystery to me, but it's a cinch she never could stand the sight or smell of clam guts again.

The malemute, an indirect descendent of the wolf, is a natural-born hunter—but not to the sportsman's way of thinking. I had to get used to the idea that once a malemute sights game, nothing on earth can stop him from running it down and swallowing it whole in the shortest possible time. When Ski was still a fairly small pup, I took her with me on a visit to the Mutch home in Homer, where, in honor of my coming, Vern had planned to butcher a couple of chickens for dinner. Vern and I got out to the chicken coop just in time to see Ski dragging a protesting hen—a hen bigger than she was—through the slats. The other chicken was nowhere to be seen, but from the size of Ski's belly we knew where it had gone. "There goes your dinner," said Vern, sadly.

Thereafter, to make up for the social blunder of my dog, I got into the habit of shooting spruce chickens along the road every time I drove into Homer to present to Vern. On one of these occasions I took Ski with me, leaving her in the car when I stopped in front of the drugstore. I joined Vern behind the counter, we got to talking and I forgot all about my chicken-killing dog. Suddenly I jumped up, knocked over a barrel and rushed outside. Just as I had suspected: Ski, her furry body covered with feathers, her jowls dripping with blood, was just finishing off the last of six spruce chickens. "There goes your dinner," I said to Vern.

Ski and the Crazy Cat

Malemutes have another undesirable trait, I discovered: They won't stay home. Ski was no better than the rest, but if she wandered away and was gone all day she at least returned in time for dinner. Eventually, however, she took to wandering in the direction of Greasy Grogan's cabin, and when he began to feed her better food than I could provide, she began to stay away for days at a time. Greasy then gave me an Alaskan name: The Homesteader Who Carries His Dog Home Over His Shoulder.

As the snow began to blanket the country and Ski grew so large she was beginning to elbow me for floor space in my shack, I built her a house of her own. It was a pretty fancy house, with 90-pound roofing on top, tarpaper upholstery inside and a wall-to-wall gunnysack carpet. No other dog, I felt, had ever had it so good. Ski, however, took one look at her new home, then proceeded to rip the gunnysacks out and tear the wallpaper off. She left the roof intact, but only, as far as I could tell, because she liked to climb up onto it and peer in through my window to see what I was doing inside. And when the snow was a foot deep, she ignored the dog house entirely and buried herself in the snow, using her big, bushy tail as a nose warmer. Only when the thermometer dropped to 10 degrees below zero did she return to her house. And even then she didn't need to: by that time her coat, with the heavy undercoat nature provides, was so thick that she could have stood—and even enjoyed—much lower temperatures than that.

During the first cold spell my dog and I had a serious misunderstanding. One particularly icy night I fell asleep in my sleeping bag with a still-burning cigarette between my fingers. Dreaming that I was fighting a forest fire, I awoke choking with smoke. I jumped up, threw open the door and tossed the flaming bag out into the snow. Then I slammed the door, and, shivering in my long underwear, looked out the window. The fire seemed to be out, but Ski was sniffing at the bag. Suddenly she grabbed it and dragged it into her house. "Oh, well," I thought. "It's no good to me anymore." I built up a fire in the barrel stove, rolled up in my two remaining blankets and tried to get back to sleep. But I continued to shiver. Cursing, I got up and built the fire higher. But it was no use: I was still cold. Finally I made a decision. Rushing to the door, I threw it open, leaped the few feet to the dog house in snow that froze my bare toes as they landed, and snatched the bag out from under the sleeping dog. Ski put up a valiant fight for her newly-acquired property, putting all forty pounds of muscle into hanging on to her end of the bag. But I was not to be defeated. With a superhuman effort, I wrenched the bag from her grasp and leaped back into the cabin. Climbing into my bed, I found that there was still enough of it to keep me tolerably warm. But Ski's howling at the moon, a heartrending song of frustration and rage, kept me awake for the rest of the night.

For exercise, Ski and I used to go hunting together, I on snowshoes, she following in my trail. These were the times when she displayed a wicked sense of humor. When I had stopped to examine a track, she would come up behind me and place a large, solid paw on each of my snowshoes. Not realizing she was there, I would take one step and fall flat on my face. And then—I'll swear it—she'd laugh. Life, to Ski, was just one long, delightful game.

There were times, though, when I tried to impress upon her the seriousness of pioneering in Alaska. I had found an old sled someone had abandoned on the beach and decided it was time Ski did some useful work around the place. Making a harness out of old parachute webbing and rope, I tied the dog to the sled, piled on all the firewood it would hold and yelled, "Mush!" Ski looked back over her shoulder at me with a pained expression. She didn't move.

Removing a few of the logs from the sled, I walked ahead of Ski toward the shack. She lunged after me, afraid of being left behind, and the sled, unnoticed, came tumbling after. At the shack, I unloaded the wood, turned the sled and Ski around and started back for another load. When Ski leaped to follow the sled catapulted forward and smacked her sharply in the rear. Yelping in outraged surprise, she rushed past me, knocked me into a snowbank and disappeared down the path leading to the highway. The last thing I heard was a yelp of pain. Then silence.

When I caught up with my dog I was treated to a ludicrous sight. The sled had gone off a bluff into the trees below, and it was hanging, caught in the branches, from one of them. And hanging from the sled, still in her harness, was Ski. Trussed up like a Christian ready for burning at the stake, she looked utterly miserable, and the eyes she turned on me at the sound of my steps were full of reproach. Never again could I lead her to within twenty yards of a sled.

Into every life some rain must fall. Returning to the cabin one day after a short absence, I found Ski tossing a small ball of fur into the air and deftly catching it in her mouth before it could hit the ground. On investigation, the ball proved to be a kitten that one of my friends—or more likely one of my enemies—had left on my doorstep. I took it into the cabin and gave it a bowl of canned milk. From the way it dived into the milk I could tell it was half starved, and when it started chewing busily on my ankle, I was sure of it.

I took the kitten outside to see what it would do. It rushed over to Ski and jumped onto her back, digging in with all twenty claws. Ski, her big amber eyes pools of astonishment, shook it off, grabbed it, tossed it ten feet into the snow. In an instant the cat was back again, asking for more. Twenty times it attacked, twenty times it landed in a snowbank. "I guess it thinks it's a dog," I said to Ski, scratching my head.

After that, to keep peace in the family, I kept the cat in the house most of the time. But I'm not as fond of cats as I am of dogs, and this one's nature proved to be almost oppressively affectionate. All night long it fought to make a bed on my face, and all night long I insisted that it would have to sleep on the floor. Finally, in sleepy exasperation, I would open the door and throw it out into the snow. There would be a few seconds of silence, and then the stillness of the night would be shattered by the howls of a cat in the mouth of a loving dog. Two or three hours later the noise would subside. And in the morning I would find the two of them bedded peacefully together, the cat cuddling up to the dog for warmth and neither of them seeming to see anything extraordinary in the arrangement.

Sunday was bake day for me. Every Sunday morning I would mix up enough dough for four loaves of bread, and every Sunday night I would put them in the oven. On one particular Sunday morning I followed my usual routine. Putting the finished dough in a bowl, I placed it on a shelf over the stove to rise. Then I went outdoors and chopped wood until nightfall. Coming back into the house, I glanced up at the bowl of dough to see if it had risen enough to bake. It had, and besides that, something new had been added. With a shout I flung myself across the room, grabbed the cat and threw it out the door. The next hour was spent in the thoroughly unhumorous job of removing thousands of cat hairs from the mixture.

One night I put the cat upstairs in the storeroom. I hoped it would go quietly to sleep up there and leave me in peace for a change. Presently I heard a scratching noise on the stove pipe which ran from my cook stove up through the second story to the roof. I looked up toward the ceiling to see an almost unbelievable sight. The kitten, using the hot stove pipe like a tree, was backing down it toward the still smoking stove. When it reached the range, it walked leisurely across the lids and jumped into my lap, where it proceeded to wash itself with no evidence of pain. "You're nuts," I said to it. For answer, the cat jumped down from my lap, crossed to the stove and climbed into the hot oven, where it curled up for sleep. After that, I could usually find it when I was looking for it by following the smell of singed hair. Truly, I had acquired a crazy cat.

Somehow, no matter how much I fed the cat it never gained an ounce of weight or an inch in size, though it ate as much as Ski—and more. Whenever it smelled food it went berserk, running madly around the shack searching for the source of supply. If I happened to be the one who was doing the eating, the kitten would dash ferociously up my leg, grab the food from my mouth or fingers and dash frantically away with its prize. Sometimes it missed the food and got my fingers instead, but this was according to the rules: fingers were considered legitimate fodder when nothing else was at hand.

When anything else *was* at hand, though, the cat got it. One day during the spring thaw I had just baked two pumpkin pies and set them on the table to cool. As I sat reading in front of the stove I heard a couple of peculiar noises behind me. Turning my head, I saw the cat standing knee-deep in the center of one pie while tearing huge chunks of filling from the other. This was too much! Grabbing the cat none too gently, I rushed out of the house, ran a quarter of a mile down the road until I came to the bridge that crossed Stariski Creek. The water was at its highest, and huge ice cakes came tumbling down the rapids. Without looking to see where it fell, I tossed the pie-eater over my shoulder into the torrent below. When I heard a splash, I walked away.

But as I walked, I regretted. "Poor little cat," I said to myself. "I shouldn't have done it. He can't help it if he's crazy. No, I shouldn't have done it."

At home I carefully cut around the cat prints and bites, and when I got through, the pies looked almost as good as new. I then felt sorrier than ever. Poor little cat . . . poor little cat. . . .

Two days later I opened the door to a plaintive mew. There stood the cat—dry as a bone and hungrier than ever. He wasn't just crazy: he was indestructible!

I kept the cat for one more day. But the ducking in the creek hadn't changed any of its bad habits. After almost losing another finger to its voracious appetite, I put it in the car and drove up the highway for ten miles. Knocking on all the doors of the homesteads along the road, I finally found a bachelor who had just moved in. When I offered him "a cute kitten" he thanked me profusely. He had been looking for something like that to keep him company, he said. "Thanks again," he said.

"Don't mention it," I said. And I got into my car and hurried home.

Ski hunted for her playmate for several days, and then, apparently, forgot about it. I did, too. But occasionally I thought about the bachelor to whom I had made a gift of the cat. There was one homesteader who would never think of me as a friend.

Chapter IX
The Snow Melted and There It Was

SPRING ON THE KENAI PENINSULA was a noisy event. The frozen creeks and rivers, thawing from the bottom up and the top down, began to flow again, and as they did, they dislodged the remaining chunks of ice and carried them, rumbling and groaning like dyspeptics in pain, toward the sea. When the ice met an obstacle—a fallen log, or a bend in the course of the stream—it jammed. Then, when the water had spread over the whole valley and built up enough pressure to break through the jams, it roared on its way to the inlet, its final home.

By then, the ground that the snow had covered only a few days before had turned into greasy mud. Underneath, only a few inches down, the earth was still frozen hard, but soon that, too, began to thaw. In a month or two the ground had dried out enough so that it could be worked and traveled, the rivers had quieted down and cleared themselves of a lot of winter debris and the mammoth king salmon had started their long, hard trip to the spawning grounds. The country became green all over, the birds returned from their southern resorts and winter was officially "kaput."

It was my first spring in Alaska, and I was financially out of the woods. I had managed to save $30 a month out of my subsistence checks, had received full payment on an old loan in the States, had taken a few odd jobs here and there, had paid all my debts to my family and gotten my car out of hock. Best of all, by building a shack and living in it for seven months, I had "proved up" on my homesteading claim.

All that remained was to make it official. With two of my neighbors acting as witnesses, I made out the necessary papers. In addition to my final filing papers, I filled out a relinquishment form which returned to the government 40 acres of my land that were too far from the highway to do me any good. This would give me a chance to file on another 40 acres some time in the future.

I mailed the papers to the Land Office in Anchorage. After my claim was advertised in the Seward newspaper for a month and no one had come forth to contest my right to the land, they would be sent to Washington, D. C., where a patent would be drawn up in my name and sent to me. From then on the 120 acres would be mine to do with as I pleased.

Anticipating no trouble along legal lines, I felt like an owner already. It was time to look over my domain and see what I had.

What was left after the 40 acres had been lopped off was in the shape of an "L," with the top of the "L" lying across the highway and extending to its foot along a north slope of high-ground timber land. The 40 acres that formed the toe of the "L" lay across the creek valley and up to—and I hoped including—the bluff on the other side. This bluff had a south slope which looked like good growing land and I hoped to be able to find the old survey line and prove that it belonged to me. While there was still a little snow on the ground, I spent a day wandering around the bluff. Finally I found the line. If my calculations were correct, I owned a strip of good flat land 250 feet deep and a quarter of a mile long. With a neighbor's help I measured from the section corner along the line and found my other corners. The strip was mine!

The first thing I did was to look for a good building location. The one I decided upon had a fine view of Stariski Creek, plus a spring which flowed about five gallons a minute only 20 feet down the side of the bluff. Water and a view! Perfect!

I was ready to start chopping down trees. Every morning I would leave my shack and walk the half mile to the new location and go to work. First I would notch 50 trees—spruce, birch and cottonwood—with a double-bit axe. Then I would saw the trees down, one by one.

The Snow Melted and There It Was

Two weeks of this and I had close to 50 large trees and numerous small ones lying crisscrossed on an acre of ground. With another three weeks behind me I had the spruce trees limbed and cut into saw logs and the birch and cottonwood, which were no good for lumber, laid in huge piles ready for the torch.

Waiting for a day when the ground was wet from a rain of the night before, I started to burn the trees I didn't want. This involved sprinkling a pile of them generously with kerosene, applying a match and standing back. The pile would blaze up quickly, the flames reaching for the sky. When it had burned down some, I would throw another batch of logs on the fire. At the end of the day I was singed from head to toe and my clothes were charred from flying sparks. The next day I returned to re-pile the half-burned wood into smaller heaps and burn it to ashes.

Now the clearing was a field of stumps sticking up four feet above the ground. There was nothing else I could do without a fairly large sum of money. I wanted to build a house I could be proud of, a house considerably larger than my shack, and what I had in mind would take more than a thousand dollars. That meant a job.

One day in June I took Ski, together with a sack of dog food, to Red Freimuth's. Red was a new bachelor homesteader who had moved onto the land that bordered me on the south, a veteran of about my own age. He was just starting to raise his own house but he would be glad, he said, to take care of my dog while I was away working. I said goodbye to both of them and headed north, towards Kenai. I had heard rumors that there was a big Army base to be built there, and that there would be work for those who wanted it.

Arriving in the little settlement of Soldotna, ten miles south of Kenai, I looked up the homestead of Howard Lee, who had worked with me at the cannery the year before. The people occupying his house were strangers, but they told me that Howard had moved to a small cabin up the road, was working on a job in Kenai and would be back that night. I found the cabin and waited.

At 8 o'clock my friend showed up. Howard was an ex-Navy fighter pilot, but I had often wondered how he had ever managed to cram his six-feet, four-inch frame into a Hell-cat cockpit and still get his hands free to work the controls. Over coffee he gave me all the dope on the job he was working on—the job about which I had heard rumors. "Gordon," he said, "this job is a cinch. We're clearing 600 acres of ground for the Army and getting paid a banker's salary."

"I've just finished clearing an acre on my homestead," I said. "That's no cinch."

"Sure it's a cinch! And it'll be a cinch to get you on the payroll. You've had *experience*, man!"

"How many hours do you work?"

"Just seven elevens." I considered. Eleven hours a day, seven days a week. It would be tough, but worth it, if the pay was good. "Can you wait a few days while I see if I can get you on?" asked Howard. "You can stay here, if you like."

"I can wait all summer, if necessary!"

Three days later Howard came home and informed me that I was to go to work on the following day. "It was a cinch," he said, when I thanked him.

The next morning the alarm went off at 5:00 and we made our breakfast, jumped into my car and drove the ten miles to Kenai. Arriving at a few minutes to 7:00, we climbed into an old Army truck that was waiting with its load of men. Right on the dot of 7:00 the truck started up and took off down the road going north from town. Five miles farther on we stopped and turned off onto a muddy track into the woods. The D-6 Cat that awaited us there hooked onto the front of the truck and hauled us through a mud-hole two miles long.

Finally we reached what was, apparently, our destination: an immense clearing, with thousands upon thousands of trees pushed into windrows as far as the eye could see. Over the whole hung a blanket of smoke,

The Snow Melted and There It Was

rising from hundreds of small fires burning in the piles of brush stacked everywhere. I later found out that the clearing was roughly over a square mile in size, and that all of the trees had been knocked down and piled up in just a couple of weeks, with a cable stretched between two Cats doing the monumental job.

In the center of the clearing was a small encampment of tents—where the contractors lived, Howard informed me. When the truck came to a stop, I jumped out with the rest of the men, found the boss of the job in one of the tents and signed up. "You're to go to the burning detail today," said the boss. "That guy over there"—he pointed—"will show you what to do."

I was handed a weed burner, five-gallon size, and told to fill it from a 50-gallon drum of stove oil. The weed burner was awkward: when it was full, I had to sit down to work its straps over my shoulders, and then crawl on my hands and knees to a drum to pull myself to a standing position. Cinch? Already this job was no cinch.

Howard, who was to be my partner that day, led me to a long line of unburned birch and spruce, piled high and mixed with dirt and brush. With a full back sprayer he was to spray oil on the base of a pile while I, following along with my miniature flame thrower, was to ignite it. Within two hours we felt like arsonists and stood back to watch the holacaust we had caused. There were about ten acres of fires going as a result of our efforts, and the wind created by the flames was sweeping through the other heaps of brush and threatening to ignite about forty more. We had been told to set fires and more fires, but this exceeded even our expectations. "This sure ought to make the bosses happy!" I yelled over the crackling of the flames. Howard grinned back at me through the smoke. "When you do a job, you should do it WELL!" he shouted.

But suddenly something seemed to be going wrong. Howard noticed it first. "The wind has changed!" he hollered. "Let's get out of here!"

We had been standing at the edge of the woods well

out of the way of the fire, but now the flames were licking hungrily toward us across the fire break. The sparks that shot up from the piles were drifting down into the woods and little spirals of smoke were curling up from the moss under the trees. Howard yelled something about seeing the boss and disappeared through the smoke toward the camp. I turned and ran through the woods, stamping out moss fires as I went while two started for every one I killed. Remembering the tales I had heard about a fire sweeping through a third of the Kenai Peninsula a few years before, I had visions of its happening again—with me—me!—as the firebug.

Then I was surrounded by men who dashed here and there with shovels and axes beating out the destructive little sparks. Four Cats which had been working at other spots in the clearing were now ranging back and forth between the woods and the fire digging up patches of burning moss. It took the entire crew of fifty men and all the equipment at hand to put out the little fires until the wind changed and the danger was over for awhile.

The rest of the crew went home that day at 6:30— regular quitting time—but Howard and I were ordered to stay until 11:30 to patrol the woods. This might have been considered punishment to some—16 hours of work on my first working day—but as Howard and I strolled around looking for errant fires we reminded each other that we would be paid for eight hours at regular time and eight hours at time-and-a-half. Since money was what we were after, why should we complain? We even made plans to start a bigger fire on the following day.

But our plans didn't go through as scheduled. On the next day I was transferred to the brush-cutting crew. The foreman handed me a heavy, double-bit axe, pointed to a patch of four-foot-high willows that stretched away to the horizon and said, "When you finish those I'll find something else for you to do."

With thirty other men armed with axes, I chopped the willows down. They were no bigger around than my little finger so I didn't have to swing my axe very hard, but even the slightest swing would make the axe bury itself in the ground. This meant that the axe had to be sharpened with a file after every hundred strokes—which gave me a rest period, at least. But resting was frowned upon. Every time I stopped to light a cigarette or stretch my back the foreman seemed to be standing only a few feet away, staring at me. A ten-minute break at 10:00, another at 3:00 and a half hour for lunch which was spent mostly in slumber was all the surcease we got from that steady chop-chop-chop, rain or shine. I had to keep reminding myself that in only a few weeks more I could return to my homestead, a tired but a very rich old man.

My first pay day came on a Saturday night. The check was handed to me in the truck and I examined it carefully. My take-home pay for my first full week was $211 out of $265—more than three times the amount I had ever before earned in a week! Gosh! Over a thousand a month for doing the work of a laborer! And if this was what an unskilled worker was paid, what, I wondered, could an experienced man like a Cat operator earn? I stuffed the check into my shirt pocket, unbelieving. It was more than I could cope with at the time. I'd think about it later.

Every day when we got back to Kenai in the truck, Howard and I would climb into my car and follow a routine we had been carrying out ever since I had been staying with him: we would drive to the nearest liquor store and purchase a bottle of Smerinoff Vodka—just about the cheapest potable you could buy in Alaska except for beer or wine. During the ten-mile drive to Soldotna, we would pass the bottle of raw, burning liquor back and forth, and by the time we got home we would be feeling sufficiently light-headed to have forgotten all about our day of grueling toil. The bottle would last us for two homeward trips, after which we bought another. Without it, we felt, we never would have had the strength to drive.

Arriving at the cabin at our usual time—8:00 p.m.—we would try to put something in our stomachs before falling into bed. Our limited supply of dishes was always so dirty that one of us would have to wash a couple of plates while the other opened a can of beans. (The mailman brought our groceries from Seward once a week but by the end of every week we were always down to beans). After dinner we would just have enough energy left to make our lunches for the next day and crawl into bed. And since it was Howard's cabin, he occupied the only real bed; I slept on the mattressless floor in my sleeping bag. At five a.m. that devil's device, the alarm clock, would rouse us, and the whole deadly routine would begin once again.

After a couple of weeks of this we made up our minds to start saving more money. We cut down on the relatively fancy food we had been buying and switched from vodka to beer. With these changes, each of us managed to save almost $200 a week. And in another week we economized still further: we switched from beer to gallons of cheap port. And that was about as low as we could sink. We were winos—filthy, dirty, capitalistic winos.

In the meantime, Howard had been put on the brush crew and we had a new foreman. When we weren't cutting willows we were piling up half-burned stumps and limbs and burning them down to ashes. The foreman was always at hand, never saying a word: just staring. Howard and I worked side by side and talked to make the time go faster, but the foreman didn't approve, and he separated us as often as he could catch us. In retaliation, we would yell back and forth in high-school Spanish, often including the foreman's name in our incomprehensible conversations. This drove the foreman wild, but it got many a laugh from our fellow laborers.

At this time some of the workers were college students up from the States "working their way through school." Howard and I liked to draw them into arguments about politics and other dangerous subjects until most of us were rushing around waving our axes in the air to prove our points. This was lots of fun—and dangerous to the foreman if he tried to break it up.

Another form of amusement was riddle-asking. One of the laborers would ask the riddle and the brush gang would go around mumbling to themselves for days until one of them came up with the answer. This slowed down the actual production but made the days, for us, go faster.

When the crew was all hard at work on the willows and the conversation had died down to zero, you knew that someone's mind was far away. Suddenly there would be a scream, an axe would crash to the ground and a man would sit down in the ashes and pull his shoe off. Another toe gone! This happened fairly frequently and nobody seemed to mind, since it usually meant a free trip to the Seward hospital and plenty of compensation pay. In fact, Howard and I had talked it over and decided that, toward the end of the job, each of us would slice off a toe. Thus we could enjoy compensation checks all winter. I don't know why we didn't do it. I guess we lost our nerve after hearing about one unlucky fellow who, upon emerging after several weeks of happy hospitalization with one less toe, slipped and fell on the hospital steps and broke his collarbone.

Well, the day finally came. No tears were shed, no one begged to be allowed to stay. Everyone just grasped his check in a soot-blackened fist and cheered. And as the truck took us back to town and freedom, I figured out what I had made: in five weeks and two days I had earned $1400, and I would return to my homestead with $1000 in my wallet.

Oh, you crazy Alaska!

Chapter X
Mansion in the Woods

I FELT PRETTY GOOD as I drove down the highway toward my homestead. Now I had enough money to start building my house! I should celebrate—buy myself a beer, or something.

Just as I got this thought I found myself passing Jackinski's Ranch, a bar and liquor store outside of Ninilchik. I backed up, turned off my ignition and went in.

The smoke-filled room was full of commercial fishermen celebrating a successful salmon season and several homesteaders celebrating nothing at all. "Hiya, Stoddard!" called one of the latter. "Join me in a brew."

The man I sat down with was a homesteader I had met at Greasy Grogan's on several occasions. "How's old Greasy making out?" I asked him, to open the conversation.

"Haven't you heard? The old——was found dead three days ago."

I stared at him, unbelieving, as he told me some of the particulars. Greasy had been doing a lot of drinking while I had been gone, and all of his neighbors had gone out of their way to avoid him. When he hadn't made an appearance on the local scene for over a week someone had dropped in to investigate. He was lying on his bunk, an empty whisky bottle in one inert hand. On his chest sat his cat, gazing hungrily into the blank, unseeing eyes.

I didn't stay to hear any more. I had had no love for Greasy, but this ——! I gulped down my beer and raced for the car.

Arriving at Red Freimuth's house to pick up Ski, I heard the rest of the story. Greasy had been buried two days before—in a simple box made of rough spruce boards—on a hill overlooking Cook Inlet across the road from Red's place. Red had officiated as one of the gravediggers and had given Greasy his last ride, using his old Army truck as a hearse. After the funeral, bottles people had been saving for a special occasion were brought out of hiding and everyone drank to Greasy's demise. You could hardly say that I mourned the passing of Greasy but I knew that I would miss him and his own particular Alaskan brand of hospitality.

Returning to my shack with Ski, I set up housekeeping again, and after a few days' rest I was ready to start work on my building project. But before I could begin, I would have to clear the clearing of stumps and take my sawlogs, somehow, to the mill.

I rented a farm tractor in Anchor Point and hired its owner, Flem Clemson, to drive it. Together, we began to pull the building logs from the clearing and stack them off to one side. It was hot work: in Alaska, where your blood thickens during the long, cold winter, temperatures like 85 degrees seem almost too hot to bear. And it was 85 degrees, that day.

We had only stacked about a hundred logs when I felt the earth shaking and heard the rumble of a Caterpillar tractor coming down the highway. "Oh, no!" I said to Flem. "I hired a Cat for tomorrow to push out the stumps. We're not ready for him yet."

I ran out to the road and flagged the Cat down. The driver told me that he had finished his work on another homestead down the road earlier than he had expected and "might as well do your job right now." At fourteen dollars an hour I couldn't keep him waiting. Showing him the start of a road I wanted him to punch through the woods 600 feet from the highway to the clearing, I rushed frantically back to the clearing to get the rest of the saw logs out of the way before he arrived. I figured it would take at least half a day for a D-6 Cat to make a road and that if we hurried we'd have plenty of time. But, within two hours, the clankety-clank-roar of the Cat and the crashes of falling timber, coming closer all the while, told us that the huge tractor was almost upon us. And it was: suddenly, knocking a large spruce tree into the clearing, the Cat came charging through.

"What do I do now?" inquired the driver, shutting his throttle down.

I told him to begin on the stumps but leave the saw logs. Starting up the Cat, he made a rush at the nearest stump, bumped into it, lifted it clear from the ground. Then he moved on to the next stump, and the next. Then, pushing them around until he had collected them into a neat little trio, he nudged them ahead of him and shoved them over the edge of the bluff.

Flem and I watched, fascinated. Then we shook ourselves and got back to the business of pulling the saw logs out of the way of the Cat. At this point Red Freimuth showed up and, like the good neighbor he was turning out to be, offered his services. With mightier muscles than mine, he lifted the smaller logs and carried them by hand to the edge of the clearing. He was a great help. By afternoon the stumps had disappeared and the logs were piled and ready for hauling to the sawmill. But before I paid off the Cat operator I had him dig a cellar for my house. This he accomplished in an hour flat, charging me $150 for the whole day's work. Boy, I thought, remembering the last time a cellar had been dug on my land and the mosquitoes and whitesox and no-see-ums that had made it such a terrible job. Boy, what a little money can do!

Renting Red's old four-wheel-drive Army truck and borrowing a flat-bed farm trailer from another neighbor —what would a pioneer in any wilderness do without neighbors?—I got to work on the logs. I had realized that I couldn't accomplish the task alone and had hired Red to help me. It was a simple job, but a laborious one. Maneuvering the trailer alongside a pile of logs, we would roll them, one at a time, onto the bed, and when we had accumulated a load of eight or nine logs of from eight to 24 feet in length we would head for the sawmill $2\frac{1}{2}$ miles away. Rolling the logs off at the mill, we would then turn around and go back for more. It was a good day when we could complete four of these trips, but at the end of the week all the logs were at the mill and we had begun to take the finished lumber back to the clearing.

Mansion in the Woods

Previously, I had given the sawmill owner a list of the total lineal feet of three-sided house logs I wanted—three sides cut, one side with the bark left on—and the dimensions of the other lumber I required. I had paid him seven cents per lineal foot for cutting the six-inch house logs, $25 a thousand board feet for the lumber; and when all of it was piled next to my cellar pit it seemed to me that I had gotten my money's worth—particularly since the use of my own trees had cut my lumber bill just about in half.

Before letting Red's truck get away, I dug up several loads of sand and gravel from a spot near the highway—more free material!—and hauled it to the cellar pit for use in the concrete foundation. All was in readiness for the hardest stage of the game: the actual construction of my house.

The Blazo lantern burned night after night in my shack as I pored over the plans I had drawn. I changed them, changed them back again, changed them again, finally decided that my original plans were the best, after all. The house I had in mind would be 16 by 24 feet, with two stories and four rooms — a living room and kitchen downstairs and a bedroom and storeroom above. It would be the biggest bachelor house within 22 miles. For a guy who had hardly ever built anything more pretentious than a chicken coop, it was going to be a tremendous task. But there's a saying in Alaska: something to the effect that a homesteader is never satisfied until he has built his third house. And here I was on my second. There was only one way to find out the truth of the saying: get going.

It was a little hard to start. I looked forward to the sense of accomplishment that would come, I knew, from watching the house take shape, but before that there would be the groundwork—the dirty work—to do: in the cellar. Sighing, I reached for a shovel.

First I had to dig the loose sand out of the bottom of the cellar pit until I reached solid gravel, which would serve as a base from which to build my foundation forms.

This I did. Then I made the pier forms, setting them eight feet apart along the sides and ends of the pit and placing two log pilings in the middle, the piers, when poured, to be a foot in diameter and extend from the gravel base to a foot above ground level. Then I built a wall form to connect all the piers; a six-inch concrete wall, I hoped, would insure a solid base for my plate.

Using a mortar box I had contrived for cement-mixing, I poured concrete into all of the forms. This took me two days. Then, while the concrete was still wet, I laid 2"x8" planks all the way around to serve as plates and outline the shape of the house, driving spikes into the wood and through the cement to hold them tight. While the concrete dried, I used the time to peel the bark off the 1400 feet of house logs.

When I had stripped the foundation forms, I was ready to start the more satisfying job of raising my logs. They were, of course, still green, and it was difficult to get them into place. I dragged them in easy stages and set them on the plate, leaving two inches of plate jutting into what would be the inside of the house to set my floor joists on. When I had the first round of logs on and nailed onto the plate, I put some more plate across the two pilings I had previously placed in position in the cellar. That center support would hold up the middle of the sixteen-foot floor joists. I then cut the floor joists and placed them on the plate, nailing them 18 inches apart. Finally I placed enough boards on the joists to make a base for putting up the rest of the logs.

Laying logs horizontally at the rate of three rounds a day, I had my walls up to ceiling height in five days. Each layer of logs was spread with a mixture of tar and asbestos before the next layer went on, and each log had been fastened to the log beneath it with ten-inch spikes. Openings for doors and windows had been left, and the whole thing was beginning to look like a real house.

For my downstairs ceiling or upstairs floor joists (take your choice) I used some of the longest house logs, laying them on the top round of logs and notching the ends so that they fit exactly between the walls and held them firmly in place. I placed them two feet apart and hoped that they would be strong enough to support my upper floor.

Now I had to put my floor boards on. Before starting the job, I looked them over. Some of them were an inch and half thick at one end and half an inch at the other, and all of them were very green. If I wanted an even floor, I realized, I would have to take them back to the sawmill and have them planed.

For two days I shuttled back and forth between the mill, taking small loads of boards in my car, having them planed to a standard thickness and bringing them back again. Nailing them down, after that, didn't take too long. I was ready to start in on the top half of the house.

I built the four upstairs walls with rough lumber. Then I built the peaked roof, using 2x4's for rafters. I should have used 2x6's instead, but I didn't think of it at the time. On each side of the upstairs room I put in a dormer section to be made up of three windows apiece —a small concession to looks which would break the monotony of the roofline. When I had finished, the whole "attic" looked messy: rough, green lumber, I knew, doesn't make the smoothest interior in the world. But as I turned from that task to another I promised myself that I would cover up all the defects with "something nice" later on.

Now that the shell of the house was done, I started seeing all the mistakes I had made in its construction. But at the same time I couldn't help feeling proud of myself for doing as well as I had. And at this point there wasn't much more I could do until the windows, roofing, back door, screen door and cookstove I had ordered from Montgomery Ward's in Portland weeks before arrived in Homer by boat. But, oh yes: a front door. Every house must have a fancy front door. I made one of three planed 2"x12"'s with plenty of knots to give it character and affixed three short peeled slabs as crosspieces.

Two weeks later a boat docked at Homer carrying, as its most precious cargo, the balance of my building materials. Red hauled it all out to my homestead in his truck and I continued where I had left off. The upstairs windows went in easily, but the downstairs windows were something else again. I had learned from other homesteaders in the area that it takes at least two years for the logs in a log house to shrink and settle into permanent position, and that if you put in your windows to stay you'll regret it later. With this in mind, I placed the windows with only nails to hold them and left a two-inch space above them filled with chinking cotton and caulking rope.

Hanging the back door was only a matter of moments, and when I had hung the screen door outside it to keep out the mosquitoes, no-see-ums and whitesox, I stood back to admire the effect. It looked pretty good, and with the back door open and the screen door shut I would have air, since none of my windows were the kind that opened.

Next I moved the cookstove — Montgomery Ward's finest wood and coal burner—into the kitchen with Red's help and put the stove pipe up. At the same time I brought in a new barrel stove with a ready-made door and placed it in the living room, putting up its stove pipe, too.

All that was left to be done before I could move into "the fanciest bachelor home on a homestead on the Kenai Peninsula"—as people had begun to call it—was to cover the roof with 90-pound roofing. Red Freimuth came to my assistance, agreeing to help me with my roof if I would help him with his. Struggling up the steep, pitched roof, we laid the rolls of green paper from the bottom up, holding on with one hand, two feet and lots of extra nerve. The tacks were pounded in every four inches, the edges were trimmed, the hot tar was applied on the overlaps—and we were through.

The next day Red helped me move all my belongings from the old shack to the new mansion. The house was still just two big rooms, bare of furniture, bare of the partitions which would eventually make it a four-room dwelling. The wind whistled through numerous unseen cracks and holes, the walls creaked and groaned and the barrel stove balked at every attempt to start a fire in it. But it was mine—all mine—and I was proud of it.

After a few days of feeling like a property owner and patting myself on the back at every opportunity, I began to worry about earning some more money to get me through the winter and pay for finishing the interior of the house. I would need plenty of cash to put insulation on the walls, cover the floor with something to keep the air from coming up through the already widening cracks between the boards, build partitions and do all the odds and ends that would have to be done. The house wasn't finished by a long shot.

While I was pondering my problem, it was solved for me in the form of a letter from one of my former fellow workers at the cannery in Kenai, George "Buffalo" Bison. "Come at once," wrote George from Cooper's Landing, a mining settlement far up the Kenai River. "There's a construction outfit building a road near here. You can probably get a job."

It was the last part of September when I regretfully locked my magnificent front door, climbed into my car, took Ski over to board at Red's and headed up the road again.

Chapter XI
Home Brew

COOPER'S LANDING consisted of a post office and three or four shacks perched on the banks of the Kenai River with the mountains looming behind. All of its inhabitants lived—rent-free, of course—on mining claims. But that didn't mean that there was any mining done. In all the time I was there, I never heard of a Cooper's Landing digging for anything more valuable than water.

No, I'll take that back: my friend George Bison, a fast man with a story, once spread the word that he had found some gold while digging the cellar for his house. Nobody ever saw the gold, but George listed his labor in digging the cellar as his "assessment work" on his claim for that year and got away with it, I'm told.

George was a stocky, dark-complected man of about 40 who owned up to being one-quarter Indian, which may or may not have accounted for the way his scalp jumped an inch whenever he experienced an emotion. He and his wife, Clara, had arrived in Alaska during the same summer as I, a fact which, because we were all greenhorns together and therefore shunned by the bulk of the populace that year, had formed a strong bond between us.

Probably the outstanding thing about George, as I look back on him, was his sense of "hospitality." Before he had completed clearing the ground for his cabin, he had prepared a 30-gallon barrel of home brew against the coming of possible guests. And when a guest arrived, everything was dropped while George leaped for a glass, dipped it into the barrel and extended it, foaming and dripping, with a bow and a smile—then filled his and Clara's glasses and continued to fill them until both hosts and guests were sodden.

Blond, thin and nervy, Clara was her husband's complete opposite in temperament and looks, and though she could empty a glass of brew with the best of them, she couldn't hold it with the least. When sober, she was a fairly gracious hostess; when drunk, she was a fishwife. Needless to say, life was never dull at the Bisons'.

After a couple of days of recovering from too much of George's brand of welcome, I made contact with the road-building outfit George had mentioned in his letter and went to work on a culvert as a laborer. My job, for ten hours a day, six days a week, involved nothing more complicated than tightening up the thousands of nuts on the thousands of bolts which held the five-foot metal culverts together. As each section of each culvert was combined, I stepped forward with my wrench, poked the bolts through their holes, spun on the nuts and tightened them. A few days at this monotonous occupation and I was ready for the nuthouse, but the bank president's salary I was receiving prevented me from bloodying my wrench on the foreman's head, as I often felt like doing. For $200 a week, I would have tightened the nuts with my teeth!

But I have an unfortunate habit: every time I do something very intensively during the day, I dream about it at night. Not good dreams, either: nightmares. In my sleeping bag on the floor at the foot of the Bisons' bed—which was the only place in their 16x12-foot cabin they could find to put me—I tossed and groaned and tightened nuts all night long. One well-remembered night something awoke me, and I rose up in fright to find myself holding a violently struggling object in my right hand. When a piercing shriek shocked me fully awake, I realized what I was clutching: a human big toe, and not my own. I dropped it as though it had been a poisonous snake and pulled the covers up over my head.

From the safety of my shelter I listened to a strange conversation. "George! George! Wake up!" That was Clara, and there was terror in her voice.

"Mmmmmm? Mmmmmmm?" That was George.

"Wake up! There's something in this bed. It bit me!"

"Why don't you shut up and go to sleep? There's nothing in this bed."

"Yes, there is! Yes, there is! It bit my big toe! George,

I'm *not* going back to sleep until you search this bed."

"All right, all right. I'll search the bed." Silence. "Well, what did I tell you? There's nothing here. You're drunk, Clara. Just drunk, that's all."

During the man-wife argument I lay as still as a corpse at a wake. And needless to say I didn't get much more sleep that night.

In the morning, after I had finished breakfast and was heading for my car, George intercepted me. "Say, Gordon," he said. "What was the idea of playing around with my wife's toe last night?" I had underestimated his astuteness.

I opened my mouth, shut it again. Then I croaked, "George, you won't believe this."

"It'd better be good," said George, looking mean.

"George, last night I was dreaming I was tightening a nut on a bolt on the culvert. Somehow Clara's toe got into the dream. I thought it was a nut, I guess. Believe me, George, I was just tightening a nut!"

George stared at me for a moment and then burst into raucous laughter. When he could talk, he choked, "Gordon, *I* believe you. But will Clara?"

Maybe Clara believed me, but from the way she treated me from then on I gathered she didn't like what she believed. Anyway, on the night after the toe episode I found my sleeping bag moved to a spot on the floor next to the home brew barrel. Heretofore, George had been unwilling to trust even his own brother that close to his liquid assets.

The Bisons spent a great many of their leisure hours in visiting their numerous neighbors—the people who lived on mining claims on the hills above Cooper's Landing proper—and testing the newest batches of home brew. Sometimes I saw them only once or twice a week, when they returned for a change of clothing. This left me in sole charge of the house, the livestock and the chores.

The most important chore was that of building a fire in the stove—a barrel stove, like mine. One night when I

Home Brew

returned from work it was so cold that I proceeded to the task immediately. To start the fire in a hurry, I poured some stove oil over the wood from a coffee can on a nearby shelf. When I threw in a lighted match, the oil flamed up but the wood didn't catch. "Not enough oil," I muttered, heading for a five-gallon "extra stove oil" container I knew to be outdoors somewhere. I stumbled around in the dark until I bumped into what felt like the war surplus gas can I was looking for. Filling the coffee can from it, I rushed back into the shack, opened the barrel stove door and slopped a generous amount of the liquid onto the still smoldering logs. Then I struck a kitchen match on the top of the stove and threw it in, too.

Phwooooooom! I leaped back, throwing up an arm to fend off the explosive burst of flame. The coffee can dropped from my hand, and the fuel in it—which I realized now was not stove oil at all but a high-pressure appliance fuel used in Coleman lanterns—spread over the floor, caught fire and started to eat away at the dry floor boards and up my trousers.

I was stupefied. I had a sudden vision of the Bisons returning to their home to find it a pile of ashes, and of me, down on my knees in abject apology, offering them my homestead in exchange. I felt like a drowning man going down for the first time. That thought reminded me of water and galvanized me into action. Snatching up two pails of soapy wash water from beside the door, I splashed their contents over the fire and myself. The water only served to spread the burning fuel over a wider area. Rushing wildly around, I entangled myself in a pair of George's wet coveralls hanging from the clothesline stretched across the room. I snatched them down and beat at the flames.

In a surprisingly short time the fire was out, but as I stood there, coughing and panting, I saw a flickering light under the floor boards. I opened the trap door leading to the cellar to find the floor joists and storage shelves ablaze. I grabbed a kettle of cold moose soup from the kitchen stove and quenched the flames.

Then, shaking with delayed reaction, I cleaned up the mess. When I was through, the cabin looked cleaner and neater than I had ever seen it before, and I was sure—or or almost sure—that the Bisons, particularly if they returned during the night under the influence of home brew, would never notice that there had been a conflagration.

But I was wrong. The next morning, the first thing George said to me was, "Gordon, was there by any chance a fire here last night?"

"How did you know, George?" I countered, playing for time.

"Well, my coveralls are missing a seat and a leg. Besides that, the smell of smoke was pretty strong when we came home last night. What happened, anyway?"

I told him the story in a few short, humorous sentences, acting out my part in the fire with violent motions. This drew a few chuckles from George, and I knew that my position as star boarder was still secure.

But when I had finished my tale George's face grew serious. "Gordon," he said, his scalp rising. "Thank God you were here to put the fire out!"

And then there was the Sunday I shall always remember as "The Great Chicken Massacre." For weeks I had been helping George with his nightly chore: putting 300 chickens to bed. This was no simple feat. It involved running each chicken down separately, capturing it amid squawks and flutterings, adding it to an underarm collection of two or three and flinging the lot into the very small chicken house and slamming the door fast. And as the chickens became faster and warier, the job took longer and longer—sometimes as much as two good, full hours.

When all the chickens were ensconced in their undersized sleeping quarters they were a sight to see. If you opened the door a crack, you got the impression of an immense mass of eyes and feathers reaching from floor to ceiling. I used to get a kick out of the idea that if the key chicken at the bottom of the pile ever lost its balance, the other 299 would come tumbling down like a flood from a broken dam.

Every night when we had finished our chore, George would go into the house and lay down the law to Clara. "Now, Clara, listen to what I say for a change!" he would shout. "Don't let those chickens out tomorrow. Leave 'em in. Gordon and I are sick and tired of chasing them all over the lot every night."

"But, George," Clara would protest. "They'll die! They'll smother to death!"

"I don't care if they do! I oughta cut all their heads off, anyway. They're not worth the trouble they cause."

But every morning Clara let the chickens out, and every evening, when I came home from work, George and I put them to bed. Finally George lost his patience. On a Saturday night, he announced to one and all that he was going to kill all the chickens the next morning and sell them in Seward.

Sunday arrived and all the preparations had been made. George began the process by chopping off chicken heads with a double-bit axe. He then dipped the carcasses in a tub of hot water and hung them upside down on nails protruding from the side of the chicken house. It was my job to pull the feathers off and transport the bodies to the house, where Clara was waiting to eliminate the pinfeathers. Our work proceeded at a good pace with the help of a jug of Cabin Still Whisky.

On my first trip into the cabin with a load of chickens, however, I found Clara seated on a stool beside the home brew barrel with a rubber tube in her mouth. Pausing only for a second in her project of syphoning home brew down her throat, she waved a hand vaguely and said, "Put 'em down. Put 'em down anywhere." I laid the chickens on the floor beside her and left.

On my second and third trips into the cabin the scene, except for the growing pile of naked chickens on the floor, remained unchanged. By noontime the number of plucked bodies in the cabin, their pinfeathers still where nature had put them, had risen to an even hundred and looked a lot like the funeral pyre of a defunct Hindu prince. And Clara, unperturbed, continued to suck on her tube.

I decided to say nothing to George of the situation. I just went back to where he was still decapitating chickens and said, "When do we eat?"

"As soon as I get through with this one," he replied. "By the way: how's Clara coming along with those pinfeathers?"

"George," I said, "you'd better go in and see for yourself."

George's scalp lifted an inch and he turned and walked rapidly into the cabin. The door slammed shut, but from behind it I could hear the sharp words of a verbal battle. Then came a thump. Then another thump. I thought I'd better go in and see what was happening.

I opened the door on a picturesque tableau. George was standing with an arm upraised, and in his hand was a chicken that he was just about to throw at Clara. On the opposite side of the room, Clara was in a similar pose —only she held a chicken in *each* hand. As I stood there, staring, they both let fly, and in a second the air was full of reactivated corpses, some of which, unfortunately, missed their intended targets and ricocheted off me. Plucked chickens were everywhere, and on the floor, where several of them had landed for the second time that day, a spreading puddle of home brew from the overturned barrel added an extra stench — and the final touch — to the scene of carnage.

Quietly I left the Bison mining claim, and on the following day I found new quarters. A couple of weeks later, having been laid off the road-building job, I returned to my homestead. I never did find out what happened to the Bisons or their chickens after that. I made no effort: I had lost my taste for home brew.

Chapter XII
Neighbors

THE BIG SNOWFLAKES drifted slowly past the window, then whirled away in a sudden gust of wind. Beyond them—if I took the trouble to wipe the mist from the glass—I knew what I would see. The ground would be invisible under its clean, white sheet—a sheet that would be, I was certain, fully one foot deep. The solid lines of spruce, standing up like groups of spun candy cones, would be broken here and there by a birch which bent precariously under its burden of snow like a fat man stretching for his toes. But there would be nothing else: no sign of life. The first real snowstorm of my second winter in Alaska was well under way.

The wind died down. It was so quiet you could have heard a rabbit drop half a mile north. Snug beside the barrel stove with a new science fiction pocket book in my lap, I did take the trouble to lean forward and wipe the mist from the glass with my hand. Gazing down on the creek valley below, I echoed the words of the song blaring from the dry-cell battery radio: "Baby, it's cold outside."

I chuckled, remembering how I had kidded my sister about the weather in Alaska. "If, as you say, it's 30 degrees below zero *outside*," she had written, "just how cold is it *inside?*" "Twenty degrees below," I had replied by return airmail.

That wasn't quite true: it was warm, there beside the stove. Or at least my front was warm, and pretty soon I would turn my back on the fire and get that warm, too. In the meantime, I had everything I needed: a house of my own, a good book, plenty of food and lots of time in which to do nothing at all. What more could I ask?

One of the nicest things about Alaska, I reflected, is the way the weather controls your life. You work hard during the summer, when the midnight sun gives you plenty of daylight hours in which to do it. But in the winter, when the snow and the cold and the lack of light make working outside virtually impossible, you can loaf through an entire season, if you want. And there's nothing you can do to change the situation, so why worry about it?

Naturally there are chores to be done: chopping firewood, emptying the garbage, cleaning up the house when there's no more walking room left. But if something more important comes up—say an invitation to a pinochle session, or an urge to go hunting—these may safely be postponed until a more auspicious time. The point is: you don't *have* to do anything.

But as it happened, I did have a couple of plans for that winter: because the walls of the new cabin were still leaking a few icy blasts from time to time, I expected to do some inside finishing. And I hoped to dig a well in my cellar. But I could take it easy. There was no hurry about it. I had the whole winter before me. . . .

When I finally got around to thinking seriously about my winter projects, it wasn't necessary to toss a coin: I decided to do the easier job first. And luckily I had saved enough money from my Cooper's Landing venture to finance the deal.

I went into Homer and bought enough hardboard—a very cheap inside finishing material made of compressed spruce fiber—to cover all the floors and walls. For a week I slapped it on, enjoying the sight of smooth surfaces growing where rough surfaces had been before. And when I was finished, and after I had erected a partition to separate the kitchen from the living room, I painted the kitchen a pale green with water-base paint and suddenly had a light, cheery room. I left the hardboard in the living room its natural brown color and it looked like what it was intended for, too. In fact, the whole house looked a hundred percent better.

But something was missing: a rug. Yes, I needed a rug for the living room, the room in which I slept and spent most of my time—a rug to keep my bare feet warm when I got up on cold winter mornings. The first chance I got, I drove into Homer and bought one—a green fibre rug, large enough to cover most of the floor. Proudly I laid it down. No other homesteader in the area had such a rug. In fact, no other homesteader owned a rug at all. Would they think I was trying to put on the dog? I didn't care if they did.

What next? Oh, yes: curtains and blinds. I wrote my mother in California and explained my needs, and very shortly some curtains arrived by air. The blinds came later—from a mail order house in Seattle.

That did it. I had used up all the money I had put aside for inside improvements for the year. But now I felt that my house was something special, something unusual for the homesteading country. I could rest in peace.

No, I couldn't. There was the well to be dug.

I picked out a spot in the corner of the cellar directly under the kitchen and started to excavate. Under the thin surface of dirt I found layer after layer of gravel, most of which could easily be pried out by hand. After scooping it up in coffee cans and taking out ten or twenty bucketfuls every morning — the work of two hours — I would knock off for the day, though sometimes I had spurts of enthusiasm and worked for three hours. And gradually the 4x4-foot hole grew deeper.

Occasionally a setback bit into my loafing time. At ten feet, I found that I would have to crib up the sides of my hole to keep from being buried alive; I did it with some birch boards I had been saving for furniture. And then, the gravel I had taken out was always theatening to slide into the hole. I would wait for a fairly good, sunny day, then start carting it upstairs, bucket by bucket, and taking it out into the snow and spreading it around the house, hoping that by spring, when the snow melted, I would have a nice gravel, unmuddy yard.

At fifteen feet I began to lose some of my enthusiasm: I had planned on hitting water long before then.

At seventeen feet I plunged my hand down after some more gravel and pulled it away wet. Eureka! The water was ice cold, and I knew that it must be from the same source as my spring. All I needed now was a pump, which I wouldn't be able to buy until the following summer. But in the meantime, would I have something to show the next visitor who happened along! The only well for miles around! Now I *did* have the fanciest bachelor establishment on the Kenai Peninsula. A house with running—well, almost running—water!

I knew I wouldn't have to wait long before showing off my improvements. The situation had changed since the winter before—my first winter as a homesteader. That year, until my success in "Henry Gubbins' Mail Order Wife," I had been an unknown quantity to most of my neighbors. Though I knew most of them by sight and name and was quite friendly with several of them, I wasn't apparently, on most of the visiting lists. But this winter I was not only apt to glance out my window at any time of day to see two carsful of families driving up, but as an eligible bachelor—even when there were no eligible daughters around—I was often besieged by invitations to dinner. In Alaska, I had discovered, the wintertime is the social time. In the summer, people are too busy working to play.

The Keelers and the Baileys, whom I had originally met through the late Greasy Grogan, were the two families with whom I exchanged visits most often. The Keelers, a family of five, had come to Alaska from Oregon in 1948, purchased eighty acres on the banks of the Anchor River and started a small sawmill there. When I first made their acquaintance, they were in the process of homesteading more land two miles south of my homestead and had moved their mill to the new location. I had gotten to know them rather well through pinochle parties, through the community doings at the Anchor Point one-room schoolhouse, and through dealing with Lawrence Keeler, a man in his 50's, at his sawmill, where his two teen-aged sons were willing workers except in moose-hunting and fishing and trapping season.

Lorna Keeler, somewhat younger than her husband, had a well-deserved reputation for being the bachelor's friend in time of need, and I had fallen into the habit of running to her for help whenever I had had an accident. During my first winter in Alaska, when I was still the greenest of greenhorns, I had been out in the woods with my double-bit axe trying to clean up some brush when the axe bounced back from an especially springy limb and hit me in the eye. I dropped the axe into the snow and put both hands up to my face. A deep cut in my eyebrow and cheek was streaming blood, but the steel frames of my glasses, which had turned the edge of the blade (and now lay broken at my feet), had saved my eye. Stumbling blindly through the drifts to my shack, I had tried to stop the flow of blood. Unsuccessful, I started for my car, remembered that it was still being repaired from the accident I had had in the fall, then staggered down the highway toward the Keelers' homestead. When I arrived there, Lorna Keeler had washed the wound and gently, expertly bandaged it with some clean napkins.

"I'm glad you came to me," I remembered her saying as she waved away my thanks. "There's no doctors around here. Folks just have to help each other." Then she told me of the time she had contracted pneumonia in the middle of the winter when she and her family had lived at Anchor Point about two miles off the main highway. Lawrence had rounded up all the neighbors and they had dug a road through the snowdrifts to the main road and dragged Mrs. Keeler there in a jeep. At the highway she had been transferred to a car which drove her to Homer, and from there a plane had flown her to the hospital in Anchorage, 200 miles away. "I recovered," she said simply, in ending the story.

At one time, Lorna said, there had been an emergency plane which, when radioed, would land on the beach at the Point to pick up people who were dangerously ill. But after one woman had cried wolf once too often with a simple stomach ache, the plane had stopped coming. That left only the hospital at Seward, 150 miles away by highway, and a doctor at Seldovia, fifty miles away across the bay from Homer, as islands of medical help, but these two spots were almost impossible to reach in an emergency because of the lack of proper transportation. "So you just come to me when you're hurt," said Lorna Keeler. And I always did.

In the food department, too, the Keelers had proved to be the special friends of the unmarried men of the community—especially to the ones who preferred good, home cooking to their own. Often they invited me and some of the others to dinner, and if I ever happened to drop in without an invitation while they were eating, it was always a case of "Have you eaten? No? Well, draw up a Blazo box and fall to." It was in the baking of pies, particularly, that Lorna excelled. She baked the best pies in the area and the most. No matter when I passed by there would always be a pile of five or six pies of all kinds on the sideboard, and Lorna always got a kick out of saying, when she saw me eyeing them, "I just knew you were coming, Gordon. You can smell my pies two miles away."

But good things must be paid for. Shortly after digging my well, I made up my mind to give a Christmas party for the Keelers and rang Red Friemuth in on the deal. On Christmas morning at my house Red and I began our preparations. The baking of a ham, biscuits and several pies, and the making of salads and other assorted dishes took up a good part of the day, and we had no more than finished when our guests arrived. In addition to the Keelers and their children—the two teen-aged boys and a younger girl—there were Mrs. Keeler's sister and her young daughter and "Old Man Smitty," who was a house guest of the Keelers at the time. I counted heads and decided that we had provided just about enough food. And luckily, there had been enough pots to cook it in and there were plenty of dishes on which to serve it: my family in California had sent me quantities of those things as Christmas presents.

Everything was in readiness. I had moved my big kitchen table out into the front room and set Blazo boxes around it for chairs, adding my bed as a davenport, bench or what-have-you. Too, there were a couple of card tables (Red's) to hold the extra supplies. The Christmas tree, a young spruce, had been decorated with strings of chinking cotton and sprinkled generously with soap chips, and there were presents underneath it for everyone.

"Oh, boy!" said the kids, spotting the tree. But Lorna Keeler had eyes for nothing but my new rug, which had turned out to be the same shade of green as the tree. "My!" she marveled. "Wherever did you get it? It's—it's beautiful! Imagine, a bachelor with a real rug to walk on. Why, I bet it's the only rug for fifty miles!"

Then she noticed my curtains and shades, and her compliments made me feel that, as far as Alaska was concerned, anyway, I was a success as an interior decorator. Encouraged, I conducted the entire party on a tour of the house to show them all the new improvements, including the dark hole in the cellar that would some day be a working well. And when I received enthusiastic congratulations from all, I knew that my Christmas party was made. The only sour note came when Lorna said, "Gordon, what you need now is a wife to keep the place clean." How well I knew it.

No one made any complaints as he wolfed the dinner down. After the meal, we cleared off the table and started another of our never-ending pinochle games while the kids drank punch and read my magazines. Suddenly I noticed that two of the children were frothing at the mouth. I took the sick looks on their faces for a slam at my cooking and their parents yelled things like "hydrophobia!" until I observed that the punch pot, my large-size pressure cooker, was sitting under the Christmas tree. Apparently someone had bumped into the tree and knocked some of the soap chips into the pot: it was full of suds—and so were the kids. This added the touch to the party that would make it an event to be talked about for years.

The Baileys—man, wife and four children—occupied

the next homestead to the Keelers'. They had moved into the area at the same time as I; in fact, in comparing notes after we became acquainted, we found out that we must have passed each other many times on the Alcan Highway while driving up from the States. Originally from a small town in Ohio, where Mr. Bailey had worked as an electrician, they had bought their homestead—complete with an already-built log house—from a bachelor who had wanted to return to the States. Immediately they had begun to build a small summer business out of a gas station, restaurant and tourist cabins. They had been successful, and there were no adopted Alaskans in the Homer area more enthusiastic about their chosen home than the Baileys. Fred Bailey said to me once: "Gordon, this is a hard life we lead up here at times. But where else can a man start out with little or nothing and end up owning his own business in just a couple of years? Why, we wouldn't trade what we've got here for the best job in the States. My business is pretty small, now, but even when it gets bigger I'll be able to take time off when I feel like it and go fishing and hunting. By gosh, this is the life!" And I agreed with him.

Looie the Goat Man—as everyone called him—was another of my neighbors. Acting as caretaker for a homestead whose owner had died, he lived a half mile away in a little one-room round log cabin. He was the most independent man in the whole region: he kept a herd of thirty goats for milk and meat, maintained a small flock of chickens for eggs and raised the best potatoes "in the whole danged country." At one time during his forty years of residence in Alaska he had raised foxes, too, but when the female mind had veered to ermine and mink he had given it up as a bad job.

The first time I met Looie was during my first fall as a homesteader. I had been hunting spruce chickens and stumbled accidentally into his domain. As I stepped into the clearing a savage malemute rushed me, snarling as he leaped out from behind a tree. For several seconds he circled me, fangs bared, trying for an opening; but my gun seemed to intimidate him. Just as I thought I would have to shoot the dog in self defense a little white-bearded man ran up and grabbed him. "Put your gun down," he said quietly in an accent which could have been German or Swiss. "He hates the sight of dem."

As soon as I had laid my .22 on the grass the dog's attitude changed, and he came over to me wagging his tail. But there was still a snarl on his face, and when I accepted the old man's invitation to "Come in," the dog followed me, growling softly as his teeth nuzzled my ankles.

As we entered the small cabin a goat, two chickens and a cat took their leave. Removing a pile of *National Geographics* from a chair, my host formally offered me a seat, and after we had talked for awhile he gave me a cup of coffee. When he handed me the cup, I took a big gulp and nearly lost my stomach; the brew was composed of equal parts of hot coffee and strong, cold goat's milk. But you don't refuse hospitality when it's offered in Alaska. Before I got away that day, I had drunk enough goat's-milk-coffee to float a small tug, and I had been completely unsuccessful in my efforts to convince Looie that I liked my coffee black. I had, however, made friends with the dog—inside the cabin, at least. Outside, he turned into a wolf again and drove me off the property.

It was during my first winter—the winter I shall always think of as "The Greasy Grogan Winter"—that I returned home from a hunting expedition one day to find the leg of an animal lying on my kitchen table. Not knowing who had left it but grateful for the meat, whatever it was, I made a stew out of it. It didn't taste bad.

A few days later I ran into Greasy. "Did you leave that meat I found at my house?" I asked him. "That leg?"

"Sure," said Greasy. "It was a coyote leg. I left it to see if you'd have guts enough to eat it." I was sick for a couple of days. Then I saw Looie and told him the story. "That was no coyote leg," he said. "I left it for you. It was a goat's leg. How did you like it?" I was sick for two more days.

Now Looie and I were good friends. He had taken to dropping in for an occasional visit, and he would sit in my kitchen drinking coffee—which, in retaliation for the goat's-milk-coffee I always had to drink at his house, I served him black—and telling me stories of his experiences in Alaska in the early days. He had been a trapper and a hunter, and he liked to tell me about the "porky-pines" he had killed by the dozen on my homestead when it had been nothing but a forest of trees. He had fed the bristly little beasts to his foxes, he said, but he hadn't seen one of them in the area, now, for years.

Sometimes we would argue about houses. He didn't think much of mine. A log cabin without moss for chinking and a roof without dirt piled on top wasn't worth living in, he said. My only defense was that I *liked* my house, and that I expected to live in it for some time to come. Luckily, the arguments always ended on a friendly note: Looie had nothing in common with the late Greasy Grogan.

Looie was almost a fanatic about animals. He talked to them, slept with them, called them his "friends." But he was practical about them, too. In addition to his ferocious dog, he seemed to own a second dog, but after awhile that dog disappeared. "What became of it, Looie?" I asked him.

"Oh, he was old and mean," he said. "I shot him, cooked him up and fed him to the chickens." Yes, a very practical man was Looie Huber.

The Rabecks, you might say, were my "farther" neighbors: they lived in Anchor Point. A young couple who had met in Pennsylvania Station in New York when she was a ticket clerk and he a Coastguardsman passing through, they had traveled to Alaska from the east coast in a jeep. They had arrived in Anchorage after a series of harrowing hardships with less than a dollar of their original capital left. (Whenever they told me the story, I thought of my arrival in Anchorage and how similar, in some ways, it had been). But they had rallied. Wiring home for money, they had existed on that until Bill got a job with the Alaska Railroad, and, living on the Anchor Point homesite they had taken, they had existed fairly well ever since, adding two small daughters to the one they already had. But "hardships" seemed to be their middle name. After driving his jeep into every ditch between Homer and Kenai, Bill Rabeck had discovered that he was going blind in both eyes. That had prevented him from working regularly, but a small inheritance had enabled him to support his family between jobs.

The only thing I didn't like about Bill Rabeck was his bad memory. Twice I invited him and his family to dinner, and twice I spent a whole day preparing some special delicacy like fried snowshoe rabbit and had to sit down and eat it myself. Bill would apologize profusely when I reminded him of the broken engagement—"I forgot, Gordon. I'll swear I forgot!"—but it would happen again. I began to think that either Bill was too blind to find my place or that the food was too terrible, and that he figured he'd had enough disasters in his lifetime without adding indigestion to the list.

My closest neighbor, Red Freimuth, was a fugitive from civilization who lived to hunt, and since I, too, was a fugitive from cities, we had much in common. We spent a good deal of the winter discussing hunting (Red), fishing (me) and our plans for the future. Red was a gunsmith and welder by trade and was making plans to put up a shop. All he needed was money. I had finally decided to build a greenhouse and grow tomatoes and do some truck farming on the side. All I lacked was money. In anticipating the coming spring, we agreed to find a job together and save enough money to fulfill our dreams and get our separate businesses going. The farm training subsistance we were both receiving was carrying us along month by month, but it wouldn't last forever. And after that — what? Jobs: Alaskan jobs, with long hours and big pay!

Chapter XIII
The Rich Homesteaders

IT WAS APRIL, 1952: the time of the spring thaw. Red's battered four-wheel-drive Army truck lurched sickeningly through one of those mud-filled trenches we call a highway in Alaska, dragging my mud-spattered, nearly disabled car behind it at the end of a long, rusty chain.

Clutching my wheel, I looked out on the bleak, cloudy landscape and slumped in fatigue. So far, it had been a tough year. In March, when the farm training program had been cancelled, Red and I had loaded up our vehicles with camping equipment and livestock (Ski, my malamute dog) and started out to look for jobs with high hopes. Since then we had traveled the length of the Kenai Peninsula following rumors of jobs, only to find out that the jobs had never existed or that the crews were already full up. Now we were heading for Kenai to make our last stand. There was an Army base going up there soon, we had heard, and the construction outfit—J. H. Pomeroy and Co. of San Francisco—would be needing men. If we couldn't get on a crew right away, we had decided, we would sit it out until we did.

"Kenai coming up!" yelled Red from the truck.

"Kenai it is!" I hollered back.

We drove through town to a homesite whose owner, a mutual friend, had given us permission to camp on his lot as long as we wished. Within half a day we had erected a tent house and parked our cars off the road where they wouldn't be run down by dump trucks or fined by the highway patrol for blocking traffic. After unloading cases of canned moose meat, fish, clams and vegetables, cases of staples and numerous sacks of potatoes, plus half a ton of coal, a coal cookstove, beds, blankets and other necessary items from Red's truck, we were ready to spend the summer if need be. "Come on, you contractors!" yelled Red. "We're ready to go to work!"

That first night in our new home Red and I were

lying on our cots discussing our chances for jobs and Ski was stretched out on the floor in front of the warm stove when two visitors turned up—homesteader neighbors who were working for the Alaska Road Commission in Kenai. In the excitement I put Ski out of the tent. After the guests had left, I looked for her and couldn't find her. "Gosh," I said to Red, worried. "Where do you suppose she went?"

"Oh, she's probably around here somewhere," said Red. "She's not used to this place. Must've wandered off."

In the morning, when Ski hadn't returned, I hunted for her through the entire Kenai district, asking questions of everyone I met, even walking the beaches to inquire at the huts of commercial fishermen. Nobody had seen her. Nobody knew anything about her. She had vanished.

For days I searched. Sometimes I saw a malemute who looked like Ski, but when I would run up to it I would see that the markings were different, the size was different, or the sex was different, and I would realize that I had made another mistake. Finally I gave up, consoling myself with the thought that maybe—just maybe—Ski had been picked up by some family that liked dogs.—A family with children, who could provide a good home. I didn't like to think that she had suffered some horrible fate. But you never knew. You never knew. (It wasn't until a year later that I heard what had happened to my dog from a friend who had known all along but had been afraid to tell me. That night when I had missed her, she had broken into a chicken house down the road from the tent and had been shot by the chicken farmer after killing several hens. It's an unwritten law in Alaska that a chicken-killing dog may be shot on sight—but that didn't lessen the blow when I heard the bad news. Ski and I had been friends, and I hated to think of her dying a death like that.)

But even the loss of my dog didn't prevent me from carrying out the main purpose of my life just then: getting a job. The hiring hall was in town. Each morning Red and I showed up there at a few minutes before 8:00 and waited, along with a hundred other desperate men, for the door to open. And every morning a little man came out and hung a sign on the door which read, "No hiring today." Cursing and muttering, the men would slowly disperse, some, if they had money, to bars, the rest of us to our shacks or tents.

Finally came the day when the little man opened the door and yelled, "Four laborers needed!" I pushed my way to the front, held up my laborer's union book and said, "I have a paid-up book and I'm a local man."

The little man gazed dispassionately over the heads of the shoving, growling crowd. "That don't make any difference here," he said. "You fellows'll have to decide among yourselves who's to go to work."

Visualizing a hundred men fighting, with only the four strongest emerging from the pile alive, their knives dripping with gore, I closed my eyes for a moment. Then I heard someone suggest that we all write our names on slips of paper and put them in a hat. "The guys whose names are the first four drawn will get the jobs," said the voice. Everyone seemed to be looking at me. Naturally. It was I who had spoken.

Borrowing a hat, I wrote my name on a slip of paper and dropped it in. Soon everyone had followed suit and the hat was held high while I mixed up the names. It was only by peculiar coincidence that Red happened to be the man chosen to pick the names, and only by another odd fluke that my name was the one picked first. Maybe the fact that, in stirring the slips of paper, I had simply given them one mighty flip, which meant that the names on top were shifted to the bottom and vice versa, had something to do with my good luck. Anyway, I dashed into the hiring office before anyone could register a protest. Immediately I was signed up as the nineteenth laborer to be hired on the job and given instructions to report to the Kenai dock. It was the last day of April and I was in.

Red, unfortunately, didn't have my luck. But three weeks later, after organizing the laborers into a first-come-first-serve list, with the men who had been waiting longest for a job and who maintained "permanent" residence in Alaska on top and the men who had just arrived from the States at the bottom, he was hired. He had a long, hard fight to maintain the "fair" order of the list, but Red was big and his temper was short then, and there had been no changes made without his O.K.

My first job involved unloading the barges arriving in Kenai with loads of construction equipment and lumber. Soon the lumber was stacked three piles high in the dock area and covered an acre of ground. After a few weeks all the other laborers seemed to have disappeared and I was the only one left to keep track of the lumber and help load the trucks when they arrived from the Army base. After five weeks I was sent out to the base, where a camp for the workers was being constructed. There I was put to work digging sewer ditches and stacking lumber for the carpenters who were beginning to swarm over the project.

A break in the monotony finally came when I was assigned, temporarily, to a "rod busting" gang. On this job I helped bend reinforcing rod into different angles for concrete forms, helped tie mats for foundation forms and draw a nice, fat check.

We were operating on a nine-hour-day, six-day week, and everyone was getting his share of overtime. My take-home pay averaged around $150 a week and I was able to save at least $125 of it. Red and I, living in the tent and cooking all our meals out of food we had canned up the year before—except for a few "hooligans," eight inch, almost transparent fish we bought from the native kids—kept our expenses at a minimum. It annoyed us a little, therefore, when various of our homesteader neighbors from Anchor Point kept moving in on us to wait for jobs. We fed them from our stock of supplies and were glad to do it, but we fervently hoped they'd become employed before our stock was down to nothing. A few did get jobs. Those who didn't returned to their homesteads to make out as best they could, or borrowed money from us to travel to Anchorage to look for jobs there.

All of our neighbors had departed when Red brought home a man he had met in town. He was down from Anchorage to look for work and would "stick around" for awhile, he said. We fed him for a couple of days, but when he gave no indication of intending to move we put our heads together to try to figure out how to get rid of him in a fairly nice way. We didn't object to feeding our friends, but a stranger was a different matter.

We tried hints of various kinds, then open suggestions. But nothing moved him. He was either very stupid or a lot smarter than we were. He seemed determined to stay with us all summer—or at least until he got a job. One night we held off from cooking dinner at the usual time, hoping to starve him out. He just sat there, waiting. Finally, when Red and I were so hungry we could have eaten *him* for dinner, we capitulated and cooked. And because you wouldn't let a dog go hungry in Alaska, we invited him to share our stew.

As far as I was concerned, there were only two things left to do: knock him over the head and dump him into the inlet, or move out and leave him in possession of the camp. "No, wait," said Red, during a whispered conference outside. "I've got a better idea. You know how people get rid of cats they don't want?"

On Sunday Red went into action. Throwing the few possessions of The Man Who Came To Dinner into his truck, he told him he was driving down to his homestead in Anchor Point. "I'll take you as far as the turnoff to Anchorage and you can hitchhike to the city from there. I hear tell there's lots of work in Anchorage now," he said.

The Leech (as we had begun to call him) showed a considerable amount of reluctance to fall in with the plan. "Oh, I don't know," he kept saying. "Maybe I'd better just stay here." But with Red coaxing from the truck and me pushing from behind, we finally persuaded him to climb in. Red gave me a wink as they drove off. He returned two hours later without a passenger. "How did you do it?" I yelled.

"Well, it wasn't easy," said Red, modestly. "He wanted to go all the way to the homestead with me, but I dumped him off at the turnoff just the same. Then I drove down the road a couple of miles and waited until The Leech had had time to get a ride in the other direction. When I got back to the turnoff, he was gone. Good news?"

"Good news!" That night we celebrated by buying a case of beer and drinking it all ourselves.

Eventually I was transferred to a concrete crew which was working in the 600-acre clearing I had worked on the year before. Base forms were scattered throughout the clearing, and it was our job to pour concrete into them, wait for it to set, then return and pour a pedestal which would support some sort of metal tower later on. My specific task was to operate the vibrator, an electric device designed to set up a vibration in the freshly-poured concrete and thus force it to settle into the form and fill up all the pockets. I was pleased with my job: it paid ten cents more per hour than most laboring jobs.

When we weren't engaged in pouring, we were supposed to be readying other forms to pour. This wasn't as simple as it sounds—not in Alaska. The muskeg in which we worked was composed of a layer of moss, a few feet of mud and about six feet of water-saturated gravel. When we came to a big hole in which we knew there was a form, we had to set up two pumps to pump out four or five feet of water before we could find it. When the form came into sight, we would all jump into the hole and clear out the mud. Then we would pile great heaps of muskeg moss around the form to keep the mud from flowing back in. With both pumps and men working at top speed, the hole would be in proper shape for pouring by the time a cat with a "Garbo" bucketful of concrete showed up. The concrete would then flow down a chute into the form to be vibrated, and we would move on to the next hole to repeat the operation.

Sometimes, however, the concrete would be delayed in its arrival. At these times, to keep from becoming bored, I would take my shovel and pan for gold in the bottom of the pit. Pretty soon the entire crew would be engaged in the same occupation. We found several signs of gold, but I'm sorry to report that no one made a strike.

After the construction workers' camp had been set up, dinners were offered at $2 per. Being slightly tired of our own cooking, Red and I started turning up at the mess hall every night. We looked forward to that meal all day. The food was good—a lot better than ordinary homesteader's fare—and you were allowed to eat as much as you could hold. It was easy to tell the homesteaders from the other men: when the meal was over, the only men left in the hall were homesteaders, busily cleaning up all the food left behind by the others and stuffing their pockets with enough food to make their lunches for the following day.

After four months of hard work I had collected $2000 in my checking account and was ready to send away to the States for the equipment I needed for my homestead. After much thumbing of catalogs and considerable careful calculation, I finally made out an order for a garden tractor with several attachments, a shallow well pump and five rolls of trans-o-glass, a glass substitute I planned to use in building my greenhouse. When I wrote out my check to Montgomery Ward's for a thousand dollars my hand was trembling. It was the largest check I had ever written in my life and there was the most money I had ever had in the bank at one time to back it up. Writing that check, to me, was like cutting off my right hand and throwing it to the wolves. But, consoling myself with thoughts of what that money would buy, I felt better after the deed was done.

In another two months I had returned the amount of the check to my account and contracted that disease known as "stake-happiness." One day the boss came up to me and said, "Stoddard, do you want to dig some post holes?"

"No," I replied. "I'd rather not."

The foreman stared at me. Then he hollered, "Stoddard, you're stake-happy! When do you want to be laid off?"

"Thursday," I said. "I don't want to make over $5000 and by Thursday I'll have made exactly $4,973.56."

"Okay. Thursday it will be."

On Thursday evening I collected my last big check from the foreman and drove through the main gate of the base for the last time, a free agent once more, a homesteader who, only twenty-five weeks before, had had a hard time raising a few dollars to buy gas for his car, but who was now the proud possessor of a four-figure checkbook. It would have taken me three years in the States to save as much.

When Red arrived at the tent that night he told me that the construction laborer who was camping on the next lot was leaving, too. "He says he's got a lot of canned goods to sell cheap," he said. "He wants to get rid of everything before he goes." This often happened around construction jobs where men who camped out had bought large stocks of food in order to save money but quit or were fired from their jobs before they had had time to eat it all up. "Let's see what he has," I said.

Red and I dickered with our neighbor until we bought everything he had at a very low figure. The food —to homesteaders who weren't used to it—was of the fancy variety: cans of tuna, roast beef, boned turkey and chicken soup, and even a case of tomato catchup. But I was feeling like a millionaire and felt I could afford a little luxury for a change—especially when it cost practically nothing. (Later on I was to get rid of the catchup by presenting a bottle of it as a housewarming present to each new homesteader who moved into my area).

The next morning, after packing my car with my share of the camping equipment, I said goodbye to Red, who was planning to work for another two months, and headed for the homestead country. It had been a long, hard summer, but I had done what I had set out to do: made money—lots of money to turn my dream of a greenhouse and small truck farm into reality. And I still had two months of fair weather before winter set in in which to build my buildings. Best of all, I would be working for myself—as contractor, foreman and crew, all wrapped into one.

I felt good. I stepped on the gas and put on some speed.

Chapter XIV
Jack of All

THE HOMESTEAD. The good old solid homestead. Was I glad to see it again! My property had never looked so good. The birch trees were losing the last of their reddish fall leaves, the creek was running clear over its shining rock bed and the evergreen spruce trees seemed greener than ever before.

Only one little detail bespoke the invasion of man. There, near the house, was a huge, deep pit, twenty feet wide and fifty feet long, the freshly-dug dirt beside it a blot on the otherwise sylvan scene. But no enormous mole had been at work. Recently, on my order, the same cat driver who had cleared the land for me a year-and-a-half before had dug the hole. It was to be the cellar for my greenhouse.

The greenhouse, I knew, must be complete before the first snowfall. I would have to work fast. Ordering the necessary lumber from the Keelers' sawmill, I hurried into Homer to pick up some supplies. I bought tools, nails and many other odds and ends. I spent money like a drunken laborer but it was going for a worthy cause, I hoped.

A few days of getting the pit into shape consumed the time until the first of my lumber began to arrive. It would have taken me until Christmas to haul the boards myself, small load by small load, in the back of my car, but the Keeler boys were kind enough to deliver them to my building site. And there was, perhaps, more than kindness in their action: I was one of the few cash customers available to them at that time, and they wanted to buy themselves a small John Deere tracter, using my money as a down payment.

Mixing my concrete as fast as I could in order to beat the winter freeze-up (when pouring concrete would be as impossible as pouring a drink from that whisky bottle full of stage tea two winters before), I began construction by placing 4"x4" posts eight feet apart around the sides of the pit to act as studs for the cellar walls, which would be sheathed later, and then erected a line of sixteen-foot 4"x4"'s in the center of the pit, cementing them in place. The latter would support my greenhouse roof.

A top layer of beams held my center posts together, and my nine-foot wall studs—five of the feet in the cellar and four sticking out above the ground—were united by 2"x4" 's. When more lumber arrived from the mill, I started work on the rafters. Using specially-cut 2x3's, I nailed the rafters every two feet, adding a line of 2x4's under each line of rafters and bracing them from my middle uprights so that the roof, with a foot of snow on top, would be properly supported.

With the shell of the greenhouse completed, I was ready for the interior. Working ten to twelve hours every day, I nailed a spruce board sheathing on the cellar walls, built growing benches which, when filled with soil, would be at ground level, and constructed walkways between the benches, using 2x12 planks on a framework three feet above the basement floor. When this was finished I stood back to survey my accomplishments. The benches running along each side of the greenhouse were four feet wide by 48 feet long, and the bench in the middle was six feet by 36 feet. Though still only covered by a naked framework, it was one heck of a large greenhouse, and when the benches were filled with soil it would grow one heck of a lot of tomatoes. I was almost in business!

Before even thinking of covering the greenhouse with glass, I considered the problem of my northern exposure. At that end of the house, glass, battered and blasted by the prevailing wind, wouldn't last any longer than a skiier in bathing trunks at 30 degrees below. What I needed was a solid wall. But wait! If I built a combination garage and workshop at the northern end, an outer wall would take the main force of the wind and I would have two walls to protect the tender tomato plants instead of one. I ordered some more lumber immediately, and within a week I had put up a building somewhat resembling a garage. It was 20 by 18 feet, included a work table, and there was plenty of room in which to store greenhouse supplies. The only thing it lacked was sufficient room for my car.

One day after the ground had begun to freeze I heard the roar of a powerful motor and a large, covered truck drove into my yard. Stopping his vehicle in a rut in the road, the driver climbed out of the cab and informed that he was carrying about a ton of freight addressed in my name.

I was delighted: it was my equipment shipment from Montgomery Ward's. "Back the truck up to the house!" I told him excitedly. The driver tried, but the truck only roared, its wheels spinning madly on ground which had frozen, thawed out a little and was too slick for traction.

"Well, we'll have to unload her," said the driver, resignedly.

Working the rest of the day, the driver and I unloaded five tons of freight from the truck, my things included, piling them in a heap on the ground. Then we tried again to move the truck. It didn't budge. It was in there to stay.

Night came on, and with it a November cold snap. We retired to the house to warm up, and after dinner I split my blankets with the truck driver. We both spent a miserable night. In the morning, when the ground had frozen solid again, the driver backed the truck out of the rut with little or no difficulty. After two hours of backbreaking work, the truck was loaded again, and the driver and I, who were old buddies by now, at last said farewell. Just another incidence of Alaska's weather and how it controls your life. . . .

Now I could look at my loot. Dragging the crates from where we had left them the night before, I managed to get them all stacked in my living room. Opening each crate was like opening packages on Christmas morning, and each bright red tractor part, as it came to light, was like finding a shiny new bicycle under the tree. When the last empty crate had been flung outdoors, I gazed with glee at the disorderly scene. Pieces of equipment were spread all over the living room rug, on the bed, and in the kitchen. Now it looked like Christmas day at about 2 p. m., when all that remains is to collect all the fancy wrapping paper and ribbons and build a huge, Yule fire.

All outside work was forgotten while I hunted up wrenches, hammers and pliers to assemble my new toys. A week later I was still puzzled over instruction books, looking for missing parts and wondering how I would get the assembled tractor out through the front door. A few days after that the shallow well pump was stuck halfway down the cellar stairs and I was searching high and low for the 20-inch circular blade that was essential to the arbor saw attachment for the tractor.

I finally forced the pump down into the cellar where it belonged and managed to drag the tractor through the front door—but not without the loss of several square inches of skin. As for the saw blade, I never did find it. The only item missing from the shipment—but after all, Montgomery Ward's, like man, is not infallible — it wasn't to turn up for at least a month, when somebody in the mail order house, apparently, found it lying around and shipped it out.

Putting the trans-o-glass on the greenhouse was no one-man job. I recruited a friend, and together we started to tack down the glass, beginning at the roof eave and working up to the peak. We had the first roll all laid out from the garage to the other end of the greenhouse when a big gust of wind whipped it out of our hands. "That stuff's worth $50 a roll!" I yelled in agony as I watched it go. "Let's get it!"

Stumbling, falling, picking ourselves up and stumbling on again, we succeeded in capturing the elusive glass. Then, holding it firmly down, we managed to nail it to the rafters. But we had learned a lesson, and after that we cut the glass into shorter lengths. We had no more trouble with the wind.

When the structure was entirely covered with trans-o-glass it really looked like a greenhouse. I was proud of it. But there was still work to be done. The benches would have to be filled with soil immediately — before the ground was frozen so hard that I'd have to break it up with a pick. I went outside and began to wield a shovel, and in two days the benches were full. Later on I would process the dirt—screen it, and so on—but it was good enough for now.

To heat the giant greenhouse I had two 50-gallon drums welded together to form a double-length barrel stove. Sinking it low in the ground at the open end of the house so that only its fire door showed, I hoped it would circulate warmth under the benches and keep the soil in them at the proper temperature. Later on I would collect slabs and cut them into five-foot lengths to feed it.

There were a few more jobs to be done, and when I had done them—hung the doors, put up a stovepipe and cleared the litter from the floors—I was ready to think about my water system.

Greenhouses were a subject I knew something about—I had helped to build several of them on my wholesale nursery jobs in California—but plumbing was a field with which I was almost totally unfamiliar. Always before I had lived in houses where the water streamed from the faucets whenever you turned the handles and you never paused to wonder why. Now I had to find out why —and how.

Reading the instruction book that had come with the pump, I made a list of the materials I would need. On a quick trip to Homer, I bought pipes and fittings and rented a set of pipe dies. My first job—and the hardest— was to sink the well point. This, I discovered, was a specially-made piece of pipe full of small holes and with a screen fitted inside to let the water in but keep all other material out. On one end was a sharp point which had to be driven into the bottom of the well. Attaching another length of pipe to the point and affixing a cap, I was ready to drive it down into the water-saturated gravel. I rigged up a homemade pile driver out of a log and ropes and got to work. Holding the log over the pipe, I would let it drop, then repeat the operation. After three days I had driven the point down three feet. Then, putting a 1¼-inch pipe inside the two-inch point pipe with a suction valve attached to the end, I connected it with the pump, which I had set on a concrete base. From then on it was easy. I ran a pipe upstairs to a storage tank in my second-story storeroom, then ran a line from it down to a faucet over the kitchen sink. Next, I ran a line from the pump to the greenhouse, burying it in the ground below the frost line. The water system was finished. All it lacked was electricity—to make the pump do its job.

But I had thought of that, too. One of the attachments I had bought with the tractor was a 2000-watt generator which would fit on the front of the tractor and operate off a pulley. A wire running from it to the pump would make the pump do everything I wanted it to do. But just as I began the task I got a better idea. While I was at it, why shouldn't I wire my entire house for electricity? Why shouldn't I have lights, as well as running water? It shouldn't be too much extra work.

Little did I know. My electrical supplies, ordered through mail order catalogs and through my brother, who was in the electrical appliance business in San Francisco, didn't take very long to arrive by air mail parcel post, but when they arrived I didn't know what to do with them: I knew even less about wiring than I had known about plumbing.

I ran into all sorts of difficulties. It was simple running two wires from the garage, where the tractor and generator were located, to the storeroom in the house, where a fuse box had been installed, but putting in the wiring for all the wall switches, wall plugs, light fixtures and the pump made me tear out the hairs in my beard, one by one. I spent a week fooling around before hiring an electrician—my neighbor, Fred Bailey—to come in and repair the results of my blunders.

Finally the great day arrived. I was ready to test all the circuits and find out if the pump would pump. Starting up the tractor, I ran to the house. With my hand on a light switch, I hesitated. Would it work? Or would there be a sudden bright flash, an explosion, and the annihilation of a house? My finger flicked the switch. The ceiling light went on. Rushing from room to room, I flicked all the switches. Every light worked. Truly, it was a miracle in the wilderness!

Now the pump. In the cellar, I pulled another switch. The pump motor started up. Dashing upstairs, I turned on the faucet over the tank. Nothing came out. Something was *wrong!* What? I clapped my hand to my head. Of course! Now I remembered: the pump had to be primed! Running down to the spring, I filled a pail with water. I climbed breathlessly up the bluff, almost running in my excitement. In the cellar, I carefully poured the water into the prime hole. Gradually the pump began to labor. The needle on the pressure gauge climbed slowly up the dial until it stopped at "40 pounds." It worked!

I turned on all the valves, then went upstairs to turn on the faucet over the storage tank. Water rushed out to fill the barrel. I went back to the kitchen, turned on that faucet. Water rushed out to fill the sink. No more Jack and Jill stuff for me!

I jumped into my car and drove up and down the road. When I would pass a neighbor's house, I would lean out the window and yell, "I have running water and lights! I have running water!" And the looks on my neighbors' faces—looks of astonishment, envy and plain disbelief—warranted all my weeks of work.

The next day people came from miles around to see my light and water system, some of them bringing along barrels and other containers to be filled with water. In Anchor Point at that time, most homesteaders were still hauling all their water by hand from creeks and rivers. A few had light plants, like mine, but none possessed a water system. And there was certainly no one else who owned a big greenhouse. It was indeed a great day for the Stoddard homestead.

Chapter XV
The Bear Facts

ALASKA'S BEARS: everybody always wants to hear about Alaska's bears. "Oh, yes, there are lots of them," I had written my family in California when they inquired about them. "I have to take my gun wherever I go; you never know when you might meet a bear."

Though this reply always pleased the inquirers—and gave them, I think, a rather pleasurable thrill—it wasn't quite true. I have tramped the length and breadth of my homestead—and other people's homesteads—tracking the small black bear (Alaska's most common bear) without ever seeing one. Either I don't hunt at the right time of day or I don't look in the right places. Neither have I the patience to lie on the edge of a damp muskeg for hours at a time waiting for a bear to come out and feed on blueberries.

My neighbor, Red Freimuth, however, is noted for having shot one of the biggest black bears ever to be seen in the community. He has its skin hanging at one end of his cabin where it almost completely covers the log wall, and he is pointed out to strangers as the "Big Bear Hunter" in our part of the Kenai Peninsula.

I remember the first blacky he shot. He came to my house late one afternoon and asked me for help in packing it out. "It's not big, but it weighs a ton—at least 200 pounds," he said. "I've hauled it on my back over a mile of juicy muskeg, and I'm fagged out. How about giving me a hand?"

We walked two miles across the broken country to where the felled bear lay in the wet muskeg. Tying its legs together, we slung it on a pole and tried to carry it out that way. But that—though I'm sure we looked like a couple of Daniel Boones as we did it—turned out to be a bad idea: at every step we took the carcass swayed violently from side to side, causing us to stagger in every direction but forward. Giving it up at the approach of darkness, we dropped the bear to the ground and butchered it on the spot, cutting the meat into chunks we could carry and leaving the hide for another trip. The next night I ate my first bear steak and had to admit it was far from perfect. We canned up the remainder and only brought it out to impress dinner guests from civilization.

Actually, bears should only be hunted for food in the fall, when the blueberries, which they love, are ripe enough to give a good flavor to the meat. Which reminds me of something an old sourdough told me early in my stay in Alaska: When you want to can up a year's supply of blueberries (the sourdough said), all you do is follow a black bear who is stuffing himself with them. When he has eaten all he wants—and before the digestive process begins—you shoot him. Then you remove the berry-filled stomach and take it home, where you have all your pint jars ready. . . . It saves you the trouble of doing all the berry-picking yourself, you see. And if there are a few stems mixed in with the berries in the jars—well, you can't be too particular when the food is free. Besides, you not only have a year's supply of berries; you've got a year's supply of bear meat, too.

There are grizzly bears in Alaska, but luckily they're not as common as the blacky. I've heard of only one being killed in my area, and that was during my second fall in the Territory. Red Freimuth and the Keeler men had been hunting spruce chickens two miles up Stariski Creek. As they approached the creek at one of its narrowest bends they spotted two bears on the opposite bank at the same time as the bears spotted them. Immediately the bears came splashing across the stream in their direction, pausing only to stand up on their hind legs for a better look at *genus homo*.

The party was armed with only 22's, except for one of the Keeler boys, who had an old 30-30. As the bears came closer, everyone opened fire, shooting wildly in an effort to stop them or turn them aside. The air was thick with flying bullets from four guns, but the bears, thick-skinned and thick-skulled as they are, paid no attention: the bullets might have been gnats, for all the impression they made.

They kept coming, and when they were only a few feet away from the terrified hunters, they circled around them as though by a prearranged plan to divide and conquer. The men whirled around, too, continuing to shoot wildly. Finally a lucky shot from the heaviest gun knocked one of the bears down. This intimidated the other bear, who ran off into the woods.

Upon examination, the dead bear was found to be a grizzly bear cub, but it was as big as a fully-grown black bear. In its hide were several 22 bullets which had gone just so far and no further—stopped by the layer of fat which is the bear's almost impregnable armor. And scattered around it on the ground were scores of ejected shells. "Geez," said one of the Keeler boys, wiping his forehead with his sleeve. "It sure takes a lot to kill a bear."

As a favored neighbor, I was given a piece of meat from that grizzly bear cub. I canned it up, but whenever I thought of tasting it there always seemed to be something better in the larder. A few months later I had a hunter guest to dinner and as a special treat served him a plate of grizzly bear stew. I learned later that he had been sick in bed for a week after visiting me. That must have been why he never returned to sample my hospitality again.

Much has been written about the great Alaskan brown, or Kodiak bear, and at the firesides of homesteaders on the Kenai Peninsula on cold winter nights, much is said. They say he's the largest and most ferocious carnivorous animal on the north American continent, standing nine feet tall—or higher—when erect. They say he lives almost entirely on salmon and moose calves, only feasting on berries in season. They say he's a most unpredictable animal and very dangerous to hunt, though unlike the polar bear, who will stalk a man and run him down, he will attack only when frightened, cornered or defending cubs—but he seems to be in one of those positions most of the time.

They say you'd better not leave your cabin door unlocked, because he's been known to enter, investigate and leave complete havoc behind him. They say that when he's wounded he'll head directly for the hunter at a high rate of speed, and that only a man who's a good shot and possesses an iron nerve can stop him with a rifle at a time like that.

I don't know: I never saw one. All I know is that whenever I see the footprints of a brown bear on my homestead—and they're easy to recognize because they're usually so big you couldn't cover them with a homburg hat—I always retire to my house for a time and leave the countryside to him. After all, he was there first.

And I'm not alone: very few of my friends will hunt a brown bear unless backed up by several guns. A good example of how wary Alaskans are about this species is the story of how the entire village of Ninilchik was once cornered by a trio of brownies. A sow and two big cubs strolled leisurely down the only road into town one day and held the river bridge for several hours against all traffic. The citizens cowered in their cabins until the bears were finally shot down by a well-armed posse.

Many are the stories told of man versus enraged brown bear. I have talked with people who came through such an experience alive but not, I can tell you, in the same old shape. One of these was a farmer from Kenai. His little dog, who apparently hadn't heard all the gruesome tales about brown bears, chased one of them one day. Then the bear turned around and chased the dog, who hightailed it back to where the farmer and his wife were standing. The bear went for the woman and the man tried to head it off with a stick. The farmer ended up on the ground with the bear on top, and when the bear departed, it left the man where it had knocked him with several broken bones and considerable less skin. He considers himself very lucky to be alive.

But there are worse stories than that. A homesteader

I knew was hunting moose along the banks of the Kenai River. Suddenly he found himself in a small grassy clearing where two little brown bear cubs were tumbling in play. Knowing that the mother bear must be close by, he started to beat a hasty retreat. Just at that moment he was knocked to the ground by a single blow from a huge brown paw. The old sow bear played with him as a cat plays with a mouse, playfully breaking most of his ribs and mauling his face until one eye was gone and most of his scalp. Then she gathered her cubs around her and left him for dead.

When he regained consciousness, the homesteader crawled painfully to where his gun was lying and managed to fire three shots—the distress signal of the woods—before passing out again. Several times, upon coming to for a moment, he repeated his call for help, and finally he was found and rushed to the hospital in Anchorage. Later on I heard that he had been flown to the States for special treatment and had died there.

I was telling this story to a fellow worker on the construction job in Kenai. When I got to the end, my listener said, "What do you mean he died? That's him, right over there." I looked, and sure enough: the man with a black patch over his eye, another fellow worker, was the hero of my story. Just goes to show you don't know what to believe.

One of the strangest bear stories I ever heard concerned a fight between a gigantic brownie and a D-6 caterpillar tractor. This battle occurred when the Alaska Road Commission was building that portion of the highway which lies between Moose Pass and Kenai. The cat was clearing some land in the Skilac Lake sector when this brown bear rushed out of the woods to challenge the trespasser. Charging the cat and growling as it came, it swung a mighty paw and dented the heavy metal as easily as a finger can put a dent in a felt hat. Then, seeing that the monster was being operated by a man, it tried to scramble into the driver's seat. Rapidly manipulating his controls, the operator swung the machine around and knocked the bear to the ground. The bear got groggily to its feet, shook itself and continued the attack. For over an hour the fight went on, with the driver always managing to turn the cat around in time to put the blade of his vehicle between himself and the bruin. He even made several attempts to run over the bear with the powerful treads of the cat, but until the bear was exhausted, the cat was almost battered to a pulp and the driver himself was nearly a candidate for an insane asylum, he was unsuccessful. Only when the bear made a false step and was squashed as flat as a bear rug on the floor of a big game hunter's room did the battle end. That section of the road is now known—to a few of the old homesteaders—as "Brown Bear Flats."

Yes, there are stories and stories. I wish I could tell one of my own, but I can't: the closest I ever got to a live bear in Alaska was when I just missed hitting a black cub with my car on the highway.

When it comes right down to it, what the homesteader is most interested in is small game. Leaving the bears, the moose (except when he's very hungry for fresh meat), the caribou, the wild sheep and the wild goats—all the record heads and record horns—to the stateside hunter who comes up, shoots his limit and goes home again, he concentrates on snowshoe rabbits, spruce chickens, ptarmigan, ducks and geese: food for his larder.

The snowshoe rabbit is an animal on which, because he's considered a rodent, there's no limit, and the law says you can kill one any time and welcome. He's easy to shoot, too: in the fall he turns white, and before the first snowfall he makes a perfect target for the hunter with a 22.

I'll never forget my first experience with snowshoes. Red Freimuth and I went up to a burned-off area near Skilac Lake where the thousands of fallen trees would have offered good cover for the rabbits if they hadn't been so white. After two hours of steady shooting, we had piled up 48 unwary snowshoes weighing from three to five pounds. Another time the Keelers, Red and I hunted around Kasilof Flats, a settlement between Kenai and Homer, and bagged 55. Two days later some of our other neighbors, hearing of our success, hunted on the same spot and killed 104. It sounds like wholesale slaughter, I know. But none of the rabbits was wasted. Some were eaten fresh (fried, of course), some were canned, and many more were taken into the cold locker in Homer and frozen for winter eating. And they made a welcome addition to the usual diet of clams and fish.

Duck and goose hunting is excellent during the fall, when, at the mouth of Stariski Creek, the sloughs and tide flats stop many a bird on its way south. Not owning a shotgun, I never did much of this kind of hunting, but my neighbors all spent morning after morning lying in the tall marsh grass waiting to shoot their limits. They were handicapped, however, by the lack of dogs with which to retrieve the birds they shot: they all owned malemutes, and malemutes, who hate swimming in cold, freezing water and would be apt to tear the birds to bits before returning to their masters, aren't much good as retrievers. Red Freimuth owned the only bird-retrieving dog in the area—a small dog of the water spaniel type—and the two of them would be invited to come along on every duck-hunting expedition.

Grouse-hunting—spruce hens in the fall, ptarmigan in the winter—is more my meat. Spruce chickens are easy game. Sometimes called "fool hens" because they can be approached with ease and knocked out of a tree with a stick if no other weapon is handy, they remind me of Al Capp's famous "schmoos," who were only too happy to be killed and eaten—who would, in fact, die of joy at the very thought of becoming somebody's dinner. Like the schmoos, spruce chickens are so unwary that a homesteader can decide in advance how many he needs, get up in the early morning, drive up and down the highway until he spots a flock of them pecking at gravel and fire away until his predetermined quota is bagged.

One morning when I was still living in my first shack by the highway, I awoke to a fusillade of shots. Looking out the window, I saw three men pointing 22 rifles at my cabin. I sprang through the door with my rifle cocked, ready to fight back. Then I realized that the men were aiming at my roof—not at me—and in a second a dead spruce chicken fell at my feet. Glancing up, I saw an entire flock of them roosting on the eaves. I pointed my rifle, emptied it of bullets, picked up half a dozen bundles of feathers and re-entered the house. The three men drove off without a word. As for me, I counted my loot, muttering, "Nobody's gonna shoot my spruce chickens but me."

The Kenai Peninsula ptarmigan are strictly winter hunting birds. They spend the summer months in the Caribous, a range of low hills running from Homer up past Kasilof; but in the winter, when the snow up there gets so deep that it covers all their usual food, they come down to the homestead country to feed on willow buds. White as snow except for two black tail feathers, they blend in so successfully with their surroundings that they're hard to see and hunt, and they have an extra advantage in being able to fly great distances when frightened. I have hiked many weary miles after the elusive birds, only to return dead tired and emptyhanded. I didn't mind the dead-tired part—I only hunted ptarmigan when I needed some exercise after sitting in the house too long—but the empty-handed aspect always bothered me. The biggest flock I have ever seen numbered twelve, and that time I was lucky: I bagged eight before they took wing.

During my second winter in Alaska I decided to try a little trapping. I had been told that the Kenai Peninsula had been "almost trapped out" several years before my arrival, but that didn't make any difference to me. I wasn't after pelts, anyway: I was after coyotes, on which there was a thirty dollar bounty.

I had a small setback when I learned that it took three years of continuous living in Alaska to become eligible for a resident's trapping license for the price of a dollar. I solved that problem by paying $50 for a non-resident's license, figuring that after nabbing two coyotes I would be money ahead. After that I was too stingy to buy myself some traps and borrowed five of them instead.

I started out with high hopes. There were so many coyotes in the area—I could hear them yipping every night and had seen many of them on my land—that I thought it would be easy to trap a great many of them before the winter was over. For this reason I didn't bother to read a book on the art of trapping, or to ask any questions of my friends. I found the partly-devoured body of a moose in a muskeg some distance across the creek from my house and set my traps around it. Every couple of days I inspected the traps, but there was never anything in them. I moved three of the traps to other locations with the same results. All winter long I worked at it, always hoping, never giving up. Then the spring thaw broke, and it became impossible for me to reach my trap line across the raging river the creek had become. After a week I was able to visit the sets at the moose carcass and found one trap gone and the other sprung. The other three traps, which I had set in various game trails and covered with snow, were now on bare ground in plain sight of any animal who wanted to step around them and continue on its way. At that point I gave up my dream of coyote bounties and turned to saner pursuits.

At hunting coyotes with a rifle I was no more successful than at trapping, my greatest failure occurring on a moose-hunting trip. As I started to cross a big muskeg I came face to face with a coyote pup. He was sitting on the game trail not fifty feet away and watching me with calm but wary yellow eyes. Carefully pointing my rifle at his head, I pulled the trigger. The pup took off like a rabbit—strange behavior for an animal who should have been stretched on the grass, dead. Another time I shot at a three-legged coyote standing on the highway beside my mailbox, but he was "one of those that got away," too. I came to be known among my neighbors as the coyotes' greatest friend and protector.

The two Keeler boys were the most experienced trappers in my vicinity. During the winter when I was making my feeble attempts at coyote-trapping, they started practically at my back door and set their assorted traps and snares for miles up the creek. If I remember correctly, their take was two coyotes, one otter, one beaver, one mink, two mink toes, four otter toes and several ermine. I'll never forget the day they clumped down into my cellar where I was working and proudly placed a beautiful black mink in my hand. While stroking the fine hair, I suddenly realized that the animal's heart was still beating. Visions of an enraged mink snarling and gnashing its sharp, wicked teeth in the confines of my small cellar while the three of us battled our way up through the trap door to the kitchen caused me to say, somewhat shakily, "Take this thing out of here—quick. It isn't dead yet." The two boys rushed outside and dispatched the mink completely, but for the rest of the day I was unable to work in the cellar: my imagination is too vivid; and besides, there was a heavy odor of musk remaining that I found particularly unpleasant.

Just as ferocious as minks are weasels. There's a saying in Alaska that if weasels were the size of dogs all the people would have to move out. I had an experience with one once that convinced me of the truth of that statement. I had shot one with my 22—at such close quarters that he should have died right away. But he didn't. Instead he came swarming up the barrel of my gun after me, and he looked so mad—and so formidable—that I dropped the gun and ran.

In the winter, the Alaskan weasel turns white and becomes an ermine. Before I had finished putting the roof on my second house, one of them moved into my cellar and settled down to stay. When I mentioned his presence to a neighbor I was told that I was very lucky to have an ermine as a house guest: he would keep my cellar free of mice. That was fine, but every time I went down to the cellar to collect some canned meat the little mouse-killer would stand over the can I had selected and, with vicious, clicking teeth, dare me to take it away from him. I usually ended up by going back upstairs and cooking up a pot of dried beans I had stored there. When he moved out—as he eventually did—I decided that I much preferred the mice; at least they ran away when I approached.

From the huge brown bear to the tiny mouse is quite a slide down the animal kingdom, but there's an Alaskan native who is even smaller than the mouse: the shrew. For appetite, this little rodent can beat the biggest and the strongest: it has such a terrific digestive system that it must have food in its stomach at all times or it's apt to digest itself. Once I set a mouse and shrew trap in my cellar by digging a hole in the ground and placing a five-gallon can in it with the top level with the ground. Three days later when I inspected the trap I found one live shrew and ten shrew tails.

With a cannibal like that at large, who's afraid of the big bad bear?

Chapter XVI
Without a Wife

ALASKA, land of snow-capped mountains, beautiful green lakes, rushing rivers, endless forests. Alaska, land of scenery galore. I was sick of it. The scenery I yearned for was of a different sort. What I wanted to see was a pretty young wife standing by the back door to call me in from the greenhouse for dinner. What I wanted to take a picture of was that pretty young wife stirring up a pot of moose stew at the kitchen stove, or making some little feminine adjustment to the curtains, or bringing me my pipe and slippers as I relaxed after a hard day's work. Such scenery would have pleased me more than the sight of a 40-pound salmon at the end of my line or the discovery of a gold mine in my cellar. Such scenery—and I would have given up pinochle for life!

There I sat beside my barrel stove, starting my third winter in Alaska as a bachelor among bachelors, with all my work done for the year and nothing to think about but the things a man will think about when he is cut off from all contact with the opposite sex—or at least from girls of marriageable age. What good did it do to own a fairly good house and a greenhouse almost ready to be put into operation without a wife to share them with?

Staring moodily out over the cold, snowy landscape of my 120-acre domain, I continued my gloomy daydreaming. And I considered my situation: the situation facing every bachelor homesteader on the last frontier. . . .

*

The bachelor homesteader's lot (I decided) is a hopeless one. In a land where unmarried women are almost as scarce as snakes—and there are no snakes in Alaska—(I laughed, bitterly, at my own feeble joke) what's he to do to prevent himself from turning into an embittered old man with housemaid's knee, dishpan hands and a stomach ruined by his own cooking?

Well, there are six possible courses open to him, and none of them could be considered ideal: he may take a child bride; he may become a squawman; he may order a wife through the mail; he may take a prolonged trip to the States in search of a wife; he may shoot one of his married neighbors and take over the widow; or—as a last resort—he can shoot himself.

Child brides are a dime a dozen, if that's what he wants. But who wants one? If he picks out a homesteader daughter in pigtails as a likely prospect for the future and has the patience to wait the six years or more it takes before she's old enough to assume even the simplest responsibilities of marriage, he's likely to find out that his intended has grown up to be taller than he: they seem to grow them big, in Alaska. Besides, marrying a child of sixteen or so would have too many drawbacks. The homesteader bachelor is an independent animal. He knows how to cook, clean house, wash clothes, bake bread—everything a wife should know. Teaching a child bride the fundamentals of housekeeping would consume too many wearisome hours—and she might make the mistake of poisoning him in the process of learning to cook. And this isn't hard to do because usually, when a girl reaches sixteen, she's grabbed off by a young male of her own age and carried—off in a manner of speaking—to the hills; the "older" bachelor just hasn't got a chance.

Becoming a squawman isn't hard. It's easy enough to lure a squaw to your lair with "squaw candy," that Alaska confection made of smoked salmon hardened to a point of chewiness which Indian girls love so well. Sometimes it's almost too easy. I'll never forget the story about the homesteader who was drinking at a bar in Kenai when he became conscious of the head of a squaw resting heavily on his left shoulder. She was sniffing at the squaw candy in the left breast pocket of his jacket. The homesteader didn't like her looks—she was old and fat—so he pushed her away. But she kept coming back, hard on the scent. Suddenly everybody began hitting everybody else, and when the homesteader emerged from the fray, his knuckles and nose bleeding and both his eyes blacked, he knew what had caused the fight: that squaw had been somebody else's squaw.

No, acquiring a squaw isn't difficult, and keeping one, when it comes right down to it, wouldn't be too bad. Usually part Russian and often good looking, the native girls make good wives for homesteaders. They were born in the country and brought up in the wilderness way of life, and they have been well trained in all the home arts. And there's a big point in their favor: not knowing anything better, they aren't always wanting to run off to the States to cities or yearning for the luxuries and comforts that cities provide. They're content, as no white girl from "outside" would be, with the homesteader's primitive lot.

And Indian girls are not averse to helping their husbands with their outside chores. There's Joe, for instance. He had the good fortune to marry a native girl who, besides being one of the best bakers in the area, turned out to be handy at peeling trap poles, cutting down trees and packing in meat on a packboard. In the social circles she's a whiz at dancing, and all in all she has the stamina of a young horse. True, she giggles all the time—all the native girls do—but to me she seems a thoroughly jolly, well-adjusted person—a perfect wife for Joe.

But not for me. A native wife might be fine in Alaska, but if I ever took her to the States for a visit, all sorts of complications would arise—complications that would be embarrassing to her. No, marrying a native girl would mean that I would have to resign myself to a never-ending life on the homestead. And then there's the question of children: native women believe in large families—sixteen or more. Children are Alaska's biggest crop. A man would have to work awfully hard to support a family like that. Take Carl. He's a college graduate, and he hoped to find some time to do some writing until he took on the responsibility of a native wife—a widow—and her five children, all in one fell swoop. She's an attractive woman and I don't blame him in the least, but

Without a Wife

now he has six children and there's probably another on the way. Oh, well. He runs a farm and will need lots of help in the future, no doubt.

As for sending "outside" for a mail-order bride—uh-uh. For one thing, my experience as Henry Gubbins in that great Alaskan epic, "Henry Gubbins' Mail Order Wife," is still too fresh in my memory. Second, I hate surprises. Third, when I receive a package of goods from Montgomery Ward's and I'm not satisfied with it, I can always send it back. Not so with a mail-order bride: when you've got her, you've got her. And of all the men I've known who have sent away for brides, only a small percentage of them have expressed themselves as "completely satisfied with the merchandise."

John's an exception—or so he says. He went so far as to order a bride from Germany, sight unseen. He got the fraulein's address from his brother, who had spent some time in Germany after the war, and he had corresponded with her for several years, he writing in English, she in German, and somebody doing the translating at both ends. Finally he became so desperate for a wife to share his lonely homestead with him that he sent her the amount of her fare to Alaska and obtained permission, after much entanglement in red tape, to bring her into the country. It cost him around $600 to get her from Germany to New York by boat and from there to Anchorage by plane. It took his last dime, in fact, and when she arrived, though she was no great beauty, there was nothing to do but marry the girl. They made an odd-looking pair: John's a great big guy and she was only about half his size. Nevertheless the groom was heard to brag, not long after the nupitals, that on the first morning at the homestead, when he had gone outside to chop some firewood, she had followed him, taken the axe away from him and pointed out, in sign language, that that was "woman's work."

Though John seems to be thriving on the sort of life he is now leading—he knows no German and his wife speaks only a few words of English so "she doesn't chatter all the time," he boasts—he still hasn't brought her over to my homestead for a visit. He says he's afraid that once she sees my house, with the running water, the electric lights and the living room rug, she'll become dissatisfied with the accommodations he has to offer. Sometimes I think I ought to start writing to his wife's sister in Germany: I hate chopping wood.

What about touring the States in search of a wife? Could be. Expensive, but could be. But what are the homesteader's chances for success? It would be useless for him to look in the cities for a girl who would be either willing or eager to assume the hardships of homesteading—though I've no doubt there'd be plenty who would look mighty good around the house during the long winter months. No, what a city girl wants—if those I used to know in California are any criterion—is a junior executive husband who can provide entertainment, pretty clothes and a rose-covered cottage in the suburbs. She might find out later that she sees very little of her husband, and that when the children come along he can no longer afford the fancy clothes. But she can't see that now. *Now* it would be impossible to convince her of the superiority of a life in which her husband would be around most of the time, the air she breathed would be uncontaminated by gasoline fumes and the whole of Alaska would be her home. It would be impossible to convince her, because you'd also have to explain that a husband with a year-'round job doesn't exist in the homestead country, that the entertainment consists of two-year-old movies twice a year, an occasional square dance and visits from the neighbors, that lights and running water are considered luxuries, and that a new parka could seem more important to her than a new dress. And that would do it.

Oh, maybe a city girl in love could become intrigued with the idea of "pioneering in the wilderness with My Man," but after a year or so she would become bored and restless and would abandon the poor homesteader to his solitary fate. I've seen it happen. There was that guy who married a beautiful ex-model and brought her back to his homestead. She made every effort to get into the spirit of the thing — wore baggy jeans and a torn sweater and smoked a corncob pipe—but within a year she was in the States negotiating a divorce. And she probably entertained her city friends with hilarious stories about the hardships she had endured.

But there are the farms: perhaps a homesteader would stand some chance of achieving success on a wife-hunting tour of the farms. Yes, when I start out on my search, that's where I'll look. And when I find a farmer's daughter who can bake apple pies that melt in my mouth, milk twenty cows before breakfast, plow a field behind a horse and still have enough energy left to keep her feet going at a square dance at night, that will be the girl for me. Unromantic? Sure. But I'll go even further: she'll be an even better bet if she wears a hand-me-down flour sack and hates the sight of shoes; then I'd be sure she'd be satisfied with my lot. It would be nice, of course if she were pretty. But she musn't be too pretty. To take a good-looking wife back to the homestead country would be to court certain catastrophe. With all the girl-hungry bachelors surrounding me on all sides, I would have to post "Keep Out" signs on all the paths leading to my house, keep my guns loaded at all times and never leave the cabin for a moment. Many a pretty wife has left her husband for greener pastures when a bachelor homesteader friend has moved in to help with the harvest. The only way to prevent this from happening would be to marry a pretty girl with three or four good-looking sisters. With all of them living at my homestead, every bachelor within a radius of a hundred miles would be hanging around offering to help with the chores. And by the time all the sisters were married off, I'd have the best-looking farm in the country. Yes, maybe there's something to that idea. . . .

As the situation now stands, the poor single man goes to all the square dances in the community in hopes of meeting a girl of his own age who is unmarried and has just, miraculously (maybe she's somebody's sister) moved into the area. Instead he finds out, again and again, that there's nobody to dance with but grandmothers, other men's wives and little girls under twelve.

And even the towns near the construction jobs on which he works in the summer offer nothing but the wrong kind of girl: a girl who is after nothing but his newly-made wealth. This type usually makes her home in the dark corners and recesses of the bars, waiting patiently for a woman-hungry man to fall into her trap. Result: the bachelor's money is soon gone and all he has gotten for it is a few hours of dull conversation and a hangover the next morning.

And then there's the other kind, the "home town" girl. Every summer there descends on the towns near the construction camps a bevy of these pretty females. They are young, fresh-faced and look just like the girls you went to school with back in the States, but their object is the same as that of the women in the bars: to shake loose some of the money from the wallets of the unsuspecting bachelors.

They come under the guise of magazine subscription saleswomen. Red Freimuth and I went into Kenai one evening to relax over a beer. As we approached a tavern we were set upon by two lovely creatures. I found myself backed up against a wall by a blonde, and when I came out of my trance I was five dollars poorer and holding a receipt for a three-year subscription to some magazine I had never heard of. Red was reeling, too, and when his girl and mine flitted off to work their deadly charms on two other suckers approaching down the street, I turned to him and said, "How much did the redhead get from you?"

"Ten bucks," he said, mopping his forehead. "But she invited me over for a chicken dinner."

"Yeah? Where does she live?"

Red's expression was one of pained chagrin. "Alabama," he said.

"Too bad," I said. "Mine invited me for a duck dinner

and she lives a coupla thousand miles closer. In Washington State."

"_____ _____ _____!" said Red.

Months later Red was still cursing: he had never received a copy of the magazine to which he had so expensively subscribed. I was a little luckier: I did get my magazine, but it turned out to be one I was totally uninterested in reading.

*

I came out of my coma by the stove in a marrying mood. "I've got to do something *quick!*" I shouted, jumping up and pounding my fist on the table.

Then I sat down again and thought more calmly. It was the first part of December and I still had a pretty good chunk of money left over from my previous summer's work. I had nothing to do until March, when I would have to get some plants started in the house. Why shouldn't I take a trip "outside" for a few weeks and make that tour of the farms? Well, maybe that was a pipe dream. What would I say when I knocked at a farm door? "Good morning, sir. Have you any daughters you want to marry off?" But I could get my sister and sister-in-law to introduce me to some girls—see some pretty faces, at least. Yes, by golly: that's what I'd do. Spend Christmas with my family, meet the *girl,* sell her on Alaska, and rush back to my homestead in the woods a happily married man. That's what I'd do!

Chapter XVIII
Civilization

"Don't come home until you've made good," my father had said when I left the enfolding arms of the family.

Well, I had proven up on a 120-acre homestead, built the biggest and finest house in my part of Alaska and was ready to go into business for myself. If that wasn't "making good" enough for my father, he could boot me out when I arrived. Anyway, I was going home: I was going home for Christmas. After two-and-a-half years in the "wilds," I was going HOME. After two-and-a-half years of loneliness, I was going home to look for a wife. Boy!

Packing my battered old cardboard suitcase with the few "city" clothes I still possessed—including four white shirts which had cost me a dollar apiece to have laundered in Homer—I carefully arrayed myself in a once-good tweed suit that had been gathering cobwebs in my storeroom upstairs. When I was ready I took one final look around the house to see that everything was shipshape. Then I stepped outside and locked the door.

As I climbed into the car, I glanced at the greenhouse and garage and breathed a silent prayer that the snow wouldn't get so deep while I was away that it would cave in their roofs. There was a lot of work involved there, and I wasn't anxious to do it again.

"Aw, what the heck," I told myself. "Stop acting like a fool. Everything's gonna be all right."

In Homer I left my car at Vern Mutch's drugstore and walked across the street to the Pacific Northwest Airlines office to buy my ticket for San Francisco, paying out $137 for the privilege. The first of the three planes I would take was the only scheduled flight out of Homer—the Kodiak plane heading for Anchorage. It would take me over my homestead, too. As it did, I said my final farewell to the tiny house, far below in its miniature clearing. Then, patting the wallet in my pocket, a wallet fat with the $400 I had put aside for "spending money,"

Civilization

I turned my thoughts to the good time I would have "outside."

At Anchorage I was told I had missed connections with the Seattle plane and would have to spend the night in the city. This was no hardship: the airlines would put me up in the best hotel, The Westward, and provide me with several free meals. I spent the time enjoying the feeling of being dressed up again—in a clean white shirt, a yellow tie, a slightly rumpled tweed suit and—I glanced down at my feet—Marine combat boots. Hmmm. Something wrong with that picture. I went into a shoestore and glanced over the stock.

"Something?" said the salesman, following my gaze floorward.

"Yeah," I said, feeling uncomfortable. "Yeah. Say, what're they wearing in the States these days?"

"All the best-dressed men are wearing suede shoes, sir."

"Suede, huh?" I rubbed my chin. "Okay. Fix me up."

A few minutes later I walked out minus combat boots and fourteen dollars. "Now," I thought. "Now no one in the States will know me from a stock and bond salesman from Sansome Street. Though what I should really do" —I chuckled, and a construction stiff I almost bumped into on the street gave me a funny look—"what I should really do is turn up at home in a parka, snowshoes and a long, long beard." I chuckled again, remembering a scene like that in a magazine cartoon. "Why Uncle Joe from Alaska," the man at the door was saying to the old trapper outside. "Won't you come in for a minute!"

The flight to Seattle occurred during the night. I would have liked to see some of the country we were flying over, but since I couldn't, and since the scenery inside the plane was much more interesting anyway, I spent the time watching the two pretty stewardesses. "Girls," I marveled, as my eyes rested on every detail of their lovely faces. "Pretty American girls."

In between their sessions of handing out paper bags to airsick women and children, I managed to draw one of the stewardesses, a redhead, into conversation. Undoubtedly she had heard all about homesteading in Alaska from the numerous homesteaders who had preceded me, but she was nice enough to give me her full, flattering attention. "Have you ever thought of living on a homestead?" I asked her, after talking awhile.

"Oh, yes!" she breathed ecstatically. "I think it would be grand—for a week or two."

That was that. "See? What did I tell you!" I said to myself disgustedly. "City girls!" But as soon as the redhead had left me to attend to her duties I got the attention of the other stewardess. I asked her the same question and received approximately the same answer. "Oh, well," I told myself. "When I get to California..."

Landing in Seattle at 3:00 in the morning, I transferred to another airline and boarded a coach plane five hours later for the last lap of my trip. From then on my impatience to get home rose as the altitude fell for what I considered quite unnecessary stops at Portland and Oakland. But as we circled the San Francisco airport for a landing, I reflected on the wonders of air transportation. Here I was in California after less than twelve hours of actual traveling, and the car trip from California to Alaska had taken me several weeks.

Yes, here I was in California, and I should have been feeling great. But I didn't: I felt terrible. My head had expanded to such an extent that I was afraid it would explode all over my fellow passengers, my ears were pounding like twin snare drums and I couldn't hear a thing. I could see, though, and when I glimpsed a familiar blue-suited figure coming toward me down the airport ramp, I ran to meet it. It was Dad. We shook hands, pounded each other on the back and, I suppose, yelled our greetings. But I was unable to make out a word of what either of us was saying.

Within the next hour, with my father hollering into my face and me making abortive attempts to read his lips, we managed to convey something of our happiness over seeing each other again. Driving back to Dad's apartment in the city, we settled down there with a few of his special martinis and had what—after my ears had cleared enough so that he only sounded as though he were talking from two apartments away—amounted to a reunion talk.

That night in bed on Dad's living room couch my ears began to pound like a pile driver gone mad. In the morning, my father called a doctor who, after examining me, told me I had "only a very bad cold." An hour after he had left the apartment my right ear exploded like a paper bag and started to bleed. Three hours later I was sitting in the office of an ear specialist who stuck a pewlike instrument down my left ear and caused another "Pop!" He then explained to me that I had a bad sinus infection in both ears—"probably aggravated by the plane trip"—and that I would have to live on a diet of penicillin shots in the arm for the next few weeks. "There goes my bankroll," I said to Dad. "I should have stayed in Alaska, where I was safe."

A few days before Christmas, pumped so full of dope that I felt like a cocaine addict, I drove down to Los Gatos with Dad. We were greeted by my brother, his wife and my two nieces and a nephew with what sounded, from a great distance, like expressions of joy. I could tell from the brightness of their eyes and the width of their smiles, at any rate, that they were glad to see me, and if I needed further evidence, all I had to do was look at the big picture window in the living room: inscribed on it, in the careful letters of a child who had just learned to print, in paint that would take weeks to scrape off, were the words, "Welcome home, Unca Gordon from Alaska." I was home at last.

On Christmas day my mother arrived from Los Angeles—though long since divorced, my parents always spent the holidays with "the children"—and my newspaperwoman sister from Carmel. The family was complete. Trying to keep my eyes off the television set—television had made great strides since my departure from civilization—I related detail after detail of my experiences in Alaska to a most attentive audience. But the more I talked, the more I built up Alaska as the greatest place on the face of the earth, the more homesick I became for my log cabin in the woods and the fishing stream at its very back door. I told them of my good neighbors, the hunting and fishing, the big-paying construction jobs and the winters of leisure, and I yearned, as I talked, to be home in Alaska again.

When I paused for breath my mother spoke. "You poor, poor boy," she said. "How terrible it must be to be up there all alone. Why don't you move back to California, where everything is easier?"

I shut my mouth and concentrated on watching television.

Between my mother's urging me to stay in the States, my father's arguing that it would be better for me to return to Alaska "to finish his job," my sister's begging me to take her with me when I went, my brother's asking me to "stick around awhile and help me landscape my place," my sister-in-law's worrying about feeding me "anything to compare to moose" and the children's bringing their friends around to stand in line and stare at "Unca Gordon from Alaska," my nerves were very quickly shattered to bits. "Oh, for the peace and quiet of the homestead," I thought. "I'm not used to families, any more."

But finally Christmas was over and I was allowed to return to San Francisco with my father for another shot of penicillin. Good for another few days, I started on the necessary rounds of relatives and friends. In addition to seeing some old acquaintances of my own, I was forced, by an increasingly difficult effort to please, to be the guest of honor at dinner parties hosted by my father's cronies "who want to hear all about Alaska" (no marriageable girls present), luncheons given by my mother's friends "who want to hear all about Alaska" (no marriageable girls present) and cocktail parties to which my sister dragged me "because there'll be so many people there who'll want to hear all about Alaska" (too many sophisticated girls). Maybe I was anti-social, maybe I had become a misanthrope, during the long winter nights in the north; but I had had enough "social life," after just a few weeks, to make me a candidate for a rest home for aged men. And my feet hurt: people never seem to sit down, at cocktail parties in the States.

The city was my undoing. Walking down San Francisco's Market Street was like swimming against a tide. People—great mobs of pushing, jostling people—were everywhere. The noise was terrific, even to my two disabled ears. It sounded like the ice tumbling down Stariski Creek in the spring thaw—but how much better was the clean roar of the river than the crying and shrieking of the metropolis!

Worst of all: with all those thousands of people pouring through the streets, there wasn't a single face I knew. I was lonelier than I had ever been snowshoeing over the frozen muskegs, miles from the nearest neighbor. On the Kenai Peninsula I knew everyone within fifty miles or more. In San Francisco, my father had lived in the same apartment house for over ten years, and the only person he knew in the 40-unit building was the manager of the place. I had to get home, home to Alaska and the homestead, where I was an individual among individuals —not just one of a thundering herd.

I was broke: my doctor's bills had taken all the money I had with me. But I could borrow money. I borrowed it from my father and said goodbye to him at the Ferry Building. It was a sad farewell this time: he was getting old, and I was afraid that I would never see him again. And I think he was thinking the same thought as he gripped my hand for the last time.

As the ferry boat took me across the bay to Oakland and the train to Seattle (I hadn't borrowed enough money to finance a plane trip all the way back), I looked back to the lighted city. It was a wrench to leave my father, but I was happy to be free once more. "I'll be darned," I said to myself, "if I'll ever return to *that* rat-race again."

My main regret, I reflected as the train headed north, was that I had been too broke and too sick to look for a wife. Well, maybe some new homesteaders would move into the area come spring, and maybe they would have one or two pretty daughters looking for husbands. You never could tell what might happen in a new year and a new season coming up. . . .

Two days later I was on the plane heading for Anchorage. It was a day flight, and I passed the long hours looking down on the rugged panorama of the spruce-covered coast, with its inlets and islands, of southeastern Alaska, thinking of my homestead and how it would look under a blanket of snow. Finally the plane landed at the Anchorage airport. I took a taxi into town and put up at a cheap hotel. On inquiring at the bus depot, I learned that the next bus to the Kenai Peninsula and Homer would leave on the following day. My money supply was running low—I still had some cash in the bank in Homer, but I wanted to save it for living expenses through the rest of the winter until spring, when I could earn some more—but there was enough for a few necessities. It was ten below zero in Anchorage and I decided to discard my thin city clothes and dress for the Alaska winter. Finding a war surplus store, I bought a new Army parka, a suit of long woolen underwear, a pair of jeans, wool socks, and a pair of paratrooper boots. Back at the hotel, after changing into my new outfit, I felt like a homesteader again.

The old-fashioned, uncomfortable bus left Anchorage at 8 o'clock in the morning, heading down the highway that had been completed only the year before to connect the city with Moose Pass, the railroad stop at which I had arrived by train two years before. After a time I got into friendly conversation with my seat companion, who was the only other passenger on the bus. He turned out to be a U. S. Deputy Marshal and a very nice guy.

The first mishap of our trip occurred about twenty miles out of Anchorage, when the bus broke down. After waiting in the little settlement of Girdwood until a relief bus came out from the city, we got started again and made it to Moose Pass without further incident.

At Moose Pass, late in the afternoon, we were told that the bus to which we were supposed to transfer had left without us because we had arrived two hours late. Nobody seemed disconcerted: this sort of thing was expected to happen—and usually did. We drove to the seaport town of Seward, the marshal obtaining accommodations with the town marshal and I spending a sleepless night in a bed across the room from the snoring bus driver in the house of the manager of the bus depot.

On the following morning, off we went again, meeting the Anchorage bus at Moose Pass, picking up a few more passengers and heading for Kenai. At Kenai the marshal got off after finishing the telling of his life story and making an offer of one St. Bernard puppy if I could come up to his home in Anchorage to get it. From Kenai southward to Homer, the bus stopped from time to time to deposit a homesteader beside the road to disappear down a lonely path leading through the snowy woods, or beside a snow-covered cabin set close to the highway with a light burning in the window to welcome him home. When we passed my homestead I didn't get off, riding on into Homer instead. After spending the night in "Homer's finest," I got up early the next morning to greet Vern Mutch just as he drove up in my car to open his drugstore.

"Howdy, Vern."

"Hello, Gordon. Glad to be back?"

"You bet!" And I meant it.

As I drove out to the homestead, I felt like pressing my foot down hard on the gas pedal, felt like yelling with excitement. Instead I drove a cautious twenty miles per hour. The highway was like glass, the glare ice threatening to spin the car around and send it skidding in the direction from which it had come if I lost control for a moment.

When I arrived at my snow-choked driveway, I parked the car in a drift, jumped out with my suitcase and, stumbling and falling through two feet of snow, aimed for my home. And when I saw my house and the greenhouse still standing though weighted down by their winter coats, I felt as though I had been away for years—not just five short weeks. I felt like a soldier returning from the wars.

Unlocking the front door, I walked inside and put the coffee pot on to boil.

Chapter XVIII
Spring Fever

THE MIDDLE OF JANUARY, 1953. The snow was piled three feet deep all around the house and the temperature was dropping to thirty degrees below zero every night. It wasn't exactly the ideal season for working in Alaska, but there were certain jobs I was determined to finish before the snow began to melt in April. In my flimsy, windswept garage, I was up to my knees in midnight oil.

I had ordered a lot of thin-cut boards from Keeler to build 200 greenhouse flats to hold the 20,000 assorted set plants I planned to set in the spring. The job seemed endless. After cutting the boards to the proper size, I nailed them together and stacked them on an ever-growing pile in a corner of the garage. In a couple of weeks the garage was so full of shallow boxes that there was no more room for me. But that was all right: I was finished. In totting up my accounts, however, I discovered that the flats, not counting labor, had cost me almost 25 cents apiece. Knocked-down flats in the States would have set me back only 15 cents apiece. Oh, well. Live and learn.

My next scheduled job was to pile up a huge supply of wood to fire the greenhouse stove when the time for firing arrived. Since the sawmills were always trying to figure out what to do with the piles of slabs left over from lumber-cutting operations, I knew this would be easy to get. All I had to do was find a neighbor with a large truck. This I did, and soon ten big loads had been dumped on the snow not far from the greenhouse door. Disconnecting my garden tractor from the power line, I moved it out to the slab pile and put on the arbor saw attachment. It didn't take me long to find out that I could cut quite a considerable number of the slabs into five-foot lengths and stack them neatly in a day, but it was several weeks before I had amassed a big enough stock pile to think of quitting.

During this same time I decided to start clearing another acre of land on the west side of the house. Each day I would set myself the task of falling at least ten trees. When they were lying on the ground, I limbed them, then piled the brush in neat piles and burned it. All through the last part of February and the month of March I kept at this job until there remained only an acre of stumps and about 200 recumbent saw logs. The trees which were too small or too crooked to be made into lumber I had cut and hauled to one side to be cut up into firewood later on.

On the first of March I planted my first seeds. The snow was still deep and the weather still cold, but my house was relatively warm, and that's where I put my first ten flats. Using the kitchen table to hold them, I moved it close to the big kitchen windows so that they would catch all the available sun. I planted tomato and celery seeds first, following with head lettuce. The soil I used was dirt I had scraped out of the cellar—the only place the ground wasn't frozen to a depth of two feet.

From then on, my function was that of a vestal virgin. To keep the house as warm as possible, I had to see that the fires never went out. The greatest danger period was in the early hours of the morning, when the thermometer would start to drop toward freezing and I would have to spring out of bed to build the fires higher and higher to save the flats from going frigid on top. Your doting father walking the floor with the baby at night had nothing on me.

When shoots of green began to show in the flats my next headache began. I would have to thaw the soil in the green-house so as to be able to plant my other seeds. For two weeks I fired the barrel stove with the five-foot slabs, keeping the fire going day and night. An inch at a time, the dirt in the bottom of the benches began to thaw. I covered the top of the soil with rolls of tarpaper so that when the sun hit the greenhouse the black paper would absorb the heat and melt the surface soil, at least. The thawing continued. Finally, the foot of soil in the benches was completely melted, but it was nothing but mud. More fire. More sun. At the end of two weeks the soil was dry enough to work. Building a screen from quarter-inch chicken wire, I proceeded to the lengthy, tedious task of screening the dirt in the benches, at the same time mixing it with sand. Then I filled the flats. When all 200 were full, I put them on boards laid across the benches. Now I was ready to sterilize the soil. Using a solution of water and formaldehyde, I soaked down the flats and left them for a week to dry out.

At this stage of the game I ran into serious trouble. The spring thaw had started, and as the snow level lowered each day under the sharp spring sun, the melted snow trickled into my greenhouse pit, rising there to a level of two full feet. Then the water entered my stove and put the fire out. From then on it was The Battle of the Bucket Brigade. Every morning I started out with a pail in each hand, filled them from the pit, climbed out of the pit, hauled the full buckets over to the bluff and dumped the water out. After repeating this operation at least half a hundred times I would have emptied the pit, but there would always come a time when I would have to bail it out again: the next morning. It seemed as though all the snow in Alaska were melting and heading for my greenhouse. What I needed, I could see, was a drain, and every time I emptied the pit of water I would try to make one by picking away at the frozen ground in front of the stove—the lowest spot—to make a hole through to the thawed ground below. After a week of bailing and digging I at last managed to break through the frost layer and the water drained through. At that point I made a notation in my little black book to hire a cat in the summer to cut a trench from the greenhouse to the bluff. I wasn't anxious to go through all that misery another year.

Planting my vegetable seeds was a job I enjoyed. It was easy, and it was nice to work in the greenhouse when the sun on the trans-o-glass had heated it up to many degrees above the temperature outdoors. I seeded about fifty flats with cabbage, cauliflower, broccoli and lettuce. Later on I would transplant the seedlings until all 200 flats were filled. As an afterthought, I planted a couple of packages of radish seed and several pounds of onion sets in one of the benches to see what would develop.

Weeks later I began the transplanting. When I was finished I had 100 flats in cabbage and the balance in other vegetables. All that was required now was to keep the flats watered and the greenhouse at the proper temperature.

By this time the snow had disappeared entirely, the ground was drying and I was ready to start putting an acre of previously-cleared land in shape to plant—the acre that had been lying fallow ever since I had cut down the trees to build my house. The Extension Service, a government agency which functioned to help farmers, had paid me $40 for clearing the acre and it expected me to use it for farming, but it had never felt the bite of a plow. It had grown, however, a two-feet-tall crop of weeds, and these would have to be removed.

The Keelers brought over their new John Deere tractor one day and plowed and disked the field, turning up thousands of tree roots which had to be picked up— by hand and by me—and thrown over the bluff. When the job was done, the field certainly looked nice: all that good, freshly-turned volcanic earth, ready for planting.

When I subjected the acre to a slightly closer inspection on the following day, however, it didn't look as good as it had at first glance: with its hundreds of holes and hills, it looked more like the highway during spring thaw. Raking the entire field over with a garden rake for a week, I managed to level it out to a certain extent and start it draining toward the bluff. Then I put my rototiller attachment on the tractor and went over the whole acre again, fluffing up the soil to a depth of six inches.

In Homer I picked up half a ton of commercial fertilizer and 300 pounds of seed potatoes. Spreading some of the fertilizer over a quarter of the acre, I mixed it into the ground with the tractor. Now I was ready to start planting. Cutting the potatoes into small pieces, with at least two eyes to a section, I planted them eighteen inches apart in the rows and placed the rows three feet apart, being careful to leave the seeds as close to the surface of the ground as possible so that they could get full benefit from the heat of the sun.

Next I planted my own, private vegetable garden next to the greenhouse—peas, Swiss chard, beets, radishes, green onions and mustard greens. There were lots of other vegetables which would, I knew, grow in Alaska—practically everything but corn—but the ones I chose were the ones I liked. Why should I grow a lot of stuff I wouldn't want to eat?

In the meantime, the set plants in the greenhouse had been growing so fast that, if I wasn't careful, the midnight sun would make them split their flats. Twenty-two hours of daylight in the spring gives a rather alarming impetus to plants in Alaska. The stove hadn't been burning for a week and I had let as much air into the greenhouse as I could so as to harden the plants off and get them ready for sale and for setting out in my own garden. As the first of them became "done," I prepared the ground in the field and planted 500 broccoli plants, 1000 cauliflower plants and 2000 cabbage plants, pressing the dirt firmly around each plant. This, I had learned from my neighbors, was the best way to get the plants growing: the light volcanic earth, when firmed, would draw all available moisture.

But there was still a great deal of ground left unplanted. Hating to see it go to waste, I bought a pound of carrot seed, mixed it with fine sand, and planted a large plot next to the potato patch. Then I was done. All that remained, for the moment, was to prepare to sell my remaining set plants to whoever came along.

I painted up a big sign and set it up next to the highway with an arrow pointing to the homestead. Decorated with a crude picture of a greenhouse surrounded by spruce trees, it read: "*Stoddard's Greenhouse. Set plants and garden vegetables for sale.*" Now I was ready for the hordes of customers who would undoubtedly beat a path to my door. My receipt books were ready, my greenhouse was ready and I was more than ready.

The first customers trickled in. They were mostly other homesteaders who had ordered plants when I had first started to build the greenhouse, and they bought only enough to assure themselves of a summer's supply of vegetables for their tables. Most of them went heavy on the cabbage plants and lettuce but light on the other plants. Some bought by the dozen but a few wanted whole flats—especially those with several mouths to feed. The money in my cash box gradually piled up and more and more flats were emptied, but there was still a large supply of plants going begging.

In the last part of June business picked up. Customers came from all the little towns up and down the road. But by this time the plants were getting much too big for the flats and I realized that I would either have to sell them faster or throw them away. One day, just on a hunch, I took a few flats into Homer with me, leaving them at a hardware store. "Sell 'em if you can," I told the woman owner on my way out. Before I got out of town she had sent a small boy after me. "She says she's sold 'em all and wants you to bring her some more," he said, breathlessly. To my surprise the hardware store sold 3000 plants in less than a week.

When at last my customer list had dropped to zero, however, I still had close to 5,000 set plants on hand. It was plainly a case of supply exceeding demand, and of the markets being too far away. Maybe next year I would sell more. I hoped so. As it was, there was nothing to do but transplant another 2000 cabbage plants from the flats to the field and throw the rest away.

In the meantime, the hundred tomato plants I had set out in the benches were doing fine with the help of lots of water, sunlight and some goat manure given to me by Looie The Goat Man. I had also planted some cucumber and squash seeds, together with a few watermelon seeds, to see what would happen.

The vegetables in the field were doing well, too, and I

was already selling radishes and green onions to grocery stores in three different communities. Broccoli was the next crop to start coming in. I cut it, weighed it up in pound bunches and took it to Homer. It sold like hotcakes—for awhile. Then the population of the isolated little Alaska town—a population which, you'd think, would be hungry for taste after taste of fresh vegetables—decided it had had enough of broccoli and stopped buying. In a way, I didn't blame them. Broccoli for dinner every night for a month can become a little boring. Anything can: I had found that out with salmon.

With each dollar I took in on vegetables three more were going out for expenses. I had discovered that there was much more greenhouse equipment to buy, and many more tools for the garden. My mistake, I decided, had been in not backing myself up with a large hunk of cash for operating expenses during my first year of being in business for myself.

From then on I concentrated on raising money, money and more money. The only thing to do, I had concluded, was to sell part of my land—land across the creek which was covered with timber and would never be any good for farming, anyway. Yes, that's what I would do .

Chapter XIX
Land for Sale

THE WORD WAS OUT that Gordon Stoddard of Stariski Creek was trying to sell part of his homestead. Some of his neighbors shook their heads sadly, knowingly. Eighty acres: the beginning of the end. Another bachelor giving up and going back to the States. Too bad, too bad. But what can you expect, of a bachelor? A man without a wife can stand the life just so long. Too bad. Too bad.

The tradesmen in Homer and Anchor Point looked up their charge accounts to see if Stoddard owed them anything. If he was planning to skip without paying his bills—well, they'd see that he was stopped at the border, all right. A man can't get away with *that* sort of thing.

My closer friends knew that I was trying to sell out all the land I didn't need in order to raise money to better the farming land I would have left when I did. They knew, too, that I was nearly broke, and that I would have to sell something—*anything* in order to live. But the rumors continued.

I didn't care. I knew what I knew: that if I didn't sell some land I would have to work on a construction job during the summer and leave the homestead, with its greenhouse and its verdant, growing fields, to fall into wasteful disuse. I *had* to sell some land.

I put an ad in an Anchorage paper listing 80 acres and a cabin—the shack I had built during my first year of homesteading—for $2500. I also listed the property with a real estate agent in Homer for a short period to see what would develop. The ad brought no results. The listing with the agent brought no results. It looked as though no one wanted my 80 acres. Things looked awfully black at the Stoddard homestead.

One day in July there was a knock on the door. The real estate agent stood on the threshold with a young couple in tow. "These folks," he said, introducing them, "would like to look at your land."

While the couple was admiring the greenhouse, the

real estate man drew me aside. "The time limit on your listing is up," he whispered. "But I'm pretty sure I can make a sale. If I can, will you pay me the ten percent commission?"

"Sure," I whispered back. "But you'll have to raise the price to take care of your cut. I still need $2500."

He agreed. And after spending the next hour walking over the land and examining, with particular attention, the shack near the highway, the people left, saying,"We'll let you know." Familiar words which often don't mean a thing. But I had hopes. And in a further conversation with the agent, who had remained behind to talk, I happened to mention that I would be willing to add another twenty acres of creek bottom land to make a solid 100 acres and price it at $3000. "Great," said the agent. "I'm sure these people'll go for a deal like that. I'll let you know." More hopes.

But when a few days had gone by and nothing had been heard from either the couple or the agent, my hopes died. And when there was a knock on the door I said to myself, "Oh, it's probably just somebody to buy cabbage plants." Nevertheless, I opened the door. There stood a young man I knew I had seen somewhere before.

He stuck out his hand. "Bud May. Land Office. Anchorage," he said.

That rang a bell. He was the fellow who went around inspecting homesteads to determine if the applicants were proving up properly. Oh-oh. What had I done now? Maybe I had failed to fill out my filing papers correctly and didn't own the homestead after all. What a horrible thought.

But his next words reassured me. "I want to buy the 80 acres you have for sale," he said. "As a government employee, I'm not allowed to homestead, you know. But I want some land. How about it?"

"Come in! Come right in!" I croaked. "Here. Have a cup of coffee. Have a seat. Have a cigarette. Have anything I've got!"

Pushing him into a chair, I rushed around collecting things to make him more comfortable, probably making him very uncomfortable, in the process. But I couldn't let him get away. I think I would have shot him down like a dog if he had made a move toward the door.

Getting down to business, I explained to him that the land for sale was now 100 acres. "I'll show it to you," I offered eagerly.

"I've already walked over part of it," he said. "But yes: show me the rest."

Returning from a grand tour of high land and low land, timber land and muskeg land, we were walking up the driveway to the house when we saw a strange car parked by the greenhouse. "That must be the people who were here the other day looking at the land," said I, thinking quickly. "They've probably come back to close the deal."

"No you don't!" cried May, growing excited. "I've got first chance at the land. Look. I've got my typewriter in the car. I'll go get it and we'll make out the papers."

After I had sold the owner of the strange car two dozen cabbage plants, I followed Mr. May into the house and we came to terms. The total price for the land was set at $2800, with $1000 down and the balance to be paid off, at the rate of $50 a month plus six percent interest, in two years. A 30-day option agreement was drawn up and $100 paid me for the option. Everything seemed shipshape and watertight. But as May was leaving he mentioned that he would have to talk the matter over with his wife. This parting shot left me with grave misgivings. Maybe his wife would say no. Maybe May would change his mind. If he did, and with the land tied up for 30 days, I might not find another buyer until late in the season. Or at all. Oh, woe!

For three weeks I suffered. Every day in which I received no word from May was a day of pain. But finally, with only a few of the 30 days left to go, I heard from May. "Meet me in Homer on Monday," he wrote. And on Monday the deal was closed, I put $1000 in the bank, the deed was placed in escrow and I bought a case of beer and some frozen frying chickens and went home to celebrate.

Before I had any prospects for selling the land I had tried to borrow money from the Bank of Homer. But being a greenhorn when it came to doing business with a bank, I had gone about it in the wrong way. I had walked in one day, hunted up the president and put the question plainly. "How about lending me $3000?" I had said.

The president had looked at me blankly. "Why, my dear boy," he had answered. "Three thousand dollars is an immense sum. Three thousand dollars is our limit—our maximum. Who do you think we are: The Bank of America?"

Then he had explained that I would have to have a very good reason for borrowing such a sum and an absolutely sure way of paying it back monthly. Besides, a 120-acre homestead wasn't very good collateral: it practically wasn't collateral at all. A bank would be taking a chance if it loaned as little as $100 on a homestead. In fact—speaking for his own bank—they'd really rather not have anything to do with a homestead.

This was a blow. I had built my house as elaborately as I had—and it was elaborate, for that area—partly with the idea of some day being able to raise some money on it. I figured it was worth between three and five thousand dollars and that I would be able to borrow on it and repay the bank on a yearly basis—even at the eight percent interest the bank demanded. Who, in a country where year'round jobs were an impossibility, could pay monthly installments on a loan? "I know. I know," said the bank president. "But we can't afford to take such risks." I had gone home discouraged and disillusioned.

After my successful sale of the land, however, I thought I would try the bank again. The down payment I had received for the 100 acres wasn't enough to pay for all the equipment I needed. This time I found the banker in a better mood to listen to my proposition. When I told him that I only required $1500 this time and that I had $50 coming in each month, he said he was sure he could fix me up. "However," he said, "you'll have to talk it over with one of our directors."

The director lived some distance north of me and I had to travel many miles to see him, but I felt it was worth the trip. He approved of "the idea" and promised to take the matter up at the bank's next weekly meeting. He was in doubt about one point, however: he wasn't sure that my homestead—the house and the ten acres that I would put up for collateral—would be enough. "Why don't you come out and see my place?" I suggested. "I'm sure it will satisfy you."

A week later the director drove into my yard armed with a formidable-looking camera. He proceeded to aim it at the front of the house. I winced. The front wasn't really finished: I had planned to cover up the upper story: which was still only rough lumber, with peeled slabs. It would look terrible in a picture. Frowning as he snapped, the director muttered, "Hmmm. I don't know. I just don't know."

"Let me show you the interior of the house," I said, grabbing him firmly by the arm. I led him upstairs and downstairs, feverishly pointing out the wonderful view from the windows, the lighting and water system, the rug on my living room floor, the "modern conveniences." Detaching himself from my grasp, the director made his escape.

A few days later in Homer, the bank told me that "everything was all set." It seems the director had been very much impressed. What he had expected to see was a tumbledown shack—the usual for a bachelor homestead—surrounded by heaps of tin cans and garbage. Instead, he found, "a really beautiful house, well equipped." "Loan granted."

The loan was consummated, $1500 was credited to my account, the payments from Bud May were signed over to the bank for my monthly payments on the loan, my household patent was put in a vault for safekeeping.

Now, I felt, I was a true businessman. I had sold land, borrowed from a bank, had a mortgage hanging over my head like everyone else and was once more a man of means. I even carried fire insurance on my house, a requirement of the bank. I was a land baron with debts.

Chapter XX
Ruination of a Sport Fisherman

THE SALMON LEAPED HIGH out of the water, shaking his head in a frantic effort to dislodge the treble hook from his jaw. Falling back with a splash, he surged downstream, spinning the line from my reel so fast—whrrrrr!—that it burned my thumb.

I let him go, waiting for his moment of exhaustion. When there was little resistance to my tug, I heaved up on my light nine-foot bamboo casting rod. Slowly I led him back to the pool on whose bank I was standing. He made a few more short, erratic runs, trying to cut the line on the rocks of the creek bottom. But gradually he became weaker and weaker. When the white of his belly showed—the white flag of surrender—I pulled him into shallow water. Reaching with my free hand into the hip pocket of my jeans. I pulled out a short gaff, placed it at a point an inch behind the feebly flopping fish's head and gave a jerk.

For several minutes the heavy salmon thrashed about among the willows on the bank, crushing whatever he came in contact with. Finally he lay still, and I was able to cut the hooks from his mouth and retrieve the gaff. He was a beautiful 38-pounder, his silver sides and back still greenish, the sea lice still crawling in his gills. A king salmon: king of Alaska.

Dragging my catch up the 200 feet to my house, I dumped it at the back door and went in for a cup of coffee. I felt no excitement. This was only one of hundreds of salmon—kings and silvers—I had caught during my stay in Alaska. This was just another morning in another summer—just another job which had to be done if I was to have plenty of fish to eat in the winter. This salmon would be in the pint jars before the day was over, and I might go down to the creek again in the afternoon after I had watered the greenhouse and tilled the potatoes and catch another one. Ho-Hum...

Ruination of a Sport Fisherman

Catching fish hadn't always been so easy for me, and there had been a time when it hadn't been such a dull, joyless task. Four years before in California, I had been as enthusiastic a sport fisherman as you'd ever hope to find: a rabid stalker of rainbow trout in the high Sierras in the summer, a feverish follower of steelhead at the river mouths in the winter, a fanatic rock fisherman on the shores of the Pacific between seasons. I had lived for fishing ever since the summer vacation when, as a small boy, I had caught my first five-inch trout in the Eel River. Every Christmas after that my family, indulging my piscatorial interest, had given me bigger and better tackle, and every year I had managed to catch slightly larger fish. I had graduated into fly fishing at ten, discovered steelhead fishing at fifteen, caught my first steelhead on my sixteenth birthday. From then on I had haunted the rivers every winter, especially the Carmel River, near where I lived. I was the first fisherman out at the opening of every season and the last to leave on the final day. But in four years I caught only three steelhead. I had to do better than that.

After the war and my discharge from the Navy, I had moved to Mill Valley, across the Golden Gate from San Francisco. From there I had fished all the streams up the California coast: the Russian River, the Gualalla, the Garcia and the Eel. I had thrown away my short casting rod, bought a nine-foot steelhead rod, bought waders and became a bait fisherman. I learned how to cast with a small weight and let a gob of salmon roe bounce over the floor of a stream—where the steelhead lie—without snagging. I learned that when a steelhead takes the bait he's as gentle as a nibbling trout, and that you have to know that nibble when it comes or lose your fish. But with all my expensive equipment and persistence, I caught only one steelhead during my last winter in California. I was disgusted. "There are too many fishermen in this state—and not enough fish!" I had complained to a friend.

All the way to Alaska I had dreamed of the fishing I

would find in the north country. And I was not disappointed. While working in the cannery at Kenai during my first summer on the Kenai Peninsula, I had driven up the highway to the upper reaches of the Kenai River before and after work to spend hours with my rod and reel. The fish I caught, one after the other, without half trying, would have been considered prizes in the high Sierras. Once I stopped by a little creek that ran under the highway through a small culvert. Standing on the highway, I tossed in my line. Its two trout hooks were baited with a single salmon egg apiece, and I really didn't expect much of a result. As fast as I could pull them out I caught Dolly Varden trout. Inside of an hour my fishing basket was bursting with fish up to 20 inches in length. It was—funny to think of it now—one of the biggest thrills of my life.

Another time I hiked up to a mountain lake which was supposed to contain an abundance of trout and, by casting from the shore with a short casting pole and a spinner, was able to land two huge, green-colored Mackinaw trout weighing a total of thirteen pounds. I lost most of my equipment in the process, besides falling into the lake a couple of times, but I considered the day an immense success.

The Anchor River, seventeen miles north of Homer, was my first salmon fishing heaven. I discovered it shortly after my arrival in town while I was a house guest of Vern Mutch. At that time, I was told, the king salmon run was over but the silvers and steelhead were still heading upstream to spawn. "Steelhead! Salmon!" I cried as I rushed down to the mouth of the river early one morning.

I had rigged up my outfit in the way I had always done for catching steelhead in California, using a gob of salmon eggs for bait. I gave my nine-foot pole a heave and cast my line far out into the center of a beautiful little tide pool. Almost at once I hooked a fish. With trembling hands and pounding heart, I played it up to the three-foot bank on which I was standing and tried to lift it. The weight was too much for my ten-pound leader: the silver salmon fell back into the water, taking my leader with him. The still morning air rang with my curses, and if there had been anyone around to hear me —well, I would have been considered a bad prospect for Alaska, for sure.

I calmed down when I took another look at the pool: it was literally boiling, swirling with fish. Wading across the stream to a sand bar, I tossed my line in again. At noon I stopped fishing—but only because I was exhausted. Lying on the sand were twelve salmon and eight steelhead, lined up from the smallest—five pounds—to the largest—fifteen pounds: more fish—and considerable more poundage—than I had ever caught in one session in all my life in California. Truly, Alaska was my natural home!

There was only one thing missing: there were no envious fishermen to crowd around me and congratulate me on my luck, no one to admire the shining beauty of the rows of fish, no people at all. Carrying the fish to my car, I drove into Homer, parked in front of Vern's drugstore and opened up the baggage compartment so that everyone could see my catch. Of all the passing people who glanced at it only one man stopped to comment. "Been fishin', huh?" he said. "You gonna sell 'em or can 'em up for the winter?"

I gaped at him.

"Say, that reminds me," he continued. "I got to get busy and catch fifty of them pretty soon or my old lady will tan my hide."

In dismay I offered him my fish. "Well, thanks," he said in a tired voice. "That *will* save me a little work." He disappeared, then, but in a few minutes he was back with a gunny sack, which he proceeded to fill with the salmon. "Don't you want the steelhead?" I asked him.

"Not on your life. They're not good for anything. Around here, we just throw them in the bushes when we catch them. The bones don't cook up in the canner.

They're not even good for dog food." I stared after him in horror as he trudged away with his heavy sack.

From then on I changed my attitude toward steelhead —toward any fish smaller than a salmon. I spent almost every day on the banks of the river, catching silvers by the dozen. I got a kick out of catching so many, and it tickled me to think that if a game warden passed by he would have nothing to say: at that time there was no limit in Alaska. Besides, I had learned the law of the land: that fishing, besides being a sport, is one of the prime ingredients of survival in Alaska, and that every single fish that isn't eaten fresh goes into a jar. (I was giving mine to Vern Mutch, and he was canning them up as fast as I caught them).

When I finally found my homestead, one of the things that helped me decide on that particular location was its proximity to the Anchor River (six miles) and the fact that the land itself had a good fishing stream running its length: Stariski Creek. Just the thought of having my own private fishing stream had made me dash off a series of letters containing snapshots of strings of weighty silver salmon to my frustrated fishing pals in the States. And on the backs of the pictures, laughing with maniacal glee, I had written, "Just a typical morning's catch in Alaska."

The following spring I got ready for the king salmon season. My neighbors seemed to think that kings were the only kind of fish worth fishing for and I was anxious to try my skill. Using the same tackle I had used for the silver salmon and steelhead, I caught my first two kings on my first day of fishing in the Anchor River. They put up a magnificent fight in the rushing water, but I landed them in the end. The other fishermen there that day had scoffed at my light bamboo pole and my small reel with the 20-pound test line. "You'll never catch a king with that flimsy tackle," they had told me. "What you need is a short casting pole with a star drag reel and plenty of 60-pound test line." "That's a lot of hogwash," I had rudely retorted—and proved it. What I had found out was sufficient to give me confidence: that the salmon would fight the bending, flexible pole instead of my arm, that the simple reel was easier to control than a heavy star-drag mechanism, and that the 20-pound line was heavy enough to land any salmon if handled properly. And while the other fishermen, with their short rods and heavy reels, used spinners with huge treble hooks baited with gobs of salmon eggs and wire leaders, I eliminated the leader and weight on my line and used only a treble hook baited with salmon roe. The weight of the bait was sufficient to keep it on the bottom, where the kings were lying, and I was able to catch them when the others couldn't.

One memorable day I appeared at my favorite salmon hole, a long, deep hole in which the stream rushed swiftly over the rocks in an unbroken line. There were several fishermen ahead of me, but none of them had had any success. Starting at the head of the hole, I bounced my bait along the bottom. Within four hours I had landed eleven salmon and lost several others. And whenever I hooked a king and followed him downstream, I would look back to see another fisherman running over to the spot I had just vacated to cast frantically into the same water. It got to be funny. I was adding fish after fish to a growing pile and nobody else was catching a thing. "You lucky devil!" they said it to me, over and over again. I tried to explain that it wasn't luck: it was the equipment I was using. But no one would listen. I was pretty unpopular that day.

After that I did most of my fishing in my own creek, leaving the Anchor River to the others. I will always remember my first king salmon experience with the Stariski. Two of my neighbors and I followed the creek to a point a mile above the bridge where there was a large hole dammed by some cooperative beavers. Throwing a rock into the pool, we watched the water churn and boil like a witches' pot, and when one of my friends climbed a tree for a better look he almost lost his balance and came near joining the fish in the creek below. "There's over a hundred kings in there!" he shouted.

For a short while we tried bait, but apparently the fish weren't interested in eating. Then we switched to snag outfits. These are made by putting a large treble hook on the end of a line, adding a heavy sinker, then putting another large treble hook above the weight. I threw my line in, let it sink, then gave my pole a jerk. The pool boiled, and out of the turbulent water leaped a king with my hook in its back. Hitting the water again, it shot like a torpedo toward the creek bank, hit it, almost caved it in with the force of its drive. Then it headed for the opposite bank. Then back again. Then, either through breaking the line or tossing the hook, it got away. But I wasn't disappointed. Snagged salmon put up over twice the fight of a fairly-caught fish — and give the fisherman over twice the thrill.

One of my friends couldn't seem to get the hang of snagging fish. "I'll snag one for you," I offered. "When I've got one, I'll hand you the pole and you can play it." He stood right by my side while I snagged a fish, but before he could start winding up the slack line in the reel the huge king salmon swam up on the beach and landed high and dry between his legs. He was so disgusted he refused to try again. "It's either too hard or too easy," he complained.

That afternoon we carried the nine large kings we had caught back to my cabin, and that night we put them up into ten cases of pint jars—food for months.

But after two years of fishing in Alaska, something sad happened to me. I was a changed man. No longer did I quiver and shake when playing a prize fish. No longer did I curse and break fishing rods if a big one got away. No longer was I the first one out in the spring and the last one to stop fishing in the fall. No longer did I send pictures of my catches home to my friends in the States: I didn't even bother taking pictures. The thrill was gone. All I did was what was necessary. When the main king salmon run was on, I spent just enough days at the creek to fill up five cases of pint jars with what I caught, and after that I would lose all interest in fishing —unless I felt like a nice, fresh salmon steak for dinner. And even then, if I fished for half an hour without catching anything, it didn't bother me: I'd just shrug my shoulders, open up a can of moose meat and make myself a pot of moose stew. And if I accidentally caught a steelhead—well, I threw it back.

Thus was accomplished the ruination of a good sport fisherman. Thus a man who had once lived to fish became a monster who only fished to live.

Chapter XXI
The Visitation

INTO EACH SON'S LIFE a little mother must fall.

I was excited when I received the letter from California: the letter that told me my mother would be arriving on a certain day in July and that I must be sure to meet her at the Homer airport. At last a member of my family was to view the results of all my labors, to see what I had accomplished in the past three years! At last I could prove that I hadn't been lying in my letters about what a wonderful country Alaska was! I must get everything in readiness, in perfect order, for the great occasion.

Scrubbing, shining, dusting and sweeping, I put the house in tip-top Navy shape—good enough, at least, to pass a mother's inspection (I hoped).

Then I turned my attention to the grounds. On the east side of the greenhouse, in the growing field, I wouldn't have to do much besides spend a day with the rototiller, cultivating between the rows of vegetables and digging the fireweed into the soil. But the west side of the greenhouse was a different proposition: there was an acre of stumps and saw logs left from my clearing work of the early spring, and in the center of the acre, sticking out like a bum at a banker's convention, stood the outhouse in all its shabby glory. I would have to hurry and clear out this blot on the landscape before my mother's arrival.

Luckily there was a D-4 caterpillar tractor in the area. I hired its owner to remove the offensive stumps and push them out of sight over the bluff but instructed him to leave the saw logs untouched. Next, I told him to move the even more offensive outhouse to a spot under a group of trees on the edge of the bluff. Then, as an afterthought, I had him ditch my entrance road and make it wider, build a new road along the government survey line back to my northeast corner, clear me a couple of spots along the bluff in that direction for possible future cabin sites, and last, but certainly among the most important, dig me a trench from the greenhouse pit to the bluff to insure good drainage during the next spring thaw. These jobs took the operator three days and cost me a large sum of money, but my homestead, when he was finished, was a thing of beauty. Mother would be pleased.

The great day arrived. I shaved, pulled on slacks and a sweater—the Alaskan equivalent to full dress in the States—and drove into Homer. After having three months of growth cut from my shaggy locks (I often went without a haircut for longer than that because of the scarcity of barbers in the area), I was ready to meet my mother. The plane landed and I was striding quickly across the field calling "Hiya, Mom!" to the small, stylish figure descending the portable stairs.

My mother was dressed as though she had just come from a tea at the Biltmore, and she stood out among the other passengers milling around us in their windbreaker jackets and jeans like a bright candle among a lot of moths. So did I, in my slacks and sweater. Or so I thought, until Mother kissed me and said, "Well, darling. You *look* like a homesteader."

Though in her middle sixties when it came to age, my mother was twenty years younger in energy. As we moved toward the car she excitedly told me all about her trip up in the plane and all the wonderful scenery she had seen on the way, and if she was tired she didn't show it in her voice. And as we drove through Homer and out the highway toward my homestead, she also tried to relate all that had happened to her since we had last seen each other at Christmas. At the same time I endeavored to point out the scenes of interest we were passing, and the result was a rather jumbled, confused sort of conversation. Good old Mother: she hadn't changed a bit. It was fine to see her again.

As we approached my place I cut in with, "Well, Mom, we're almost there. There's the old shack where I first proved up on my homestead. We are now crossing Stariski Creek, the creek that flows through my land.

Here's the road into my place. And there: there's my house and homestead." I stopped the car in front of the house. "What do you think of it?"

"Why, it's all very nice, dear," she answered in what I felt was a slightly disappointed voice. "It's not exactly as I pictured it, but it looks as though you've done a great deal of work."

Not permitting her to say any more, I caught her hand and led her through the house, the greenhouse and the garage, then out across the fields. She exclaimed at most points with appropriate words of praise, but finally she said, "Son, do you mind if I take off my best coat and change my shoes? I'm afraid these high heels are making big holes in your potato hills."

Cursing myself for my selfish enthusiasm, I gave my mother a little time to unpack her bags and get settled a bit. Then, thinking she would be hungry after her trip and anxious to show off my well-stocked larder, I said, "What would you like for dinner, Mom? You can have your choice of canned moose meat, rabbit, bear, spruce chicken, clams or fish. For vegetable I can offer you fresh-out-of-the-garden broccoli, cauliflower, cabbage, swiss chard or mustard greens."

"Well." She hesitated. "If you don't mind, Son, I'd just like a cup of tea and some toast. I had a good meal in Anchorage when the plane stopped there."

I was disappointed in her reaction to my menu, but I tried not to show my feelings. Across the table from my plateful of moose meat, fried potatoes and boiled mustard greens, I eyed her cup of tea and wondered, sadly, if she would ever get used to homesteader's fare. Maybe I should have put in a supply of canned corned beef hash or boned chicken or something. Maybe. Oh, well; probably the clean, fresh air of Alaska would improve her appetite . . . .

After dinner Mother gave the house a second scrutiny. "My, this floor is dirty," she commented. "Don't you ever clean it, Son?"

"Sure, Mom. I sweep it every two days. I gave it an extra lick in honor of your arrival."

"Why don't you mop it?"

"I don't own a mop. Besides, you can't take the time to keep a house perfectly clean when you're working out of doors all day long."

She frowned, meditatively. "I suppose not. But tomorrow I'm going to do something about it. You can buy me a mop in that town we passed through. Living in the wilderness shouldn't mean that you forget the way you've been brought up. You never saw our home in California looking like this."

"No, Mom."

Later in the evening Mother expressed a desire to take a bath. I filled a bucket with water and put it on the stove to heat, saying, "Bucket bath coming right up, madam!" She looked at the bucket. "Well," she said, "I guess I won't take a bath tonight. Maybe tomorrow."

The outhouse was also a shock. When she returned from a late-evening trip, she remarked. "At least you could have built the toilet a little closer to the house, Son. I nearly got lost in the dark, trying to find it."

When it was time to go to bed, I fixed Mother up on an iron cot with my thickest mattress and warmest blankets. Knowing that a comfortable bed had always been one of her prime requirements in life, I was dubious about the whole arrangement, but it was all I had to offer. And all night long the cot squeaked and groaned as she tried to find a sleepable position. "Poor Mother," I thought, as I listened. "She's going to have a hard time, roughing it up here with me." I pounded my pillow, buried my head in it. "But then," I told myself as I sank into oblivion, "a sourdough was never made in a day."

In the morning Mother offered to take over the cooking, as I had hoped she would. She was an excellent cook, and my mouth was already watering with the thought of tasting some more of those good meals I had loved as a boy.

And I would have tasted them, I'm sure, had it not

been for my coal cookstove. Mother had never seen one before—or, at least, not since the days of her own childhood—and she was aggrieved when it turned on her like a big, black monster. First it was too hot. Then it was too cold. I would start it up and have it working normally by the time I left the house for the fields, but the minute Mother found herself alone with it she would lose all control. "I can't *understand* it," she would cry. "I watch this little gauge in the oven door, but the oven doesn't act at all like my gas oven at home." She was right: it didn't. All the meals came out overdone or undercooked. And, irritated over her failures, Mother begged me to buy a better stove. I explained to her that though a butane stove would give better results, a coal stove was more practical in a country where coal was free, and it would have to do. Thereafter, the coal stove stayed solidly in place—as did all of Mother's meals in my stomach.

Poor Mother: there were so many things that bothered her about life in Alaska—about life, particularly, in the Stoddard homestead cabin. For one thing, she was afraid of the cellar. I had made the mistake of telling her the story about the ermine who had occupied it one winter and snarled at me every time I went down to get some supplies, and of how I hadn't shot it because it kept down the hordes of mice and shrews which lived there, and that did it, I guess. I assured her that the ermine was gone, now, but she argued—most reasonably, I'll admit—that the mice and shrews were still there, and she flatly refused to set foot in "that hole." As a consequence, she called me in from the fields several times a day to fetch cans of food for her. This bit into my working time and annoyed me a little, but I really couldn't blame her, I told myself, for not wanting to meet my little cellar friends.

Mother's only vice was ice water. When she learned that I owned a spring that supplied five gallons of ice water every minute of the day, she was overjoyed. And from the way in which she raved over the coldness of the water and its flavor, I knew that at last there was something on my homestead that pleased her. She insisted on my going down the hill to the spring every evening before dinner and bringing back a pitcherful of it. On certain days when I was tired from a tedious day's work I would try explaining to her that I had gone to great trouble and expense to put a water system in the house in order to eliminate the hill-climbing, and I assured her that the water which came from the kitchen faucet was exactly the same as that which came from the spring. "But the spring water is colder," she would inform me. So off I would go, down the hill like Jack to fetch a pail of water.

It was mid-July, and the weather, to my mind, was warm. During the days the temperature would often rise to as high as 80 degrees. To an Alaskan who is used to sub-zero temperatures, this seemed as hot as a blast from a furnace. It seemed warm to Mother, too, but when the temperature dropped to what I thought of as a still-warm 70 degrees at night, she would begin to shiver. "Build a fire in the barrel stove, Son," she would say.

"But Mom," I would protest. "There's plenty of heat coming from the cookstove."

"It's not warm enough for me," she would reply, pulling her sweater over her shoulders.

Then I would build a small fire, and for the rest of the evening I would suffer in a sweat-dripping undershirt while Mother, in a thin house dress, would sit as close as she could to the stove. I watched, with some dismay, the dwindling of my winter's wood supply, knowing that I would have to build it up again before the snows came. But I understood: Mother and I were inhabitants of two different worlds, now, and never the twain would meet.

After Mother had been with me a week I decided to drive my car up to Anchorage and trade it in on a jeep truck. Leaving the greenhouse in the care of the Keeler boys, Mother and I started out, heading north. Our progress was slow. Mother had brought along her 35-mm. camera, and every few miles or so she asked me to stop so that she could take a picture. I didn't mind, but as the day wore on, I began to worry about reaching the city before late at night. The Sterling Highway, even in the daytime, isn't very safe to drive, and at night there's always the danger of hitting a moose or skidding off some sharp curve. I pleaded with her. "Mom," I said. "We've still got 150 miles to go. If we stop any more for pictures we'll never make it."

She seemed to understand, but at the next point of interest she said, "Just this once. Please?"

And so it went. Alaska is cluttered with scenery—too much of it, to my way of thinking—and besides, I was familiar with it all. But to Mother it was "magnificent, breathtaking, awesome." I tried to see her point of view, but it was difficult. This was a business trip for me, and I wanted to get to Anchorage as soon as possible and back to the homestead even quicker. As it turned out, we made Anchorage at about 9. p. m. without mishap, except for one flat tire and three broken valve springs.

On the following day, after stopping in a hotel overnight, I ran around town looking for a good trade-in on my car while Mother investigated the shops. I was finally able to get a 1950 jeep in poor condition by turning in my car and $600 in cash. I also bought a new short block for the jeep—just in case the other motor wasn't any good—picked up Vern Mutch's chain saw, which had been repaired, and bought a Buick axle for the Keelers. Then I met Mother at the hotel. "I want to see some sights," she said.

I was too tired to want to do anything but go to bed, but I took her out to dinner. We had to wait in line an hour before being served, and that didn't please her too much. Nor did the food. That finished Anchorage for Mother, and we were able to return to the hotel and retire.

The next day I picked up the jeep and we started back. Driving on the paved portion of the road wasn't too bad, but when we hit the gravel it was like taking a ride in a concrete mixer. The truck jolted and reared until my mother was shrieking for mercy. To make her feel better, I stopped every few miles to let her rest and take pictures,

The Visitation

hoping and praying that the pile of junk I had bought would hold together until we reached home.

About ten miles from the homestead the truck stopped. The motor was still running, but that was all. The time was midnight and it was so dark I could hardly see Mother sitting beside me on the seat. With no flashlight, it would be impossible to determine the source of the trouble. "Wait here," I said to Mother.

Walking half a mile in a direction I knew well, I routed a friend out of his warm bed and borrowed a flashlight, a screwdriver and some baling wire. But back at the truck, with my head under the hood, I still couldn't locate the trouble. "Well," I said to Mother. "It looks—"

"Gordon!" she said. "Here comes a car!"

As lights approached, I stood in the middle of the road and flagged the car down. I had an idea. Mother, who was freezing in the truck, could get a ride with whoever it was. In a whispered consultation, I explained the plan to her.

"Go with a strange man in the middle of the night?" she cried in a scandalized voice which I was sure the strange man could hear. "Oh, *no*, Gordon."

"But, Mother," I pleaded. "I might be all night fixing the truck. In the meantime, the man can drop you off at the homestead and you'll be home, at least. Please. The man won't hurt you."

After much discussion she agreed, the man agreed, and off they drove. Pretty soon more lights showed. It was a jeep, and I flagged it down. "Let me look at your engine. Maybe I can find out what's broken in mine," I said to the driver.

It didn't take me long, after that, to find out that there was something missing in my gas feed. I fixed it with a piece of wire and hurried home. Mother was still up and very voluble. She spent the next several hours telling me about the nice man who had driven her home and what an adventure the whole experience had been.

A few days later I went into Homer and down to the dock to pick up a load of groceries I had ordered from

Seattle a month before (buying groceries in quantity that way was a big money-saver, though it did take time) and two drums of gasoline. Mother had wanted to go in with me—she was finding the quiet of the homestead irksome—but I had convinced her that with a big load and an unfamiliar truck it wouldn't be safe. On the way home I stopped at the Keelers' and picked up a surprise for her: a malemute puppy, a kitten and two bantam chickens. Mother was delighted with the kitten, tolerably interested in the dog and openly frightened of the bantams with their two-inch spurs. Promptly she named the kitten "Happy" and carried it into the house, barring entrance to the dog, whom I named "Attu," and to the chickens, who became "Mom" and "Pop."

At four o'clock the next morning the rooster crowed —loudly and long—and the puppy joined in with typical malemute howls—which sound, I admit, a little like a wolf. I turned over in my bed, figuring that the noise would soon stop and that I could get back to sleep. But in her cot across the room Mother was wide awake. "How do you expect your poor old mother to sleep through a racket like that?" she said.

"But, Mom," I replied. "You live in a city where it's much noisier than this at all hours of the day and night."

"Yes, but here it's so quiet all the time that any noise at all awakens me. Please, son: can't you do something about those animals?"

From then on until my mother left the homestead I shut the puppy and the chickens in the garage each night in lidded boxes, and in the morning, after Mother was fully awake, I let them out. The kitten? Well, the kitten was allowed to sleep in the house: it didn't make any noise, though it did use the back of my head as a claw-sharpening post every night.

The Keelers had built a large addition to their house and were holding a square dance for the community in it every other Saturday night, providing "canned" music and plenty of fun for all comers. When Mother heard about the dances, she wanted to go to one: she loved to dance.

"They're pretty strenuous," I told her. "They last all night. Do you think you can take it?"

"Pooh!" she said, scornfully. "I can outdance anyone there!"

And she could. She danced until midnight, ate her fill of the midnight supper brought by all the housewives of the area (bachelors were never asked to bring anything but their appetites), then danced some more. "My," said Lorna Keeler, watching Mother weave in and out among the fifty or sixty dancers on the floor. "Your mother sure has a lot of pep."

"More'n I've got," I answered, mopping my brow.

By 3 o'clock in the morning, after twirling Mother through all the squares, I was so worn out that it was all I could do to hang onto the wheel of the truck during the two-mile drive home. "That was fun!" she said, as we entered the house. "Let's be sure to go to the next one!"

"Yes, Mother," I said as I crawled painfully into bed.

On the following day she was still full of zip. "Let's go blueberry picking," she suggested, gaily. "I've seen lots of them out there in the woods, and they look beautifully ripe."

A few minutes later, however, after falling down at almost every step in the thick moss carpet that serves for terrain on most of my land, and after picking only a handful of berries, she said, "Let's go home."

I gave her a wicked look. "No," I said. "Not until we fill all the pails. When we go dancing, we dance; when we go berry-picking, we pick." At that point it started to rain, but we picked and picked—until, at least, she had filled a little half-gallon pail and I a four-gallon bucket.

From the day she had arrived Mother had been kidding me about salmon. "Where are all those salmon you wrote me about?" she'd say. "I'm not going to leave Alaska until you catch one for me."

I explained to her that the king salmon run was over and the silver salmon run hadn't begun yet. "I'll catch you one in a few weeks, when the run begins," I promised.

"I certainly would like to have one now," she said. "You'd better catch me one, or I'll tell everyone at home that you've been telling fibs."

To keep Alaska's fishing legend alive, I devoted a couple of hours each day to fishing fruitlessly at the mouth of the Anchor River. Maybe, I thought, I could catch the first salmon of the season—the advance guard of the run to come.

The fish I finally caught was a little one—only eight pounds—and I hooked it in Stariski Creek. Carrying it triumphantly into the house, I dumped it into the sink. "Here's your salmon," I said to Mother. "Are you happy now?"

She smiled, looking at the fish. "You'll have to clean it," she said. "I don't know anything about those things."

I ended up cleaning it, frying it and eating it. Mother had found out that she really didn't like salmon, after all.

One day Mother decided to give a dinner party. When I had taken her around to call on some of my friends they had usually invited us to dinner, and she felt obligated, she said, to return the favors. Her guest list included Mr. and Mrs. Vern Mutch and Ken Rickly, who was the postmaster at Anchor Point and a good pinochle friend.

Shortly before the Mutches and Ken arrived, Mother asked me to put on a suit for the occasion. "But, Mother," I protested. "No one gets dressed up for dinner in a homesteader's cabin. Nobody wears a suit, up here. You saw how they dressed at the dance the other night."

"But you look so terrible in those jeans and that ragged blue work shirt."

I went upstairs, found my tweed suit hanging up in the storeroom, found a shirt to go with it, found a tie. "There!" said Mother as I came downstairs. "Now you look *civilized*."

But the party was not a success. I was overdressed and embarrassed about it, Mother was overdressed and embarrassed because the coal cookstove had turned on her again. After the guests had gone, I explained to her that people do not judge other people by the clothes they wear in Alaska—but simply by what they do and accomplish. "I see," she said in a small voice. But I don't think she did.

At the end of five weeks it was time for my mother to return to California. As we stood on the veranda of the Anchor Point store waiting for the bus that was to take her to Seward and a boat heading for the States, we had our last talk. "I think it's fine, what you've achieved on your homestead," said Mother. "But you're wasting your life up here. You weren't brought up for this kind of—of... well, I think you'd be much better off to come back to the city and get a good job. I hate to think of a son of mine living up here in this wild country, wearing dirty clothes, not taking a bath every day, not shaving or brushing his teeth regularly, becoming a sort of savage. Won't you sell out and come back home?"

"No, Mother," I said rather vehemently. "I can never go back to that old life. I might go back for a visit now and then, but I could never live in a city again. I like Alaska. I like the feeling of independence I have up here. I wouldn't trade it for anything!"

The bus drove up and we kissed each other goodbye. Then I drove slowly back to the homestead, glad to have my freedom once again. But when I entered the house and saw some of the things Mother had discarded in her packing—pictures of California, pieces of clothing, a heelless mule under the cot she had used for a bed—and a note she had tacked over the kitchen sink ("Gordon! A reminder! Comb your hair and brush your teeth!"), I felt suddenly lonely. Striding out and slamming the front door, I jumped back into my truck and drove down the road to the nearest bar. Mothers! You can't live with them, but as soon as they're gone you find you can't live without them! What's a poor homesteader to do?

Chapter XXII
Pets and Livestock

I LAID MY BOOK DOWN and chuckled. Then I roared. Watching Attu, the malemute puppy, and Happy, the kitten, as they tussled together on the living room rug was one of my favorite indoor sports—much more entertaining than reading the latest batch of pocket books brought by a neighbor in exchange for some of mine!

Clumsy, fat Attu, not yet grown-up enough to be entirely sure of his footing but full of determination just the same, would stagger across the floor toward the twitching Happy whining in a brave, high-pitched tenor. The tiny black-and-white kitten would wait until he was almost upon her. Then she'd leap straight up into the air, land in back of Attu and skitter under the bed.

"Where'd she go? Where'd she go? She was here just a minute ago," Attu would seem to say as he whirled stupidly around, lost his balance and fell ungracefully on his head. Then, just as he had hauled himself to his feet with his forehead wrinkled as though in concentration on some new course of action, he would be knocked to the floor again by the flying kitten.

With only a few variations, this game would continue until both dog and cat were exhausted and I was exhausted from laughing. At that point they would curl up on the rug for a nap together—Attu on the bottom and the kitten, lying outstretched across the puppy's balloon-like stomach, rising and falling with his heavy breathing. What a pair!

Life was not all play and fun, though: there was serious business to be done. When Happy and Attu were outdoors, they looked upon themselves as hunters, and they spent all their waking hours stalking the two bantam chickens. The chickens would be peacefully pecking the ground for stray bits of grain when suddenly Mom would look up, emit a frightened squawk and run pellmell for the garage, with Pop, valiantly defending her rear, only a few steps behind. A stumbling, shuffling Attu would follow as far as the garage door, peer into the dark interior, change his mind about pursuing the chickens any further and stumble back into the sunlight to wait further developments. Happy, in the meantime, would have ceased her pre-springing twitching movements and turned her attention to a passing bee. But pretty soon the chickens would be back in the yard again, and the hunting party would start all over. The only thing that bothered me about the whole performance was the fear that the dog and cat might catch the chickens some day—and learn, to their chagrin, that bantams with two-inch spurs are well able to take care of themselves.

When Keeler had given me the chickens he had told me, frankly, that he wanted to get rid of them. The hen, he said, laid very few eggs, and what eggs she did lay were impossible to collect because the rooster always put up a fight for them. Besides, they were both seven years old and too tough to eat. I took them because they were free, and because I thought they might amuse my mother, but the time very shortly came when I began to feel that I had gotten the worst of a very bad bargain. Although they weren't expensive to feed, they filled my garage with feathers and covered my tools with droppings, and when the hen stopped laying entirely all I had left was the dubious luxury of a non-winding alarm clock. And even this grew tiresome—especially when daylight began at 3 o'clock in the morning during the period of the midnight sun.

When I had first introduced Mom and Pop to their new home they had acted like a couple of displaced children. They had perched atop my slab pile through days of wet weather, their feathers dripping, their heads drooping, their eyes closed as though in pain. They looked as though they had lost their last friends—which they had, in the form of the Keelers' 500 other chickens. And there was worse to come. One day I heard an excited barking and looked out the kitchen window just in time to see the two bantams flying down into the willow-covered creek bottom pursued by a neighbor's dog. Calling the dog off and sending him home, I waited for the chickens to return. There was no movement in the creek bottom for quite awhile. After two hours, the rooster came trudging tiredly up the bluff, his head down, his feathers in complete disarray. He staggered to the top of the slab pile and started to crow—obviously to call the hen. But no hen appeared, and after crowing himself hoarse the rooster gave up. He was the most dejected chicken I have ever seen. He slumped down on the slab pile, and though I put out the choicest grain for him he ignored it, continuing to gaze forlornly down into the creek valley for some sign of his mate. It was almost dark and I was inside, cooking my dinner, when I heard the rooster crow. And there was a new note in his voice: a note of happiness. Rushing out the door, I beheld the hen staggering wearily up the bluff trail, and when the two chickens met in the yard there was a reunion scene I'll never forget. With new bursts of energy, the two little birds jumped madly about, actually doing a dance of joy. I had wisely named them "Mom" and "Pop."

Life in Alaska can be dangerous for domestic animals. One day I was in my usual position by the barrel stove reading a good book and drinking endless cups of warmed-over coffee when I heard Attu whimpering in pain. The sound seemed to be coming from a long distance away. I dashed outside, but there was no sign of the dog in the yard. I rushed out to the garage. No Attu. I loped back to the house, listened again. Then it came to me: the pup was in the cellar.

Grabbing a flashlight, I went outside and down through the outside entrance to the cellar, cursing myself for having left the door open that morning. I flashed the light around. Still no Attu. Then I heard the whimpering again. Moving over to the well, I saw that one of its covering boards was missing. I directed the light down the seventeen-foot hole. There, standing in a foot of ice-cold water, was Attu, gazing piteously up at me. Apparently he had been playing in the cellar, stepped on a loose board and plummeted, like a big, heavy rock, to the bottom. It took me only a few seconds to climb down the well, pick up the puppy—who was now wriggling with such excitement that I could hardly hold him —throw him over my shoulder and climb out. He wasn't hurt: only scared out of the few wits he had. Before I rubbed him down I made the well cover so safe that even a shrew couldn't have fallen in.

A few days later I leaned my salmon pole up against the house and went inside to clean my morning's catch of silvers. Just as I applied my knife to the second fish I heard a series of frightened yelps from Attu. Dropping everything, I rushed outside. Attu, on his belly, was crawling across the yard with the big treble hook I used on salmon affixed to his mouth and the fishing pole trailing behind. Catching him, I broke the line and carried him into the house. No fish had ever been hooked so completely. Two of the hooks were caught in the roof of the poor puppy's mouth, and the third protruded from his lower lip. He was so trussed up that he could neither open nor close his jaws.

Rolling him in a blanket to keep him from kicking me while I operated, I took him out to the garage, where I looked for something with which to cut the hooks. The big tin shears I found were clumsy and not too sharp, but I stuck them into the puppy's mouth and tried to cut off the bottom hook. Each time I put the pressure on, Attu gave a yelp and tried to wriggle out of the blanket, jamming me forcefully in the stomach and addling my aim with every kick. It was awful. Finally, though, I made a lucky snip, and off went the hook. Then, with a pair of pliers, I pulled what was left through the lip and removed the other two hooks from the roof of the mouth. Released, Attu gamboled happily around the yard as though nothing had happened. As for me, I stumbled into the house and collapsed on the bed. After that I was careful to put all fishing gear out of the reach of curious animals.

Cats, in general, seem to stay out of trouble more than dogs. Whether it's because they develop faster, or whether the predatory animal in their makeup makes them less clumsy and more cautious I don't know. At any rate, while Attu was courting disaster at every turn, Happy was spending her time keeping herself immaculate, learning to catch mice and looking more and more like the self-sufficient little animal she would eventually become. But there came a day:

I was working out in the cauliflower patch, cutting the over-ripe heads down so that they would rot more quickly. The kitten had accompanied me to the field and was having a fine time stalking me from cauliflower to cauliflower. I didn't pay much attention to her: I was working steadily, swinging my butcher knife from right to left in measured rhythm. Suddenly, as I took a mighty swing at an unusually big head, I saw another head—a little, furry head—peering out at me from between the leaves. It was too late to arrest the force of my arm. The cat leaped high into the air, then landed and shot down the rows, her life's blood spurting in all directions.

I was petrified. What had I done? And what should I now do—now that I had almost murdered a trusting pet? I ran into the house and grabbed my loaded 22 rifle. At least I could put the poor little cat out of its misery.

I found Happy sitting on the edge of the bluff. Her head still seemed to be intact, but when she shook it, the blood spattered the ground around her. I put the rifle to my shoulder and took a bead on her. Then I lowered the gun. I couldn't do it. Even if she was suffering, I couldn't do it. And maybe . . .

Apparently unaware of the imminence of death, Happy had begun to apply her tongue to her coat. Where had I heard that when a sick cat begins to wash it can be considered on its way to recovery? An old wives' tale, maybe. But then there was that one about a sick cat's eating. When a cat eats, they said, it can't be very badly off. I made a resolution: "If Happy eats," I told myself, "I won't shoot her. I'll wait and see what happens."

Returning to the house, I filled a bowl with canned

milk. When I placed it before the kitten, she gave me a dirty look. "I know," I said. "I'm a dirty, stinking murderer. But do you want some milk?"

She lowered her little half-severed head to the bowl and began to lap. When she had licked the bowl clean, I carried her into the house, wrapped a clean cloth around her neck, and padded a box with a sweater of mine which she had always seemed to like. For the next two weeks her every mew was my command. And in that period, she washed the two-inch wound in her neck and shoulder until it was completely closed, and very soon hair began to cover the scar. Cats are amazing creatures.

As Attu grew he gained in appetite. I had bought a 100-pound sack of mink and fox food and was feeding it to both the dog and chickens: it was much cheaper than regular dog food and just as cheap as the grain the chickens liked. But Attu wasn't satisfied with his rations. After he had wolfed his own meal, stolen the cat's dinner and rifled the garbage can, he would head for the garage to see what the chickens had left. Day after day I would see the chickens flying out of the garage to leave Attu in complete possession, and I wondered, as I watched, just how long it would be before the worm started turning.

One day Attu disappeared into the garage as usual, only to erupt a second later howling in terror. Riding like a bronco buster on his back was Mom, her beak affixed to the back of his neck and her two-inch spurs driving through his fur toward his flesh. Behind came Pop, flying through the air and aiming his spurs at the enemy's rear. I never saw a dog run so fast. Putting on an immense surge of speed, he dived down into the cellar, and his persecutors, almost visibly dusting off their hands in triumph, strutted back to their unfinished dinner.

The puppy cowered in the cellar for the rest of the day, refusing to come out until dark. And ever after that, when he stuck his inquisitive head into the garage, a single indignant squawk would send him — yipping, scrambling, tail between legs—to the cellar. Not only that: the bantams became so brave as a result of their vanquishment of a dog that they seemed to feel that even a man wasn't too big for them to tackle, and I had a hard time getting my tools from the garage from then on.

Attu's growth was something Happy never learned to accept. When they had been a puppy and kitten together, just a few weeks before, she had always been able to knock him down with one of her flying tackles. But as he became bigger and heavier and steadier on his feet, she would charge and charge and nothing would happen. It was like throwing herself against a stone wall, and every time she picked herself up and prepared to try again, there was a look of puzzlement on her face.

That was one of the new games that filled my evenings with entertainment. The other was played when Attu, with a huge, capacious maw full of sharp, curved teeth, would pick the kitten up, drop her at my command, pick her up again. "What's going on here?" Happy would seem to say—but she would always come back for more.

I chuckled, I laughed, I roared. It's good for a man to have pets, on a homestead.

Chapter XXIII
The Season's Work

It was early August. The garden looked good. Standing in their neat, cultivated rows, the cabbages were green and plump. The white cauliflower heads were fairly bursting from their coverings of leaves. The potatoes were in full bloom, their white blossoms tossing in the breeze and forecasting a good crop. The carrot tops were thick and sturdy, and underneath them, the carrots themselves bulged impatiently through the soil. The broccoli had sent out new flower shoots and would have to be cut again and taken to market.

In the greenhouse, too, there was abundance. The cucumbers and squash were ripe and the tomatoes were losing the last of the green on their skins.

Yes, I had a good crop: all I had to do now was turn it into profit. And this, I had found out, was more easily said than done. My greenhouse produce, without any competition to speak of, would always have a ready sale, the demand still far exceeding the supply. But the truck garden vegetables? Well, they were a different matter. My closest market was the town of Homer, my main customer the one grocery store out of four which specialized in fresh vegetables. But the vegetables this store bought from me were hardly enough to pay for the gasoline it took to take them into town. The other stores in Homer either imported their vegetables from the States by boat or plane or didn't handle them at all. The restaurants dealt, mainly, with regular suppliers in Anchorage. I had realized that I would have to seek other markets or go broke.

For awhile I had sold to a store in Ninilchik. Then I had made the rounds of the stores in Kenai—but with little success. I had thought of contacting the "city" markets in Seward and Anchorage but had discarded the thought as quickly as it had come: there was the transportation problem, and the fact that I couldn't leave the greenhouse long enough to call on the markets there. I had thought of the Army bases with their thousands of soldiers to feed, but I knew that that was out, too: I was too small an operator to supply them regularly in the quantities they would require.

I sat down and mulled the matter over. Truck farming, without a market—and what had ever made me think there would be one, in this land of scattered homesteads and sparsely-settled communities?—was plainly a losing proposition. At least *now* it was. But what if I stored some of my vegetables during the winter and sold them in Homer and Ninilchik when no one else could supply them—and when I could ask a higher price?

Yes, that was it: storage. Proper storage. By rough estimate, I figured that I would have three tons of cabbage, two tons of potatoes and half a ton of carrots to store. The cellar of my house would take care of the potatoes, but the cabbages would require a much bigger place. I had heard of a thing called a root cellar . . .

Driving into Homer, I went in to the Farm Extension office and asked for a government pamphlet on building a root cellar. They had one, and they gave it to me.

In America's pioneer days, I suppose the farmers used shovels and the muscles of their arms and backs for the kind of job I had to do. I was luckier: I could hire a caterpillar tractor to dig me a deep pit. When that was done, and when I had figured that my root cellar would be 30 feet long and 14 feet wide, I peeled 35 six-inch spruce poles, set them upright in five-foot rows $3\frac{1}{2}$ feet apart and imbedded them in a gravel base at the bottom of the pit.

My next job was to get some planks with which to make the walls and roof. With my jeep truck I hauled some 200 of the saw logs from my extra acre clearing to the Keelers' sawmill, where I had quite a few of them cut into two-inch planks. I used 6"x6" timbers on my upright poles to hold up the roof, and when I had finished nailing the planks to them I had a very solid and substantial building, strong enough to bear the three feet of dirt that would cover it and keep its contents from freezing. The roof I finished off with a layer of 90-pound roofing paper; I would need a good roof, one that would neither leak nor rot. But I would need ventilation, too: I cut two holes in the roof and stuck lengths of stovepipe through them.

When I had built an entranceway with two doors and had had the Keelers, with their tractor, cover the roof with dirt, I stood back to examine my handiwork. My root cellar was a structure six feet high in the middle and five feet high at the sides—big enough to stand up in and large enough to store all the vegetables I might harvest. I was all set.

It was fair time in Alaska, and all the little towns on the Kenai Peninsula were sprucing themselves up for the yearly occasion. I selected the little fishing and homesteading village of Ninilchik, which had been a Russian penal colony in the days of the czar, as the best place in which to show off my garden products. It was the closest to my homestead; and besides, the fair officials had invited me to enter. "Bring as much as you like," they had said. "We need plenty of entries."

On the opening day of the three-day fair—the day of judging—I unloaded my truck at the schoolhouse where the event was to be held. I placed three cabbages—in reality big ones which I had peeled down to a manageable size—on a table beside several gigantic cabbages weighing 30 and 40 pounds apiece. Seeing the other heads, I changed my mind and started to snatch my puny entries away. But I was too late. Before I could go into action, an attendant had asked me my name and given me my exhibitor's number: my cabbages were there to stay.

I wandered over to another table and dumped the rest of my vegetables. Sizing up the competition, I decided that my only chance to win lay in my cucumbers and tomatoes, since hardly anyone else—mine was the only homesteader greenhouse for miles around—would be entering anything like them.

I went back to the truck and got out a box of canned goods I had brought along, placed them on a table labeled "Home Canning Displays." I didn't have much hope for my assortment of jars, though. How could I compete with the woman canners of the district?

That afternoon, when I was told that the judges had awarded all the ribbons they were going to award, I entered the produce display room with a trembling heart. Surely I had received at least one ribbon—one ribbon, for all the entries I had made. I saw my cabbages first. On one lay a first prize ribbon. On another, a second prize ribbon. On the third, a third prize ribbon. Boy! My cabbages had beat out all the 40-pounders!

I moved over to the tomato table. Here I was in for a shock: my entries had received only a second and a third prize ribbon. The blue ribbon had been awarded to a native woman who had raised one tomato plant in a sunny window in her house. I had spent hundreds of dollars building an expensive greenhouse, hundreds of hours of labor. I had fertilized my plants with the best fertilizer and chosen my tomato entries from thousands of beautiful examples—only to be beaten by one little plant with half a dozen tomatoes on it, a plant grown in a dishpan in a window. Phooey!

But my disappointment was assuaged somewhat when I looked at my canned clams, salmon, vegetables and berries. On half of my jars lay ribbons of various colors—blue, red and white. I had won out over a bevy of homesteader wives who had spent weeks in the preparation of their exhibits. Won, with a few jars I had canned up in a hurry!

Loaded down with my many ribbons and cash from vegetables I had sold on the spot, plus a few prizes I had won in games of chance at the fair, I drove proudly back to the homestead. The Stoddard honor was intact. And maybe next year I would win ALL the prizes!

With still a month to go before I would have to put my crops into storage, I decided to start another building project. When I had borrowed money from the bank, I had set aside some of it to use for building a cabin for sale at some future date. I had even figured on dividing

The Season's Work

up the ten acres of woodland up the creek from the clearing into four pieces and building a cabin on each lot. But that would have to come later: now I would concentrate on just one cabin—the model for the rest.

The site I had selected—a piece of the ground on the bluff point which had been cleared by a cat just before my mother's arrival—commanded a wonderful view of Stariski Creek, almost better than that from my home. And the road leading to it—made by the cat at the same time—would facilitate the transportation of materials. I plunged cheerfully into my task.

After drawing up plans for a cabin 16 by 20 feet, I gave Mr. Keeler a list of the dimensions I required, and within a few days he had cut all the lumber I would need (from the saw logs left over from the root cellar project) and I had hauled it to the site.

To form my foundations, I buried wooden pilings four feet deep, setting them on solid gravel and surrounding them with gravel on all sides so as to prevent them from being forced up out of the ground during the winter freeze-up. There were twelve of these pilings altogether: four along each length of the cabin and four through the middle.

Next came the plate and the floor joists, which ran crossways. Then I was ready to lay my first round of eight-inch house logs. This cabin would differ from my house in that I would only lay the logs horizontally up to window level, making the top half of the cabin of frame—boards nailed on 2x4's. It would be what was called a "half and half" cabin. In discussing building problems with my neighbors, I had learned that "half and half" cabins were much easier to build when you were using green wood—which I always did—since you didn't have to allow for log shrinkage over the windows as you did with a "whole log" cabin. True, each of the logs beneath the windows would shrink a quarter of an inch or more in thickness as it settled, but the 2x4's on the upper frame wouldn't shrink in length and the window frames could be nailed in permanently at the outset. My big house had given me lots of window trouble and I wasn't anxious to go through it again.

The frame walls went up in a hurry and I was soon working on the roof and ceiling joists. When I had covered the roof with boards and completed the walls I began putting the windows in. And there were lots of windows: almost the entire south wall (facing the creek) was solid with them, there was a window on the east end which actually opened—an oddity in Alaska, where windows are for light and seeing through, not for ventilation or for letting in the icy winter blasts—and there was a window in the front door.

For the floor I had had some of my best boards planed and sized, and, being almost identical as they were, they were fairly easy to lay. The roof I covered with the usual 90-pound roofing tarpaper, leaving a hole for a tin smokestack.

To finish up the exterior of the cabin and to make it as good-looking as possible, I nailed on hundreds of vertical peeled, edged slabs, cutting each one separately to make it fit between the top layer of logs and the gables. Then I applied a generous amount of linseed oil to the whole to protect the wood from the weather and give it a glossy mahogany color. Finally I painted the window frames.

Next job: the interior. I covered the walls and ceiling with sheets of celotex—expensive material in Alaska but a lot cheaper than plywood, which I would have preferred to use. I crossed the ceiling with imitation beams made from peeled, varnished slabs. I made mop board and other molding for around the windows from planed spruce, nailed it down and varnished it. Then, as an added feature (this house was getting to be too fancy!) I made a sink with drawers underneath and cupboards above. Finally, I moved in a little airtight Montgomery Ward wood stove. The cabin was done: all it lacked was furniture. Furniture, and a buyer.

The project had taken me a month and cost me close to $700, and the result, to my way of thinking, was a perfect little Alaskan wilderness cabin. Set on the bluff in a patch of birch and spruce as it was with its ideal view—from the south windows you could look down the creek for half a mile—it had many features which could be considered unusual in a country where the main thing was to get a roof over your head. I liked it so much that I was almost tempted to move into it myself. No, my big house had all the conveniences. But one thing I knew: anyone who wanted to buy my new cabin would have to pay a fairly large price—a price that I would figure out later.

By this time the first frosts of the season had made their appearance, and the ground had begun to freeze an inch each night, thawing out in the heat of the day. The first hard frost had done my cabbages no harm—they were cracking and splitting, but only because they had grown so fast—but it had killed my potato vines, which lay back black and dead on the ground. It was time to harvest my crops.

I made a series of bins in the root cellar out of six-inch boards and left an air space on each side and underneath. Then, after cutting the cabbages and carting them from the fields in the truck, I used a washtub as a carrier and threw load after load of the firm heads down into the bins. Finally I had the last cabbage under cover.

The potatoes were next. Using a hay fork for digging, I laboriously worked down the long rows, lifting the spuds clear of the dirt and letting them lie awhile in the air to dry off before putting them into gunny sacks. Then, loading the sacks into the truck, I took them down into my house cellar and dumped them into two bins I had built in a hurry. When I was finished I had two huge piles—enough to last me through the winter and enough, besides, to sell. Later on I would sort them, keeping the smallest for my own use.

My next step was to build some shelves in the house cellar to hold all the quart jars of vegetables I had canned up during the summer—broccoli, cauliflower and Swiss chard which I had been unable to sell. When potatoes and jars were all in place, the cellar was so crammed from top to bottom that I felt like a squirrel surveying his winter hoard of nuts.

The last crop to take in was the carrots. I had waited just a little too long and had to dig them out of two inches of frozen ground with a pick. Breaking their tops off, I stored them between layers of sand in the root cellar—almost 500 pounds of them. Then I shut the two cellar doors and heaved a sigh of relief: the field harvest was finished.

But the greenhouse harvest was still going on. The big glass nursery, with the barrel stove supplying the heat, was still turning out tomatoes and cucumbers by the bucketful, and I was still selling them in Homer for a good price and would continue to do so for as long as they lasted: people, it seemed, were hungry for tomatoes and cucumbers. And although I had had trouble selling my other vegetables, I had proved to myself that I could grow almost anything that would grow in Alaska. Maybe next year I would have better luck, find more markets. Anyway, my season's work was done.

Chapter XXIV

Tourists

IT WAS THE MIDDLE of October and the last tourist had disappeared down the road. It was quiet again. Boy, how quiet it was!

Until this year I really hadn't had much experience with Alaskan tourists. Always before I had been away from the homestead, working on construction jobs, during the tourist season. But now I knew all about *genus tourist*, and the memory made my head ache as though someone were using it for a tom-tom.

Starting in May, the stillness of my peaceful woods had been shattered by a series of sounds. These sounds had had nothing in common with the familiar sounds—the call of a bull moose to his mate, the yip of a coyote at the moon, the howling of a malemute dog. And as the strange sounds had increased, the local sounds had seemed to die out. Had all the wild game fled to the hills—and my homesteader neighbors with them?

You can imagine how Robinson Crusoe might have felt if a jet plane had suddenly buzzed his isolated island. That's how I felt when the seldom-traveled highway began to roar with high-powered cars, the air began to vibrate with masculine shouts and feminine shrieks and the hinges on my cabin door threatened to buckle under repeated knocks which preceded repeated requests for water, gasoline, directions or "permission to park in your front yard."

As I got to know them, I began to divide the tourists into two distinct types—both of which made me think of packing up and moving much farther north—to the almost impassable Brooks Range, if necessary.

I'll call the first type the Motel Tourist. This species, a resident of the States or Canada, travels in a late-model car and brings his family—his wife, his mother-in-law and two or three kids—along with him. He's more of a machine than a man: the main impression you get, as he drives by at a rate of speed inspired by his determination to see the greatest number of sights and collect the largest amount of conversation material in the shortest possible time, is of a guided missile whizzing past faster than sound.

Though he's the darling of Alaska businessmen like Fred Bailey who have the proper accommodations with which to trap him—after all, he must eat, drink and sleep—the Motel Tourist raises the mortality rate among the pet and livestock population of the homesteading country to an alarming degree. And even the homesteader isn't safe on the roads: every time he drives down the highway he takes his life in his hands. The road has become almost invisible under the curtain of dust thrown up by the flying cars and his windshield is often shattered by the bits of gravel of which the dust is composed. And he has to be very, very careful on the curves: Motel Tourists are under the impression that there are no traffic laws in Alaska.

When he visits his local general store to pick up some supplies, the homesteader finds himself pushed and jostled by hordes of strangers who are buying up all the fishing tackle he had planned to buy himself when he got hold of a little cash. Then he takes a look at the prices on some of the other goods and sees that, since the first tourist was sighted coming down the road, they've all been doubled. And worst of all: some Motel Tourist's child with a chocolate-smeared face is apt to point at the homesteader with a grimy forefinger and say, "Look at that dirty, funny man, Mommie."

The unlucky homesteader who has erected his dwelling close to the highway is in for a rough time, as I soon found out. My house was located just 600 feet off the highway. There were trees between, and it couldn't be seen by the most observant driver. But that didn't mean that I was safe from invasion: my private road proved to be an almost impossible-to-be-resisted lure. Many's the time I heard a car drive into my yard and saw it turn around again and drive off, the driver apparently realizing his mistake. But if I happened to be quick enough to get the front door open in time to look out, the Motel Tourists would stare back at me as though I were some kind of a freak, and how had I dared to build a house at the end of a road on which they had intended to park their car while they were fishing in my creek?

Some of the Motel Tourists went to all sorts of ridiculous lengths to fish in my creek without my knowing anything about it. One day, I remember, a car parked in my growing field and an entire family made a furtive dash across my vegetable garden, crushing cabbage plants underfoot as they ran. Desperately they tried to descend the bluff at the edge of the garden, but they got so tangled up in brush piles and fallen trees that they were soon whirling in circles looking for an easier way down to the creek. When they found one, they fished openly, boldly, moving downstream until they had collected directly below my house. Training a pair of high-powered binoculars on the courageous little band, I could see them looking up in my direction with expressions of triumph and scorn. "Boy, we sure put it over on that guy," I could almost hear them say.

"All you had to do was ask my permission and you could have walked down my path to the creek," I muttered. A few minutes later my uninvited guests were in full retreat. Calmly I watched them stumble and fall through the willows as I cradled my hot, empty 22 in the crook of my arm. I had aimed over their heads, but my barrage had been enough to send them scattering, in terror for their lives. It takes a lot to make a homesteader mad—but very little provocation to make him lose his temper.

And then there are the Litterbugs. These are the weekenders, the fishermen and hunters from other parts of the Territory who rush down to the Kenai Peninsula on the long holidays during the moose season and the salmon runs. Their object is to fish their fish and bag their game quickly—and with the least possible expense. They are armed with sleeping bags, Coleman stoves, bread, beans, beer and enough nerve to put a carnivorous brown bear to shame. Nothing is sacred to them, and no property is private. They camp along the highways in gravel pits, ditches, homestead driveways and homestead yards, and occasionally a homesteader will find that they have moved, bag, beans and beer, into his house. And when they leave—well, a garbage dump is what a homesteader could call the formerly untouched wilderness he used to call his home.

When I saw the Litterbugs coming and heard about the damage they could do, I seriously considered locking up all my farming equipment, hiding my dog and cat in the cellar, putting my fishing tackle away for the year and departing for the north—and I was sure that the fish and the moose had beaten me out by a couple of weeks, at least. Instead I decided to take the line of least resistance, figuring that if I was nice to The Litterbugs, they might be nice to me. Asking only that he take his beer cans with him when he left, I gave anyone who asked for it permission to park his car in my yard while he joined the legions thrashing the creek with their poles below. And it worked pretty well.

There were times, however, when I saw red. When I heard bullets whistling over the house and thumping into my log walls, I would crawl to the edge of the bluff facing the highway and trade shot for shot, emptying my heavy rifle and the 22 in the general direction of the trigger-happy target shooters to let them know that there were people in their line of fire. Sometimes that stopped them, but more often they fired back as though it were some sort of game, and I would have to give it up. And when, on quieter days, I dared to walk out to the highway to see if I had any mail, I would find my mailbox and business sign so punctured with holes that they looked like pieces of English lace.

Once in awhile—a very great while—I invited a complete stranger, or a whole carful of them, into my house. This practice turned out to be a big mistake. One Saturday afternoon at the height of The Litterbug season three soldiers from Fort Richardson (Anchorage) drove into the yard and asked my permission, very politely, to fish. "Sure," I told them. "Good luck."

That evening the soldiers came back with no fish and asked if they could put their sleeping bags on the ground near the house and stay the night. Since the mosquitoes were at their worst that day—and the Alaskan mosquito's worst is worse than a bedbug's best—I took pity on them, invited them to sleep in the house and told them that they could cook their dinner on my stove. They were a nice bunch of guys, and they were so grateful for my hospitality that when they departed, they left me with enough "C" rations to last me for a week. In the meantime, I had shown them my secret fishing holes and they had been able to catch their limit of salmon.

From then on the word was out. Friends of the three original soldiers—more soldiers—showed up every weekend during the fishing season, and gradually my homestead took on the appearance of a servicemen's rest camp, with pup tents sprouting in my fields like a new kind of crop. It looked as though I would have to take that trip to the Brooks Range, after all. Fortunately, however, the fishing season ended before I could take any sort of drastic action, and when it did, peace and quiet descended once more. The Litterbugs were gone for another year.

There's a third type of tourist which invades Alaska in the summertime—the Rich, or Millionaire Sportsman—but luckily this type sticks pretty close to the towns, and I had no experience with one on my homestead. The only one I ever met was the one I encountered during my first summer in Alaska, when I was a guest of Vern Mutch's in Homer. A wealthy lawyer, he wore a gaudy Hawaiian sports shirt, Palm Beach slacks, a Panama hat, two-toned shoes and a "Alaskan" belt bought in a souvenir shop in Anchorage, and he was armed with an expensive moving picture camera and enough money to hire someone else to do all the tasks he might find too onerous—such as changing 16-mm. film or baiting a hook. He turned up in Homer one day, checked in at the best hotel and expressed to Vern a desire to "see the sights."

Vern is a friendly man and a strong Alaska booster besides. He put himself—and me—at the lawyer's disposal. "How would you like to dig some of our giant razor clams? The beaches about thirty miles north of here are famous for them," Vern said.

"Let's go!" enthused the lawyer.

When we arrived at the beach the tide was out, but not far enough out to insure good digging, and Vern and I didn't expect to get our regular quota of ten gallons apiece. Nevertheless, we showed the lawyer how to use the short-handled shovel, how to look for a hole in the sand no larger than a penny, how to dig a single scoop of sand away from beside the hole, how to reach down and grab the fast-disappearing neck of an eight-inch clam before it got away. But the lawyer soon lost his enthusiasm for the sport: his stomach protruded so far that he couldn't bend over fast enough to catch the elusive bivalves.

Meanwhile, while he was straining and grunting and cursing, Vern and I each dug about ten good-sized clams and decided to call it a day. "Wait a minute," puffed the lawyer, as we started to collect our gear. "Somebody's got to take a movie of me digging clams."

I loaned him my shovel while Vern stood ready with the camera. But after a few minutes of fruitless digging, the lawyer gave up. "I've got a better idea," he said to me. "You bury your clams in the sand and I'll pretend to be digging them. My friends in Kansas City'll get a kick out of that."

"But it won't look realistic,"I started to protest. "You have to pull the neck—"

"Oh, nobody'll know the difference," the lawyer scoffed, somewhat annoyed. Then he put on a winning smile. "Come on, let's try it."

The camera whirred, the lawyer stood on the spot where the dead clams were buried, he pointed down to the spot, he dug his shovel in and proudly lifted ten clams from the sand with one asthmatic heave. Grinning, he looked toward the camera without a trace of shame on his bland, round face. I fervently hoped that some of his friends in Kansas City were expert clam diggers and would be able to see through the little farce.

As we were preparing to leave, Rex Hanks, the homesteader whose land we had crossed to get to the beach, left his water-powered sawmill and came down to say hello. After awhile the talk—led by the lawyer—got around to gold.

"Want to try panning some gold in my creek?" offered Rex. "I'll show you how." Scraping some sand out of a crack in the coal ledge beside the stream, he carefully, slowly washed it out in a gold pan he produced. In a few minutes he showed us the pan with three tiny specks of gold in the bottom. "Give me that pan!" cried the lawyer, grabbing it unceremoniously out of Rex's hands. And "Start the camera!" he yelled at Vern.

Kneeling by the water, he began to swish the gravel and sand around in the pan with great energy and inefficiency, and before the little play came to an end the gold Rex had panned was lost forever in the bottom of the creek. But that didn't seem to bother the lawyer at all—nor did he apologize. Instead, he spent the next half hour posing an enraged but still polite Rex Hanks in the various motions of running a sawmill, causing him to lose much valuable working time and ruining—because Rex was no actor and posing made him nervous—much of his hard-to-come-by lumber. The only reason we didn't allow the lawyer to pretend to be running the sawmill himself was that we all hated the sight of blood.

As time went on, the lawyer further endeared himself to the local populace by chartering a plane to fly up to the Caribou Hills in back of Homer and shooting himself a moose and a brown bear with the assistance of several experienced guides—then bragging all over town about what a terrific feat he had accomplished singlehanded. The moose rack and bear hide, after being proudly displayed to sourdoughs who had bagged twenty like them in their time, were sent back to the States to grace the lawyer's pine-paneled trophy room, and the meat—as it usually was with Millionaire Sportsmen, I heard—was wasted.

After that, I took to departing by the back door whenever I saw the lawyer barging through the front door of Vern's drugstore. The last I heard of him, he was trying some salmon fishing at the Anchor River, the salmon were cooperating marvelously and a cameraman was recording the scene for posterity and Kansas City. Since then some of my friends have informed me that "all rich tourists aren't like that—some of them are real sportsmen." But how should I know? He's the only one I met . . .

*

Yes, the tourists were gone for the year, driven away by the approach of winter. And luckily for us homesteaders, there would be no winter tourists in our part of Alaska: the skiing wasn't good enough on the Kenai Peninsula.

But as I stood listening to the silence, I was struck by a sudden thought: what if I should build some tourist cabins some day, and make some money during the annual invasion? Would I like the Motel Tourists and The Litterbugs any better then? Would I welcome them with an open hand? You bet your life I would!

Chapter XXV
Fire! Fire!

As I TURNED the truck off the highway into my road, I noticed a layer of blue smoke hanging low over the creek valley. It looked kind of nice, kind of pretty, and it was a couple of minutes before its awful significance penetrated my tired brain. When it did, I went cold all over. "My God!" I yelled. "The house is on fire!"

I rattled into the yard and brought the jeep to a sickening, lurching stop. Then I just sat there and stared. It wasn't the house: it was the greenhouse.

Smoke was pouring out through ripped holes in the plastic glass. The front half of the structure had caved in. The flames, having done their dreadful business here, were now licking hungrily toward the garage. Too late. I had arrived too late.

I tottered out of the truck, peering through one of the holes in a side wall. The benches had all collapsed, and those charred, blackened, twisted masses were the tomato plants on which I had lavished so much tender care.

And the sound—the sound was like an inferno. Above the crackling and popping of the flames themselves I heard a high, whistling, sizzling noise—something like the sound a tomato makes when you hold it over a gas jet to loosen its skin. Sure, that's what it was: only there were hundreds of tomatoes losing their skins.

I turned away to see Attu the puppy and Happy the cat, their forefeet tucked neatly beneath them, calmly watching the show—an enthralled audience of two. The sight of them brought me out of my shock. Yelling, "Got to save the garage!" I raced to it, took a quick look at the 100 gallons of gasoline and cases of appliance fuel stored there, and started the power plant. From there I ran to the house to start the water pump. Not waiting for the pressure to build up, I rushed to the greenhouse to see if I could turn its water faucet on. The faucet was buried under a pile of glowing ashes and the hose which had been attached to it wasn't there any more.

Dashing back to the house, I found another hose in the cellar, carried it outside, dropped it. Finding a bucket, I filled it at the kitchen sink and ran back and forth pouring water over the ember-covered faucet in the greenhouse until it was cool enough to attach the hose. I had the fire under control in a matter of minutes.

Then I inspected the damage. My whole crop of tomatoes—about 500 pounds of them—was lost beyond recall. Half of the greenhouse roof was gone. All the benches were ruined. In two short hours—I had been gone from the homestead just about that long—I had lost a business. The uninsured greenhouse would cost hundreds of dollars to replace. I was broke. It was late in October. I had been counting on the money I would receive from the sale of my tomato crop to carry me through the winter. Now I would have to depend upon the stored cabbages, carrots and potatoes — and who knew how much they would bring? From where I sat on my doorstep, my prospects looked pretty bleak.

In a day or so the news got around. My neighbors came to stare with me at the blackened frame. "We'll help you rebuild it, Stoddard," they said. "If we can get enough guys together, we can finish the job in a week."

"No, no," I said. "I haven't any money to buy any glass, or lumber, or anything."

"I'll loan you the dough," said one.

"I'll let you have the lumber," said another. "You can pay for it later, when you're on your feet again."

"No, no," I said. "Thanks, fellows. But no. It's no use."

I don't know why I refused their offers of help. Maybe it was because of my pride, a stubborn pride that made my independence, right then, seem more precious than gold. Maybe—even though, like America's first pioneers, Alaskan homesteaders always help each other out in times of stress—I didn't want to feel obligated to my friends. Maybe the shock of seeing all my hard work and plans go up in smoke had broken my spirit.

I don't know. Anyway, it was weeks before I could

think calmly—or think at all—about the matter. I spent hours sitting on my front doorstep doing nothing—nothing but stare. And when thoughts returned, they weren't good thoughts: they were bitter thoughts. If I had had a wife or a partner to watch the greenhouse while I was away, I told myself, the fire wouldn't have occurred. But I didn't want a partner, and a wife was almost impossible to find. Okay. I would sell my cabbages and other stored vegetables little by little, enough to live on through the winter. In the spring, I would sell the homestead, and in the summer I would return to the States, admitting defeat. The hell with it all. The hell with Alaska.

My fire seemed to have started a chain reaction. Within a month, another bachelor was burned out. This time it was Wayne Jones, a homesteader whose place was a few miles from mine. He was visiting a neighbor when it happened, drinking a friendly cup of coffee. Suddenly the door flew open and another neighbor dashed in, yelling, "Wayne! Your house is on fire!"

His face white, Wayne started for the door. Then he stopped, turned around. "Just how bad is it?" he asked the friend who had brought the news.

"The whole place is in flames!"

"Well, there's no hurry, then," said Wayne, going back to his chair and picking up his cup. "I might as well finish my coffee."

By the time Jones arrived at his homestead the frame house had been reduced to coals, the coal pile stacked next to the house—his fuel for the winter—had become a fiery furnace and exploding ammunition was whizzing in all directions. "That's why I wasn't in any hurry," he explained. "No sense in getting shot by your own house. There were too many bullets in there."

Jones had lost everything he owned but a heavy tractor which had been out of range and another small cabin he had built. He moved into the extra cabin and his neighbors contributed enough kitchen gear and food to last him through the winter. "I'm fine," he would say, when anybody asked. "Just fine. I'll build a better house in the spring."

One night I was playing pinochle at the Baileys'. The door opened and in walked two of my friends from Anchor Point: Ken Rickly, the postmaster, and his partner Tony.

"Glad to see you," everybody said. "Join the game."

"Naw, naw," said Rickly despondently. "We'll just sit awhile."

We all turned to stare. If there were two more avid, more enthusiastic players in the whole Territory of Alaska than Rickly and Tony, we didn't know them. "What's wrong?" I inquired.

"I just don't feel much like playing tonight," said Rickly. "My house just burned down."

Gradually we got the whole story. Rick had been away from home at the time—just like Wayne Jones and me. Tony had been preparing dinner. A piece of insulating paper had dropped from the ceiling to the hot coal cookstove, burst into flames, blazed up and ignited the ceiling. In two seconds the whole house was afire. Tony had had just time enough to get out the front door, and when he found himself outside he had run confusedly down the highway shouting for help. Then he remembered that his truck and Rickly's jeep were parked beside the burning house. He ran back and managed to move them just before the house collapsed.

As in the case of Wayne Jones' fire, everything was lost —clothing, guns, bedding, furniture, an expensive movie camera, and even a coffee can full of money. The two trucks and the clothes they wore were all Tony and Rickly salvaged. But on the following day they found an empty cabin in Anchor Point, and on that same day people began to look through their supplies and see what they could spare. All morning long homesteaders trooped into the postoffice carrying boxes and bags. By noon Rickly was worn out saying "Thanks." "I wish they wouldn't do it," he told me when I dropped in that afternoon. "It's embarrassing. It's awfully kind of them, but it's embarrassing. They've brought clothes, bedding, groceries—everything. What's a guy to do?"

My contribution was outside in the truck: a sack of potatoes, a box of cabbages and carrots, some dishes and silverware and two almost-new packs of pinochle cards. Now I knew I couldn't give any of it to Rickly without embarrassment to us both. When I left the postoffice, I took the sack and the boxes over to his new cabin and dropped them on the doorstep. For weeks Rickly kept saying, "I wonder who left that stuff at my door. Why don't they come forward and be counted?" And finally, my tongue loosened over a glass of vodka, I admitted the crime. "Oh," said Rickly, looking away. "Yeah," said I, looking away. "Let's not talk about it."

After Jones' and Rickly's fires, mine began to seem very insignificant. I still had my house, at least, and it was heavily insured: in spite of the high rates charged in an area where there is no fire protection, I had scraped together enough cash for that. But because none of our burned buildings was insured, none of us was able to rebuild. Much later, Wayne Jones was to convert a greenhouse into a liveable home, and Rickly was to build a store next to the postoffice with living quarters in back, and by that time both of their tragedies were forgotten. But just after the fires, we were all so despondent that we cracked jokes. Whenever the three of us got together we did nothing but kid each other about the fires. "It's funny how three *bachelors* should get burned out," one of us would say. "Yeah," someone else would reply. "Must've been some frustrated old maid done the deed." And "Yeah," the third would agree. "Some old maid from the States who went right back again after she did it. She must've been from the States! there ain't no old maids in Alaska." Then we would all roar and slap each other on the back as though we had just heard the funniest joke in the world.

However, bachelors weren't the only victims: several other fires occurred during the latter part of the year. At Clam Gulch, midway between the towns of Ninilchik and Kasilof, a warehouse burned to the ground. At Kenai the bakery burned up. In Homer a garage burned down, a total loss. At Anchor Point another family was burned out. None of the buildings except the last was fully covered by insurance.

How did the three fires start? Well, I blamed mine on my dog, Attu. On the morning of the fire, I had checked the double-barrel stove in the greenhouse and had left only after satisfying myself that its doors were closed up tight. The fire in the stove had been burning since the previous night and there should have been nothing remaining by morning but a bed of coals. Attu had a habit of sleeping in front of the stove on the warm sand, and my guess was that, after my departure, he had gotten up, stretched, brushed against the stove's draft door and knocked it open. This would have caused the fire to flare up, and it had probably gotten so hot that the stove pipe melted, setting the building on fire. No other explanation has occurred to me.

With the Jones fire a similar thing happened. The coal cookstove had gotten too hot and the pipe had collapsed, the sparks from the firebox igniting the rest of the room. Rickly's fire could be laid to cheap building: bare insulation paper—two layers of paper with a layer of tar in between—isn't very fireproof when tacked to a ceiling.

A couple of years before, Bill Rabeck had started the fire which had burned his house down and thrown his family out into a snowstorm by bringing a gallon jug of gasoline inside and placing it next to a hot stove. The gas had expanded, popped the cork and filled the room with fumes. The fumes had collected under the roof, and when a spark from the barrel stove had ignited them, the house burned down in a very few minutes. The Rabecks stood in the snow in their pajamas and watched it go. The next day, true to tradition, the good people of the community had rallied around. Within a week, loads of clothing, bedding, foodstuffs, toys for the children and even contributions of cash were bursting the seams of the new house someone had offered the burned-out family. I remember Bill's saying, not long after, that he'd never had it so good. "Before the fire I could only afford one pair of shoes," he said. "Now I've got sixteen."

We had all learned lessons from our fires: the value of safety precautions and of fire insurance, no matter how much it cost. And we had learned that no one—not even in a wilderness—can be totally independent. And we had learned—though we all should have known it before—that no one knows how many friends he has until he gets into trouble.

But friends or no friends, I was discouraged. Without my greenhouse I was lost. I had no ambition to start over again, no further projects to dream of. All I wanted to do was to get through the winter, somehow, and sell out—lock, stock and barrel stove—in the spring.

What a lonesome, hopeless sort of winter *this* was going to be!

Chapter XXVI
Winter, Art and Pinochle

SOMETIMES WHOOSHING BY like a train in a hurry to get to its destination on time, sometimes knocking on the doors and windows like a traveler who has lost his way in a storm, the cold north wind blew a sad, ghostly refrain. Overhead, flights of sandhill cranes and geese headed south. Underfoot the frozen ground waited for the first touch of snow, while the muskeg ponds, almost as you watched them, glazed over with thin skim ice. Another seven months of cold Alaskan winter was beginning.

I was ready for it. My root cellar was full to bursting with vegetables to eat and to sell. My house cellar was stuffed with potatoes, cases of canned vegetables, jars of salmon, clams and berries. The storeroom over the kitchen was piled high with lard, canned fruit and sacks of flour and sugar. By Alaskan standards I was pretty well off: by the standards of my relatives in the States—the States, where a full wallet was the measuring stick—I was poverty-stricken.

It was the first of December and I was starting my usual winter routine of sitting by the barrel stove reading endless pocket books and drinking countless cups of coffee. A dull routine, but it had never really bothered me before, when my mind had been full of plans and dreams for the coming year. But this year, without any plans except to sell out, get out in the spring, and without anything to think about except my troubles of the past fall, the winter stretched ahead in a bleak, unbroken line. I'd get a good case of "cabin fever" if I wasn't careful—might even end up by talking to myself. True, there were Attu, the malemute, and Happy, the cat, for company; but what I needed was a *human* companion—someone to talk to who would answer when I spoke!

My problem was solved a few days later. A new homesteader who lived up the creek about a mile above my place, Smitty, offered the perfect solution. When he had come down from Anchorage to build a house on his homestead during the summer he had brought with him an old man to help on the job. Now he was returning to Anchorage for the winter, but the old man, he told me, preferred to "stick around on the Kenai Peninsula." Would I take him in? He could help me around the house in exchange for room and board. I jumped at the opportunity, and when Smitty left for the city I acquired a combination companion and "valet."

The old man's name was Art Sorenson. Though about 60, he was heavy-set and strong for his age: he had been a blacksmith in his youth, turning to welding when the machine had replaced the horse. He had come to Alaska in 1947 to work on construction jobs and had never returned to his native state. Every summer he had made good money—big money—every winter he had "lived high," and every spring he was broke. He was a prime example of what was known as a "construction stiff."

The previous summer, feeling that he was getting too old to hold down a construction job, Art had come to the Kenai Peninsula to help Smitty build up his homestead and had hoped, maybe, to find one for himself. Now, without even enough money on which to live frugally in the city during the winter, he was only too anxious to do my chores for his room and board.

I fixed up a place for him upstairs and we settled down like a couple of squirrels to eat our way through my winter stores. A typical day—after the ground was covered with snow and we were more or less confined to the house—would begin at about 10 a. m., when I would open my eyes to find the living room warm and a fire burning merrily in the barrel stove. Art, who would be sitting by the stove, would come to attention at my first sleepy yawn. Springing up, he would pour me a cup of coffee from a steaming pot and hand it to me as I lay at ease in my bed. What a contrast from other winters, when I had had to jump out of bed onto an icy floor, build a fire quickly with a generous amount of stove oil, hop back between the blankets to wait an hour for the room to warm up—and then get up and brew my own coffee!

After a breakfast of pancakes and more coffee—prepared by me—Art would wash the dishes while I drank still more coffee and read by the fire. Then Art would sweep the house, empty the garbage, check the water tank to see if it needed filling, feed the dog and cat and bring in a day's supply of wood. Meanwhile, the master of the house would do nothing but loaf.

When the chores were done, Art would join me in the kitchen. Then would begin a series of two-handed pinochle games which would continue until we were both tired of the game. After that we would retire to the living room to read for awhile, Art a Western and I an adventure novel.

At 2 o'clock in the afternoon we would both be hungry again and I would make more coffee and some salmon sandwiches. After eating we would have another pinochle session, or—if there were a few sunny hours left before the winter night closed in—I would put on my snowshoes and go ptarmigan hunting while Art stayed home to split wood or shovel snow from the driveway. When I returned from my hunt—usually unsuccessful—there would always be a fresh pot of coffee awaiting me, along with a greeting apiece from Art and the pets. After a dinner of clam chowder, cole slaw and apple pie (our menu hardly ever changed), Art and I would each relax with a book until it was time to play pinochle again.

There was only one variation in our daily routine: on Mondays and Thursdays I would walk out to the mailbox on the highway and pick up the mail, which had been brought out from Homer by truck. On these afternoons Art and I would answer letters and devour all the new magazines. And somehow, these landmarks in the course of every dull, similar week, to be looked forward to in advance and discussed when they had passed, helped the days go faster. . . .

The evenings were a little more exciting, though they

had their element of sameness, too. "Going pinochling," as the late Greasy Grogan had called it, had become the favorite indoor winter night sport of all the bachelor homesteaders on the Kenai Peninsula—or at least in the vicinity of Anchor Point and Stariski Creek. It was the perfect cure for "cabin fever," that malady which seems to afflict everyone who has lived too long by himself or in too close quarters with someone else. This winter there were four of us who had banded together for our mutual health: Art and I, Ken Rickly, and Ken's partner, Tony. We had formed the habit of playing virtually every night until the early hours of the morning. Half the time Rickly and Tony came to my house to play and be fed and half the time Art and I would go over to their cabin at the Point.

When it was our turn to visit our antagonists, Art and I would have to start getting ready two hours before the time when we were expected to arrive for the game. Right after dinner, while Art did the dishes, I would plow out through the snow to the garage and start up the light plant. Attaching one end of a long electric cord to the head bolt heater on the engine of the jeep, I would affix the other end to a wall socket in the living room. For an hour I would let the plant run to heat up the truck's engine block. Then, turning the juice off, I would retrieve the truck's battery from its place beside the barrel stove—where it was kept to keep it from freezing when not in use—and put it in the jeep. Then I would put gasoline in the tank; check the oil and water (making sure that there was enough anti-freeze solution in the radiator); put a few drops of Band-ice, a liquid which was supposed to prevent condensation, in the gas tank, and, at the last, start the motor, to leave it warming up for half an hour. Then, donning parkas and leather, wool-lined mittens, Art and I would start out for Rickly's cabin, six miles away. At Anchor Point the temperature was usually ten degrees colder than at my homestead—sometimes 30 to 40 degrees below zero— and when it was time to go home Art and I would almost always have to get Rickly to tow us in his jeep, which was easier to start. For these reasons I much preferred to stay at my place on the coldest nights and let our partners come to us. And they were usually glad to, mainly because mine was the bigger, more comfortable house, and because I had electric lights. When they didn't show up, it was a sad, gloomy night at the Stoddard homestead.

As Christmas approached, all the bachelors in the area got the holiday blues. You can scoff all you want about Christmas, and about how commercial it has become, but it *is* one time of the year when you regret being thousands of miles away from your family. Feeling this way but not putting it into exact words, Art and I had a talk a couple of days before the important day and made plans to have a party at my place on Christmas Eve. We would invite all the bachelors in the district and try to cheer each other up or drown our sorrows in holiday spirits.

The Eve arrived, cold and clear. The house was ablaze with lights, and in the living room there was the usual spruce Christmas tree with its usual trimming of cotton and soap chips. Everything looked pretty festive.

First to show up were Rickly and Tony, with Rickly carrying a basket of food and Tony clinking two bottles together over his head. Then came Red Freimuth, bearing two pies and a case of beer. Finally arrived Chuck Randall, a one-armed veteran who had a place on the beach, with his contribution of beer and beans. The party was complete.

Art and I were ready for our guests. The kitchen table was piled high with food, with a turkey occupying the seat of honor. I buried the beer in a snow bank by the front door and broke off a three-foot icicle from the eave of the roof for highballs. The festivities could begin.

Tony had brought along the makings of a Christmas punch, the rather alarming recipe calling for adding two baked oranges with cloves to a quart of flaming brandy, the fire to be put out with a gallon of burgundy wine. We couldn't seem to get the cookstove hot enough to bake the oranges, so we abandoned that plan entirely, simply mixing all the ingredients together and bringing them to a boil on the Coleman stove.

As host, I was awarded first chance at the punch. "Just wait until you taste this, Gordon," said Tony, smacking his lips as he proudly handed me a cup. I lifted the cup carefully to my mouth, took a small sip, and dislocated my jaw. The mixture was bitter and the fumes were as deadly as a dangerous poison gas.

"Whatsa matter, Gordon?" asked someone.

"I dislocated ma jaw," I answered, pointing to my distorted face.

I made another unintelligible remark. Finally the guests caught on, and there was a rush toward the steaming bowl. "Boy, what a powerful punch! Guy takes a sip and dislocates his jaw! Lemme at it!" they yelled.

During the rest of the evening I was unable to talk, but I managed to drink enough of the lethal mixture to deaden the pain in my jaw. When the first pot of punch was gone, we mixed up another, using Spanish brandy and port wine this time. This tasted much better, but by the time we got to it nobody cared.

Art, being the oldest bachelor there, beat the rest of us to immobility. He had spent the evening sitting on the floor with several half-full beer cans arranged in a semicircle around him. In one hand was a highball, in the other a cup of punch, and he had developed quite a talent for mixing his drinks. Presently he stood up, bent on restocking his supply. Staggering toward the punch bowl, he stumbled, fell, knocking himself out on the edge of the bookcase. When he had been quietly laid away in his bed upstairs, we finished the party off on a sentimental note by singing Christmas carols to which we all remembered the words only too well, trying not to remember, as we sang, the Christmas Eves of better—or at least childhood—days.

The guests departed at 4 a. m. on Christmas morning. In the afternoon, when I awoke, I discovered that there was enough liquid refreshment left over for another party. and I collected Red, Rick and Tony for a pinochle game. The game lasted until the last drop was gone, and the holiday season was over for another year. Art's season didn't end until two days later, however—when he was sober enough to come downstairs.

Winter dragged on. One cold January night Art and I were driving home in the jeep from an all-night pinochle game in Anchor Point. Four miles from the homestead the jeep stopped: all the water had boiled out of the radiator. The temperature was 30 degrees below, it was five o'clock in the morning and it was obvious that we would freeze if we lingered to do anything about re-starting the truck. There was nothing for it but to walk home. Two hours later we arrived at the house half frozen and almost collapsing from fatigue.

Awaking at noon, I had breakfast and then walked out to the mailbox. Sorting the letters, I came across one from my older brother in California. There were special delivery stamps plastered next to airmail stamps. It looked ominous. I tore it open with trembling fingers. "Dear Gordon," I read. "Take hold of yourself, kid. It happens to us all. Dad passed away in his sleep — — "

With tears running down my cheeks and freezing as they ran, I walked slowly back to the house. "I've got to go," I muttered. "I've got to go down there." But how could I? I was broke—too broke to attend my father's funeral, thousands of miles away. Looking again at my brother's letter, I read further: "We know that you're broke and can't come down. If I had the money I would send it to you, but I haven't just now. Don't try to come down if it means you'll have to go further into debt to do it. Knowing how fond you were of Dad, we're all thinking of you and hope — — " Go into debt? Why shouldn't I go into debt to pay my last respects to my father, the father who had been so hopeful for my success in Alaska. Sure! I could *borrow* the money!

Then I looked at the postmark on the envelope of the letter and lost all hope again: my father had died over a week before. Because there wasn't any special delivery service in my part of Alaska, the special delivery letter had taken a week to reach me. It would be no use to go now. My father had already been buried, the funeral was over. Darn Alaska! The hell with the whole Territory! How was I to get through the rest of the winter without Dad's letters to give me the encouragement I needed? Why had I ever left California? If I had never come to Alaska, I wouldn't be in this fix right now. Poor Dad!

In the house, I threw myself on my bed to think of the good times, the good talks my father and I had had together, to feel sorry for myself, to curse the country that had kept me from being with my father in his last days and with my family at a time when we should have all been together. "I know one thing," I said to Art, who was hovering, embarrassed, over the barrel stove. "Now, for sure, I'm getting out of this rotten, lonely country."

During the next two weeks I tried to throw myself into work—good, hard, physical work. I spent hours sawing up logs into two-foot lengths and splitting the lengths into cords of firewood. Then I decided to drive into Homer and up to Ninilchik to try and sell my stored cabbages and potatoes—to raise money with which to buy cigarettes and a few supplies, and to keep myself busy.

And I kept busy, all right. On examining the cabbages in the root cellar, I found that most of their outside leaves were rotting, and Art and I labored several days and nights under the light of a Coleman lantern to peel the thousands of heads and reset them in the bins. Next, we washed and sacked my surplus of potatoes. Finally, we turned into salesmen. The potatoes we were able to unload on other homesteaders who hadn't grown any during the previous summer, but the cabbage sales, which started out fairly briskly, slowed, dwindled and finally came to a standstill. By this time the remaining heads were starting to rot again, and in desperation I contacted a neighbor up the road who had some hungry cows to feed and delivered two and a half tons of cabbages to him free of charge. Thus ended the fiasco of Stoddard the Truck Farmer. With the root cellar empty, I figured up my gross take for the summer. In the entire year—counting set plants, greenhouse produce and truck crops—I had taken in a total of only $450. It had certainly been a bad year. My only consolation was that I wouldn't have to go through it all again.

But the winter wasn't over yet: there were still a few more disasters to come. A couple of days after getting rid of the cabbages, I got careless one particularly cold night and left my house cellar trap door open. Result: all the remaining potatoes froze, to rot later on when the cellar was warm again. Result No. 2: the pump froze solid and all the pipes burst, and it took me three days with a blow torch to thaw the ice in the pressure tank and put in new pipe. It seemed that even the forces of nature were against me.

And even food was becoming a problem. There were still a lot of vegetables on hand, but the canned fruit was all gone, the canned clams had long since been eaten up and there were only a few jars of salmon left in the larder. And there was no money with which to buy meat or other supplies.

"Fresh meat," as a matter of fact, had become our sole topic of conversation.

Chapter XXVII
The Moose and Me

MY HERD of wild livestock had returned from the Caribou Hills. Everywhere we looked we could see the dark brown forms silhouetted against the white of the snow, standing, hip-deep, in poses of profound rumination, as they cropped the tender green shoots of the brush willows. Everywhere we looked, our mouths watered, our stomachs growled and visions of thick, juicy steaks swam before our meat-starved eyes. Now was our chance to restock the larder, to forget, for a time (and over a large moose filet) the mishaps of the previous weeks!

Seated on a Blazo box beside the barrel stove with a cup of coffee in one hand and a pair of powerful binoculars in the other, I watched the movements of the moose for hours at a time. It was difficult to pick out the one to shoot and the moment to shoot him. What I had in mind was a young, tender bull, but these were few and far between, and the one I chose would have to be separated from the rest of the herd and far enough from the house so that no suspicious neighbor would witness the deed.

The younger bulls were easy to single out—their horns were still intact—but the huge old bulls, who had shed their cumbersome racks weeks before, were indistinguishable from the cows except by the horn marks on their heads. Every morning Art would come down from his sleeping quarters above and tell me how many moose he had counted from his window, and we would discuss at great length the age of each young bull and the sex of the larger animals. One day, in order to get a closer look, I cut down all the birch trees surrounding the house. The next day the herd had moved to within a hundred feet of the window and was feeding with obvious delight on the birch twigs scattered about on the snow. Another morning I opened the front door to find five moose standing within forty feet. They looked, as they turned hastily away, as though they had been about to knock on the door. Another day I was reading by the kitchen window when a shadow fell across my book. Glancing up, I saw a big cow staring in at me. Before she disappeared, the two of us exchanged a long look, our noses within inches of each other.

None of these experiences could be considered unusual. Apparently more curious than afraid, the Alaskan moose descend from the hills and back country every winter to congregate close to human habitation. Every homesteader has his "own," private herd, and it is only when dogs are running loose or the homesteader gets too aggressive for comfort that a herd will leave the vicinity of the cabin of its choice.

It is in the wintertime, too, that the moose are almost as harmless—as docile, as friendly, as skittish, as dumb—as domestic cattle. It's only in the rutting season, in the fall, that a bull will attack a man or vehicle without provocation, or in the early spring, when a cow, always ready to make a stand to protect her newborn calf, is really dangerous. I have come face to face with a bull in the winter and watched the bull, abashed, walk away, but I have tried to take a picture of a bull during the rutting season and had to run for my life.

The one real danger from moose during the winter is the possibility of hitting one on the highway. Headlights blind them and send them into a panic of confusion, and they'll often run ahead of a car for miles before turning off into the woods. However, I had had an experience two winters before that had proved the exception to all the rules. Red Friemuth and I, in his big truck, were taking a ton of a neighbor's potatoes to Seward when we encountered one of the biggest bull moose I have ever seen on the road. He was trotting along the highway a few yards ahead of us and didn't seem to be aware of our approach. Suddenly he turned around and lowered his head to charge. The hair stood up on his back, his eyes flashed, and we could see that he was really mad.

"Guess I'd better stop," said Red, slamming on the brakes. The moose stopped, too, but he stood in the center of the road just in front of us, his head towering so far above the truck that it was out of sight in the windshield.

It was 40 below zero that night and we had to get the potatoes to Seward before they (and we) froze. "Come on. Come on. Let's stop playing games," said Red, leaning on his horn.

The noise startled the moose into moving up the road. But every few feet he would turn and charge, and every few feet Red would slam on the brakes. If we had hit the moose, or he had hit us, our trip would have been over: the moose would have made mashed potatoes of the truck and we would have made steaks of the moose. Eventually, though, in a sudden burst of speed, we passed him, leaving him still angry, still looking for trouble far behind.

But as I said, that was an exception to the rule. On the whole, the winter moose is a very tame animal, and shooting one, I had always thought, would be like going out to the barn and slaughtering your favorite milk cow. For that reason I had never shot one—up to now. But this winter it was different. Fresh meat was not only a necessity: it was an obsession. I would *have* to turn big game hunter for awhile.

There was only one drawback: the illegality of killing a moose in the wintertime. But there was also a loophole: the law of the wilderness states that anyone who is hungry and without sufficient provisions can shoot game anywhere, any time. There was the case of the woman at Anchor Point whose husband was away and whose four children, if not starving, were at least very hungry. A moose happened to pass through her front yard and she went out and shot it. Word got around and the game warden hopped right over. Upon learning the facts, he patted the woman on the shoulder. "Look," he told her. "If you ever find yourself in a fix like this again, just let me know. I'll shoot you a moose and bring it to you. We can't let kids go hungry."

Similarly, homesteaders in my area who shot winter

moose were never bothered too much by the authorities—mainly because it was known that they never wasted the meat (and because, perhaps, they took such elaborate precautions to avoid being caught in the act). The main culprits, according to both the game warden and the homesteaders, were the city dwellers who traveled the highways looking for game. These types would shoot a moose alongside the road regardless of sex, and then, afraid of being caught, would leave the meat to rot. One early spring, I remember, a cow met her death in this way about a mile from my place. Inside her were twin unborn calves. Incensed at the waste of three good moose, all the homesteaders in the area were up in arms to find the man who had committed the crime.

But in spite of what looks like a look-the-other-way-while-the-deed-is-done policy, the game laws are very strict in the Territory. A person who is caught with illegal meat in his possession is liable to a $500 fine, six months in jail and the confiscation of his rifle and the vehicle in which he is transporting the meat. I remember the case of the two men who were apprehended with illegal moose meat in their small plane: they lost the plane, their guns, considerable cash and their liberty for several months.

Though some of the natives of the Territory—Indians, or half-breeds, as a rule—allowed themselves to be caught by the game warden in order to enjoy the comforts of a nice, warm jail during the long, cold winter, every homesteader went to great pains to avoid incarceration. This involved keeping an illegal kill an absolute secret from all but the other homesteader who helped him pack it in and got his share of the carcasses as hush money. If word of the kill came to the ears of a neighbor who was flat broke and just a little bit "dishonest," the moose killer was apt to find himself turned in for the $100 standing reward for such information. The traitor's name, in such cases, was never revealed by the authorities, but somehow he was always found out. And when he was, it behooved him to pick up and leave the country: he was through, as far as his neighbors were concerned. . . .

Art and I grew hungrier day by day. And practically every day Art would point out a young bull about a hundred feet away and say, "Let's get that one."

"No," I'd say. "He's too close to the house. Besides, he's standing out in the open and the game warden could spot the remains from the air. We can't take a chance like that, Art."

But finally I made up my mind. There was a small bull feeding on the willows in the creek bottom and he looked just right for eating. "This is it." I said to Art. "You circle around and come up below the moose and drive him upstream into the woods. I'll be waiting for him. We'll be eating steak tonight if we're lucky."

I left first. Wearing our only pair of snowshoes and carrying my heavy rifle, I mushed up the bluff and crossed the ice-bound creek a half mile up the valley. Using the trees as cover, I slipped down into position in a clump of spruce where I could see the bull still calmly feeding 300 yards away. I waited nervously, hoping I would have the guts to shoot him when he came into range. Suddenly Art appeared down the creek from the moose. Without benefit of snowshoes, he was having a hard time of it. Struggling through the deep snow covering the ice, he was falling down every time he made a move. The bull raised his head to observe the clumsy approach, then returned to his meal as Art passed within 30 feet of him without seeing him in the tall willows and climbed the hill to the house. Damn! Our strategy hadn't worked!

Gradually the bull started moving in my direction, pausing every few feet to feed. Then he disappeared behind some trees. Damn again! I arose from my cramped position, began creeping cautiously forward. I hadn't taken three steps before the bull appeared from behind a spruce not fifty feet away. We stood watching each other, the moose with his body turned sideways to me but with his head swiveled toward me for a better look. Slowly I lifted my heavy rifle to my shoulder and took aim at his left ear. Should I shoot him? Or should I let him live? If I pulled the trigger I would be killing an animal over five times my weight, but a peaceful animal, who had never done me any harm. If I pulled the trigger I would be guilty of killing an animal out of season, and my nights and days would be filled with worry over being caught. Every time there came a knock on my door I would be afraid to answer it. I would be a fugitive from justice, if I pulled that trigger.

But if I didn't pull the trigger Art and I would go hungry for the rest of the winter. I pulled the trigger.

Boom! The gun stock jammed into my shoulder, the moose dropped like a rock to the snow, lay still. I had done it. I watched him for a moment, ready with another bullet in case he got to his feet. And I listened, the silence gathering around me. To me, the shot had sounded awfully loud in the clear, still air. Maybe a neighbor had heard it. If he had, he would be at my front door that night, his hand out for his share of illegal meat. But as soon as he had eaten some of it, he would be as guilty as I. Yes, it was better if a neighbor had heard the shot—better, anyway, than if there was a game warden stalking through the woods, or driving down the highway, or circling above in a plane. But there was no sound of cars on the highway, no sound of a plane engine above. There was no sound at all, except that of my heavy breathing. I was safe—for the moment, at least.

Suddenly I felt funny. My legs began to shake. The blood rushed from my head. I went cold all over. Things were going black. I started to fall. So this was what they called "shock." Quickly I stooped, scooped up a handful of snow and plastered it on my forehead. The dizziness receded. I opened my eyes. It was all over. I had better stop worrying and get to work.

Removing my snowshoes, I walked over to the fallen moose, who was quite dead. It would be better, I knew, to avoid leaving a snowshoe trail around the body: this would be a sure sign of a crime committed to a game warden in a plane. Taking my knife from its sheath,

I cut the bull's throat and drained the blood. Then, retracing my steps, I put the snowshoes back on and carefully followed my previous trail back to the house. Now a game warden wouldn't be able to tell whether I had been coming or going.

Art was waiting for me. "Did you get it?" he asked eagerly.

"Sure," I answered. "It was easy."

At about 8 o'clock the two of us were ready to sally forth and butcher the moose. Wearing parkas, we collected packboards and butchering tools and started out the door. Suddenly the headlights of a jeep showed up in the driveway. Slamming the door, we shed the parkas, threw the packboards down the cellar and grabbed a magazine apiece. When the visitors—a party of friends looking for a pinochle game—knocked and entered at my shouted "Come in!" they found two innocent men peacefully reading by the stove.

The pinochle game lasted until midnight. When the tail-lights of our unwelcome guests finally disappeared down the road, we sprang into action. Redonning our parkas and retrieving the packboards from the cellar, we loaded up the gear and plowed our way to the kill without the aid of snowshoes or flashlights. We worked fast and silently, skinning the moose, cleaning it, and cutting it into quarters. Covering the entrails with the hide and then shoveling snow over all, we stood up, ready to carry the meat back to the house. We made three trips, falling and crawling through the darkness, trying to make tracks like a moose but not succeeding in our efforts. At last the meat was piled in the snow near the house. Putting it into gunny sacks, we carried it over into the thick woods on the north end of my clearing and hung it up in a brushy spruce tree, arranging the branches around it in a very natural way after slicing several pounds of steak meat from a hind leg. Then we returned to the house for a midnight feast. To heck with hanging the meat until tender! We were hungry NOW.

On the following morning I arose early and returned

to the scene of the crime to finish covering up any telltale evidence I might have overlooked in the dark. Then I returned to the cabin to sit and worry until the next snowfall. A few days later Attu located the kill and dug up the head. When I got it away from him, I took it to a spot far away in the woods and set coyote traps around it, thinking that I might as well make a little money on coyote bounties on the side. I also set traps under the tree in which the meat was hanging, but this turned out to be a bad idea: Attu followed me one day when I went out to get some meat and almost got caught for a coyote himself.

After a week a heavy snow fell and I felt a good deal safer. But there was still the problem of keeping the secret of the moose meat from the neighbors. Whenever I brought a hunk of meat into the house to thaw it out I hid it in the basement. When I put the meat on the sink to slice off steaks I kept one ear open for the sounds of approaching visitors. And when my pinochle friends came over for dinner they had to be satisfied with fish chowder: for all they knew, salmon was the only kind of meat I possessed.

Sometimes a friend would drop in unexpectedly and catch Art and me with moose meat on our plates. "Heh-heh," I would laugh. "Think you caught us with illegal moose meat, huh? Sorry, friend. This is some meat left over from last season. Someone gave it to me."

And so it went. Until the last piece of meat was consumed, until the hide had been torn to bits and scattered to the winds by the coyotes, until the bones had been spread to the far corners of my homestead, I never felt completely at ease. Crime may fill your stomach, but it certainly doesn't pay off in peace of mind.

Note: If, by any chance, a game warden has read the foregoing words, I must ask him to check with my neighbors. They will tell him that Gordon Stoddard is the biggest liar and the best story-teller on the whole Kenai Peninsula.

Chapter XXVIII
Spring, Tenants and Sandy

THE THAW HAD BEGUN. Each day the snow level around the house was dropping an inch or so, each night freezing temperatures brought the melting process to a stop; but all in all the sun was making headway. And when the ice in the puddles and ditches began to turn to water and start on its journey toward the creek, Art and I began to shake ourselves out of our winter lethargy. We continued to beat each other at pinochle and read our pocket books—but always with one eye apiece trained on the growing patches of uncovered ground. The time was approaching, the time was approaching. . . .

My plans—insofar as I could make them—were made. Having set a price of around $10,000 for my remaining twenty acres, my house, the new cabin and all my equipment, I had painted a large "For Sale" sign and set it up next to my mailbox on the highway, and I had invested $20 (borrowed) to run an ad in an Anchorage paper. That was fine, but I had also figured out that I would have to take a job. It might take me all summer to get rid of my property, and in the meantime I would have to make enough money to live on and pay off my pressing debts. And if, by any chance, I shouldn't be able to sell my real estate, I could at least save enough money on a high-paying construction job to pay my way "outside." That was my only goal: to go "outside."

One day I made the decision. "Art," I said, "today's the day we go up to Kenai and get squared away with the labor union and see what's available in jobs."

With our pockets filled with just enough borrowed money to pay the labor steward for our yearly dues, we started off in the truck. Arriving in Kenai, we drove out to the steward's homestead. He wasn't home. We returned to town to eat and wait and then went to a bar for a beer. After awhile I left Art in the bar and took a walk around town to look up friends and find out what was doing in the construction line. Returning an hour later after hearing "Nothing, right now," at least twenty times, I found Art surrounded by empty beer cans and in no condition to accompany me on another trip to the labor steward's homestead. I went alone, found the steward home, paid Art's back dues and my own and entered our names on the hiring list. Because I had not worked during the previous year and had lost my place, I was, I noted, the sixtieth man on the list. The outlook was black: we were in for a long wait. Maybe we wouldn't get jobs until late summer. Discouraged, I returned to town, dragged Art out to the truck and drove home.

By the end of April we had had no word from Kenai and felt like forgotten men. And if something didn't happen pretty soon we were apt to be starving men. But just before I was about to take some desperate measure— I didn't quite know what—Johnny Hansen, a bachelor neighbor who lived down the creek, offered me a week's work. "I'm putting in my fish trap and need extra help during the spring tides," he said.

I jumped at his offer. The next morning I was up at 4 o'clock and driving the ten miles up the highway to Johnny's trap site. After climbing up a hill to the edge of the bluff, sliding down 200 steep feet to the beach and walking a mile along the sand to the site, I was ready to call it a day and crawl under Johnny's beach shack and go to sleep. But it was not to be. Johnny, Red Freimuth and Wayne Jones were waiting for me, ready to go to work.

Drawing on a pair of hip boots, I followed Johnny and his tractor as they pulled a trailer piled high with 25-foot trap poles down to the water's edge. The tide was far out and the water lapped gently at the outermost end of the trap, which, I saw, was already in place. Our job was laid out for us. While two of us grabbed a pole and stood it up next to an iron stake sticking up two feet above the sand, Johnny would pound four large spikes into the pole and then bend them around the stake, thus fixing the pole in a vertical position. In an hour the trailer was empty and the tide was snapping at our heels. But there was still a lot to do. Working feverishly against time and tide, all four of us tied the wires hanging from each pole—Red, standing on a stepladder, had put them up just before—to stakes on either side. When we had finished securing the last pole we were as soaking wet as a cluster of sponges. My job, for the day, was done, but Johnny and Red would have to wait for a high tide so that they could take a skiff out and tie smaller poles to the tops of the verticals for crosspieces and tie on wire to be secured to the iron stakes on the following day.

Freezing in my dripping clothes, I made my way home, determined not to show up for that miserable kind of work again. Was it worth it, for any amount of money? I thought not. However, after a good rest and an afternoon of foot-warming by the barrel stove, my interest in money got the better of my reluctance to go swimming in Alaska's icy seas, and I reported for duty on the following day. In five days the job was done. The trap, except for the chicken wire that would be stretched along the lead, the line of poles from beach to pot, was finished. I had worked only two hours a day, but Johnny paid me $100 in nice, crisp five-dollar bills—the usual pay for that type of work. Not bad. . . .

With a little cash in my pocket, Art and I were able to return to Kenai in the middle of May. We had decided to "wait out" our jobs in Red Freimuth's old tent —a decision which had meant that I had to find good homes for Attu and Happy so that they would be well cared for in my absence, sad though it made me feel to part with them.

We stayed for a week. Nothing happened in the job department. We moved back to the homestead. Then we moved back to the tent. Then back to the homestead. Then back to the tent. And so it went. By the time our money ran out we were fifteenth and sixteenth on the labor list, but from the way the list was moving—like a snail undecided as to whether to go backward or forward —it looked as though we wouldn't be going to work until autumn. At this point I called on my relatives in California for monetary help. It was immediately forthcoming, though not in any great quantity. Art also wrote to relatives, and when he received a little money he decided to use it to go to Anchorage to look for a job. I saw him off on the bus and wished him the best of luck.

The next thing that happened was that Red let me know that there was a small job waiting for me near my homestead. For about the twentieth time, I packed up and closed the flaps of the tent behind me in Kenai. At the homestead I set up housekeeping again and contacted Red. In a few days I was helping to build a large log cabin for a Mr. Edris from Anchorage. But after a week I quit the job and prepared to return to Kenai. My break had come at last.

It had all come about through Alaskan hospitality. One Saturday afternoon a car and a pickup truck had driven into my yard and several men had climbed out. "You Stoddard?" one of them said.

"Yeah."

"We noticed your sign out on the highway—about the cabins and property for sale. Want to tell us about it?"

I gave them my usual sales talk but I saw through their scheme. They were all loaded down with fishing gear, and they just wanted an excuse to fish in my creek. It had happened before. Finally came the question I had expected: "Mind if we wet our lines in the creek while we're here?"

"Don't mind at all," I answered. "I'll even show you the best holes."

I took the party a half mile upstream to a fishing hole boiling with salmon and left them to have their fun. When they came back past the cabin on their way out, I invited them in for coffee. We talked until midnight. One of the men, as it turned out, was a contractor who was building an addition to the Kenai School; the rest were workers on the job. Feeling friendly, the contractor slapped me on the back as he left and said, "Stoddard, if you need a job, come up to Kenai on Monday. I'll put you to work."

Two days later—it was the last week in June—I began my first real job of the season. It had been a long wait.

At the Kenai School, however, I found myself in the doubtful position of being the only Indian among an assortment of chiefs: in other words, the only laborer on a job which employed nothing but skilled carpenters besides. This meant that I was given a lot of hard, back-breaking work to do. But I wasn't unhappy: I was paying off my debts at the rate of $100 a week.

Returning to the homestead one Saturday night after two weeks of work, I found everything still in order. I felt myself very lucky to have a weekend in the woods in which to relax, and I set about relaxing with a great deal of vigor. Sunday morning I awoke early and went to the creek to catch a salmon for dinner. In the afternoon I was lolling on my bed with a good book when a car drove into the yard. Out of it stepped a man, a woman and three little girls. The man introduced himself as Bob Bertelle of New York City. "We've been looking everywhere for you," he said. "We went clear to Kenai to find you."

"What did you want to see me about?"

"We saw your 'For Sale' sign on the road and we want to buy the place. Would you take $6000—$5000 in cash and the other thousand in payments?"

I was speechless. This was my first real offer. What I couldn't do with $5000 in cash! Wow!

Just the same, my answer to Mr. Bertelle was, "No. Thanks. But no." I went on to explain that my price was $8000 for the house plus ten acres and another $3000 for the smaller cabin upsteam with its ten acres. I couldn't go any lower.

After two hours of talking I had come down to $7000 for the house but Bertelle hadn't gone up. "It's too bad you didn't catch me two weeks ago," I told him. "I was broke, then, and I would have grabbed at your offer.

Now I'm making money again and I can afford to wait for my price."

I never saw two people more anxious to buy. Bertelle kept trying to get rid of his $5000 and I kept refusing it—but with greater reluctance, I might say, each time. Finally Mrs. Bertelle asked me if I would rent the homestead. Now *there* was a solution. If I rented the house to them, possibly Bertelle would find himself a high-paying job like mine and come up to my price. And if I changed my mind about accepting their offer, I would know where to find them. We settled on a token sum of $20 a month, they paid me a month's rent in advance and said they would move in during the following week. I was a landlord.

Every other weekend during the summer I drove down from Kenai to see my tenants. While I stayed at the homestead, I slept in my new cabin and ate all my meals at the house, courtesy of the Bertelles. I liked the Bertelles, and it was good to see some life around the place. Their three little girls, who very soon began to consider themselves "real Alaskans"—even to making several skirt-wetting attempts to fish in the creek—were just what a homestead needed.

One Saturday night I walked into the kitchen and stopped in amazement. Sitting at the kitchen table as though he'd been sitting there for years and it was his own kitchen table was "Sandy" Smith—Alexander Malcom Smith. Sandy, the famous prospector and explorer who had spent most of his long, eventful life in Alaska. Sandy, who had been one of my father's most treasured friends. But the last I had heard of him he'd been living in southern California.

"Hey, Sandy!" I shouted, grabbing his hand. "What are you doing here?"

"Sitting here getting acquainted with your verry nice tenants," he answered calmly, sounding just as Scottish as ever. "Sit doon, Gordon lad. Have a cup of coffee."

I gazed in wonderment at the grizzled little man. Ninety-three years old, he was. I knew: my father had written me about Sandy, again and again. He was a real, honest-to-Pete, 93-year-old sourdough. As a boy, I had read about him in a book on explorers and daring men of modern times, and I remembered that the telling of his adventures had taken two pages to Robert Peary's one. He had found a mountain of jade, fallen into an Alaskan lake of oil and sold it for an astronomical sum, discovered an island of ivory and had barely escaped with his life after prospecting for gold in Siberia. The last time I had seen him was when my father and I had visited him in Vancouver, B. C., one· summer. He had been a young 85 then, had been married for five years to a woman half his age and was the father of a four-year-old son. He had told us while we were there that he had had a physical examination only the week before and the doctor had informed him that he had the constitution of a man of forty.

Apparently he still had the constitution of a man of forty. As he sat there at my kitchen table he looked and acted like a man of sixty in very good health, at least. His voice was strong, his fist, which he banged on the table to emphasize his points, was like a ball of iron, and there was nothing about him to indicate a man well past his prime who should have been toothless, wizened and feeble.

And he was still ambitious. His plan, as he unfolded it during a long evening of talking, was to go uranium hunting in the far north. "In the meantime I'm seeing a few friends—like you, Gordon (and incidentally I took the liberty of moving into your cabin up the creek) —and playing some golf."

"Golf!" I said. "Where would you play golf?"

"Oh, there are links, near the cities," he replied. "Don't you know that much about Alaska by now, Gordon lad?"

I sat there, open-mouthed. It was still impossible to believe that the famous, fabulous Sandy Smith was sitting at my kitchen table, drinking my tenants' coffee. It was as though the president of the United States had dropped in for a chat.

After the Bertelles had indicated that they would like to go to bed before morning, Sandy and I climbed into my truck and drove over to the cabin. When we arrived there the truck crashed into it. "Oh," I said, in the ensuing silence. "I forgot. My brake line is busted."

Sandy laughed. "It's lucky the cabin was therre, Gordon lad," he chuckled. "Otherwise we'd be sitting in the creek right now."

Shakily I climbed out, found no damage to either house or truck, got out my sleeping bag and followed Sandy into the cabin. Sandy had already made himself at home: the room was full of luggage—suitcases, boxes, a couple of duffle bags and a bag of golf clubs. "Y'see, Gordon, I'm prepared for any emerrgency," Sandy explained.

"Wasn't it expensive to ship all this stuff up here?" I asked him in awe.

"No, lad. I brought it with me when I came up the Alcan. I got a ride with two boys in Los Angeles and we drove up in four days."

This, like all of Sandy's stories, was hard to believe. But I believed it, remembering what my father had always said on the subject: "Sandy's tales may sound fantastic, but they always turn out to be true. He usually has some newspaper clippings to back them up."

As we lay in our sleeping bags on the floor, Sandy told me about how sorry he had been to hear of my father's death. When he had received the news, he said, he had felt his true age for the first time in his life. "Your father was so proud of you, Gordon," he added. "He would have been so proud to see the fine place you've developed here."

"Thanks, Sandy," I whispered, choking up. "It's almost like having Dad here to have you, his best friend, here to see what I've been trying to do."

"But you say you're leaving Alaska, Gordon. You might think so, lad, but it isn't true. Alaska will always

Spring, Tenants and Sandy

have a hold on you. You may go 'outside' now, but you'll be back. They always come back. Look at me."

I looked at him in the darkness, marveling. Yes, Sandy Smith had came back—at 93. But not me. No, sir; not me. I was getting out for good. . . .

I got only three hours' sleep that night. Sandy, much more energetic at 93 than Gordon Stoddard at 30, was up and about early, hungry and "rready to get goin'." I persuaded him to wait for his breakfast until after the first tendril of smoke could be seen curling from the Bertelles' kitchen chimney. That afternoon I had to work on my truck and didn't have much chance to talk to him before heading back to Kenai and my job. But I remember his saying, as we shook hands in farewell, "Stick to Alaska, lad: it'll stick to you."

When I returned to the homestead on the following weekend the Bertelles told me that Sandy kept them company for five more days before taking off for the north. "My, what a lively man," said Mrs. Bertelle. "He ran us ragged." Then the story came out of how Sandy had hustled the Bertelles around to the point of exhaustion. He had shown them how to pan gold, instructed them in the sourdough way of catching salmon and in general talked them to death. And he had eaten quantities of their food.

I laughed and laughed. "I don't know who was showing whom what true Alaskan hospitality can be," I said.

Chapter XXIX
Goodbye, Alaska!

FOR EIGHT WEEKS I worked on the job at the Kenai School. Then, one evening after work, a friend of mine who was a labor foreman on a construction job at the Army base came to tell me about an opening for a hod carrier. The job paid more per hour than the one I was on, offered at least a nine-hour day, and, as far as he knew, would last a lot longer than my present job. Would I take it? I sure would, if I could get a release from the school project. The next day I approached the contractor and explained my reasons for wanting to change jobs. He was more than fair: he would hold my job open for a week or two in case I didn't find the new job to my liking, he said. On the following day I reported at the main gate of the Army base and was signed up as a hod carrier.

I had always thought of a hod carrier as a man who carried a small, concrete-filled trough at the end of a long pole. Maybe so, but during my entire experience as a hod carrier I never laid eyes on one of those contraptions. My duties, instead, consisted of wheeling wheelbarrows of concrete and concrete blocks to the place where the two blocklayers to whom I had been assigned were laying a wall. Piling up the blocks within their reach, I would add mortar to their boards as they needed it. They worked fast, and it was a running race to keep up with them. And when they called for other materials —wall ties, clips, steel web, jumbo bricks, jam blocks, half blocks, bricks, steel rods—it was a case of "Hey, Stoddard! Get the lead out of your pants!" as I and my wheelbarrow trundled constantly. After a few days of this I began to wonder why I wasn't asked to feed the blocklayers their lunches bite by bite and pour their beer down their throats, too—so that they could become living examples of the theory of perpetual motion. I felt like a freed slave when, after two weeks of the hardest work of my lifetime, I was told that my two blocklayers were to be laid off, and with them, me. But I was a little worried about my future until the foreman who had gotten me the hod-carrying job informed me that I was to be transferred to a grading crew without the loss of a day's pay.

My new job, however, threatened to be even harder than the last: I was to work fourteen hours a day, seven days a week. But was I disheartened? No! My pay would come to at least $350 a week! For that amount of money I'd have poured beer down the throat of an elephant!

As for work, there was plenty of it. Wielding rakes, picks, and shovels, a corps of laborers—me included—prepared numerous streets and parking lots for asphalt paving. It was a monotonous job, and meeting the Army Engineers' requirements of "not more or less than 3/-16ths of an inch from final grade" was no cinch. After the big five-yard dump trucks had dumped their loads of crushed rock and gravel on top of a sub base, the huge graders had leveled the mounds off and worked the gravel down to within half an inch of "final grade," and the heavy rollers had packed the whole until it was as hard as concrete, we would swarm over the street to take out the big rocks, carve off the humps and fill up the hollows. Then, stretching strings from crown to gutters, the foreman would tell us how far we had come from the requirements and direct us to grade the whole thing over—literally by hand—to the different pitches indicated.

Suddenly I was made a labor foreman, at two bits more per hour. The promotion came as a shock—like my fellow workers, I had had little or no idea of what I was doing, merely taking orders from the foreman of my gang and pocketing my large check at the end of each week—but I accepted it. And after worrying for awhile as to whether or not the other laborers would take orders from a foreman who obviously didn't know any more than they did about grading streets, and after working side by side with the men for a week in an effort to gain their respect and cooperation, I began to relax and enjoy it. I relaxed so thoroughly, in fact, that I soon found myself standing around doing nothing but bawl commands.

But after five weeks I had had enough. With all my debts paid off and $1500 left over (I had saved $1100 during those five weeks alone), I was stake-happy again. I fired myself, collected my pay and dashed for my truck. Driving back to Red Freimuth's old tent, I packed up my gear in nervous haste and drove as fast as I could toward my homestead. It was almost the end of September, my tenants would be leaving for the States for the winter, and if I didn't catch Bob Bertelle before his departure I might never get another chance at his $5000. Maybe I could talk him into coming up to my price of $7000 for the house and ten acres and giving me the $5000 as a down payment. If I could, I'd have a stake for returning to California. I pressed my gas pedal to the floor and the old truck rocketed over the rough gravel road leading south.

Pulling into my front yard, I was relieved to see smoke curling from the stovepipe of the house. They were still there! I barged inside and found the living room piled high with packing cases. I had arrived in the nick of time!

I got right down to business. Asking the Bertelles to sit down around the conference table—the kitchen table—I inquired about their plans. "We're heading 'outside' tomorrow," said Bertelle. "We love Alaska, but we're leaving."

I presented my proposition. They politely rejected it. I argued. They argued. I pleaded. They demurred. By nightfall all I had secured was their promise to "stay a few more days and think it over." I helped them unpack their bedding and retired to my other cabin to rest up for the campaign of the morrow.

In the morning I got out my biggest guns, and for three days and three nights thereafter I talked. Finally, when I had accepted the fact that the Bertelles would never meet my price, I changed my tactics. "Why don't you buy my new cabin?" I said. "I'll lower that price to $2500." I went even further: I told them that they could live in the bigger house rent-free until they had built the necessary additions to the cabin, offered them my jeep truck rent-free for hauling logs, coal and lumber throughout the winter, offered them, free, two weeks of my services as a logger. "Well, now, maybe," they'd say. "Yes, maybe that's a good idea. All right." And the three little girls would shout, "Oh, boy! We're going to stay in Alaska!" and start doing an Indian dance around the living room. Then the Bertelles would change their minds. The stumbling block—the one we always came up against in the end—was Mrs. Bertelle's arthritis: she wasn't at all sure, she said, that she could stand the long Alaskan winter. And in the end, I saw their point. I had seen it all along, but I had wanted that cash.

Finally, after we had all talked ourselves hoarse, the Bertelles packed their car, assured me of their intentions to "return next year and buy the place," waved goodbye and drove out of my life. The house, after they had gone, was as empty as it had seemed after my mother left. I got out my own suitcases and began to pack. With or without the necessary money, I would return to California. I would go right away. And I didn't care if I never came back. Alaska hadn't been kind to me and I wouldn't be kind to it. What was there here for me, anyway? A little hunting, a little fishing, a few good times, an annual opportunity to make a lot of money fast in order to be able to loaf for the rest of the year. But what future was there in a life like that? I had proved to myself that I couldn't make money on farming here—not with the markets so scarce. And life on a homestead was lonely—undeniably lonely. No more Alaskan winters for me. I was going home.

Two days later, as I walked out to the garage to get some nails with which to batten down some shutters over the windows to protect them from the winter storms, I took a long look at the house. It was beginning to show its age. The logs really needed a new coat of linseed oil before I left. I must see to that. But on the other hand—why bother?

My house. I thought back to the time of its building. How much work it had been, and how proud I had felt on the day it was completed! But in just a few years people would wander through the overgrown grounds and say, "That's the old Stoddard house. Used to be quite a place in its day. I wonder what ever happened to Stoddard?"

Gazing out over the field, the field in which I had dreamed my dreams of becoming a successful truck farmer, I could see nothing but masses of dried-up fireweed stalks, though I knew that here and there, buried among them, were the stems of cabbages gone to seed. The jungle was already taking over. Would that fertile volcanic ground ever be planted again with vegetables—vegetables which grew so fast and large in the rays of the midnight sun?

I passed the blackened shell of the greenhouse with hardly a glance. It was hard to look at, and I didn't have to look, anyway, to find out what was there: where, the year before, there had been a shining new structure filled with ripe tomatoes and cucumbers, now there was only a gutted wreck filled with nettles. I didn't want to see it.

I stared down into the empty root cellar. Mold was growing on its damp ceiling and sides, but I could see it as it had been, in its prime: stuffed with cabbages and carrots, and with me, huddled in a parka on a cold winter night, weighing produce under a Blazo lantern for delivery in the morning. Those days were gone forever; no use thinking about them now.

The house, the field, the greenhouse, the root cellar: these were what I would leave behind me in Alaska—the only tangible evidence of my ever having been in Alaska. And what were they? Relics: relics of the failure of a man.

But wait: there were other things I would leave behind. My friends—those good friends with whom I had shared my sorrows and triumphs, with whom I had hunted and fished, with whom I had played endless games of pinochle. Yes, and I would leave behind the square dances at the Keelers', the Ninilchik Fair, the card parties in the Anchor Point schoolhouse. I would be leaving them behind for a city, where you could live for ten years in an apartment house and never get to know your neighbors.

When I had arrived in the homestead country, I reflected, I had been a stranger, a greenhorn, a "cheechako," a new bachelor who hadn't been encouraged to settle. Now I had friends from Kenai to Homer. "Hi, Stoddard," "How are you, Stoddard?" "Good to see you, Stoddard," they said when they saw me. And they had urged me to stay when I had told them I was leaving. And when they hadn't been able to persuade me, they had said, "You'll be back in the spring. A few weeks in the States and you'll be sick of it. I know. I tried it once." Yes, it would be hard to leave my friends behind.

In the empty house I took one last look at the view from the kitchen window before boarding it up. I could see the creek, snaking toward the house, disappearing from sight, then coming into view again to flow toward Cook Inlet. How many times I had lounged on the window seat and watched the salmon working their way up against the current to vanish around the bend! And that old beaver who had tried to make his home by the log that crossed the pond: I had watched him, too. Every fall his house had been swept away in the heavy rains, and every year he had returned to try again. Maybe that ripple out in the water was the little devil starting this year's construction project.

And the moose. I would miss seeing my own private herd feeding in the willows in the winter. And how I would miss the taste of moose steak! How I would miss —

Well, no use thinking about all that now. I went outside, nailed on the last shutter, went back into the house, picked up my suitcases, walked out the front door, locked it. Then I walked slowly down the road to the mailbox to wait for the bus to Anchorage.

As I sat there on my suitcases, I found myself staring

at the new power line poles that had gone up during my absence in the summer. Electricity was soon to come to my part of the Kenai Peninsula. All my neighbors would have it, but the linemen would bypass my empty house. It sure would have been nice to have steady power for my well pump—nice not to have to run out to the garage every time I needed water. It sure would have been nice to have continuous electric lights. Oh, well.

There had been rumors, too, that the old highway was to be paved all the way to Homer inside of two years. What a pleasure it would have been to drive the truck over a nice smooth road when I wanted to go to town! And I could have sold the Highway Commission some of the gravel on my land, too—and probably gotten a job on the grading crew, to boot.

And those rumors of oil. More than rumors. On the Keeler homestead during the summer one big oil company had been digging test holes, and there were several other oil companies coming in. And with all the coal lying underground throughout the area, it was reasonable to suppose that there might be oil under my homestead, too. Boy! Gordon Stoddard, the Oil King!

I began to dream. With a little cash, I told myself, I could fix the house up—put a cement-block basement in, build a fireplace, panel the inside walls, buy some comfortable furniture, have the power line hooked on, buy a deep freeze for my fish and game. And I could rebuild the greenhouse—right, this time, with thermostats and safety devices to prevent another disastrous fire. Maybe I'd even build one or two extra greenhouses—really go into the business. Greenhouse tomatoes would always be something I could sell. And I might build the three extra cabins up the creek as I had once thought of doing —to sell, or possibly to rent out to people like the Bertelles.

Maybe I could make the place kind of a millionaires' fishing lodge—take a party of four or five paying guests at a time, during king salmon season!

Of course, oil wells all over the place might spoil the

scenery a little: the millionaires wouldn't like that. But I could dream, couldn't I?

But wait! What was happening to me? I was becoming ambitious again! I was making *plans!* Was I crazy? I had burned all my bridges behind me. I *had* to leave Alaska. I had stored up no food for the winter, I had given my dog and cat away, and my jeep was at Red's up for sale. But—and I knew it now—I didn't want to leave Alaska: Alaska was in my blood; Alaska was my home.

What to do? I tried to think calmly. Well, this was what I would do: I would go "outside" for the winter— I had enough money to last me for awhile—but I would return in the spring. Maybe I'd even find a wife in the States this time. That was what was really the matter: I'd had no one—no one *close*—with whom to share my life, good or bad as it was. That was all I needed to keep me happy in Alaska: a wife!

Whew! Lucky thing I hadn't talked Bob Bertelle into buying! Yes, I would come back. The beaver had come back. Sandy Smith had come back. And I'd come back.

"I'll be back," I said aloud.

Homer Spit and glaciers are visible as you approach Homer, Alaska, on the Sterling Highway.

Fishing off Homer dock. In the background are Kachemak Bay and the Kenai Mountains, with glaciers.

The fishing village of Ninilchik, former Russian penal colony. Russian church can be seen on hill at right.

The Walli homestead is one of the earliest homesteads on the Kenai Peninsula in Southern Alaska.

Left: Author Stoddard does some grocery shopping at Homer.
Right: Postmaster Ken Rickley of Anchor Point, seventeen miles from Homer.

Fred Bailey shovels gravel for his Alaska gas station. His hobby is making plaster-of-Paris molds of wild animal footprints. Wife Vi operates a cafe.

Left: Stoddard cutting down trees on his homestead.
Right: The first little cabin he built.

A homestead near Stoddard's on the Kenai Peninsula. Here is a good example of a "stump farm" in the clearing process.

Left: Fishing for King and silver salmon on the Anchor River, about six miles from author's homestead. Right: Stoddard and neighbors gather free-for-the-taking coal at rocky Cook Inlet.

Panning for gold on Stariski Creek, which runs through the homestead. Most local gold is too fine to be worth the trouble, says Stoddard.

The author gaffs a silver salmon at 9:32 a.m. at Anchor River, about six miles from his homestead. This may look like recreation, but for homesteaders it's all in the day's work. Every King salmon caught in the Spring, every silver salmon caught in the summertime, is canned for winter food.

Left: The author and a friend from the States, George Walton, happily display a half-hour's catch of Kings from Stariski Creek. Right: Straight to the pressure cooker go the salmon, until 48 pints are stored away.

Tourists may dig razor clams for fun but homesteaders do it for food. Those on Cook Inlet beach are delicious fried and make excellent chowder. Stoddard cans most of his, to be stored for winter in his attic along with canned moose and a few spruce hens.

As a do-it-yourself homesteader, Stoddard peels a three-sided log to be used on the new house.

Left: Starting construction of the storm porch. Note the fancy electric installation.
Right: Stoddard puts finishing touches on the roof.

Anchor River, near Homer. Here there are accommodations for campers, as well as cabins to rent, near the bridge. Anchor Point, seventeen miles from Homer, has population of under a hundred.

Left: Summer 1955: unexpected arrival of friends from the States.
Right: At home with Stoddard, Attu and Happy, the cat.

Red Freimuth takes time off from work in gunsmithing and welding shop to tease his dog, Ike. An enthusiastic hunter, former Iowan Freimuth arranges his Alaskan life to include plenty of idle hours for his favorite recreation.

Left: Raising goats in Anchor Point reminds Louis Huber of his native Switzerland.
Right: Former Oregonians Laurence and Lorna Keeler enjoy their chicken-raising on the Kenai Peninsula.

Homesteaders Bill and Janet Rabick add a stylish improvement—a wardrobe—to their wilderness home. Two daughters, a neighbor child and Nushnik the sled dog look on.

Illustrations 251

The new homestead, from across a growing field in late summer, 1955. Notice greenhouse and garage to the right.

Stariski Creek from the kitchen window of the homestead. It furnishes plenty of backyard fishing for this lucky Alaska homesteader.

Left: Attu greets master with day's bag of ptarmigan.
Right: Early Spring and a moose pauses by the garage.

Using a light sled he made from a pair of skis, Stoddard trains Attu to be a sled dog.

"Living off the land" in high style. Stoddard comes home with a moose quarter and is joyfully greeted by Attu. The two will have a proper homesteader's banquet, then the master will busily can moose for the long winter to come, and for neighbors who drop in.

The third house that Stoddard built, this time to sell.

Stoddard picks up his mail, which arrives only on Mondays and Thursdays. Road entrance to his homestead has become part of the Sterling Highway. Notice homemade sign proudly announcing readiness of above cabin.

Illustrations

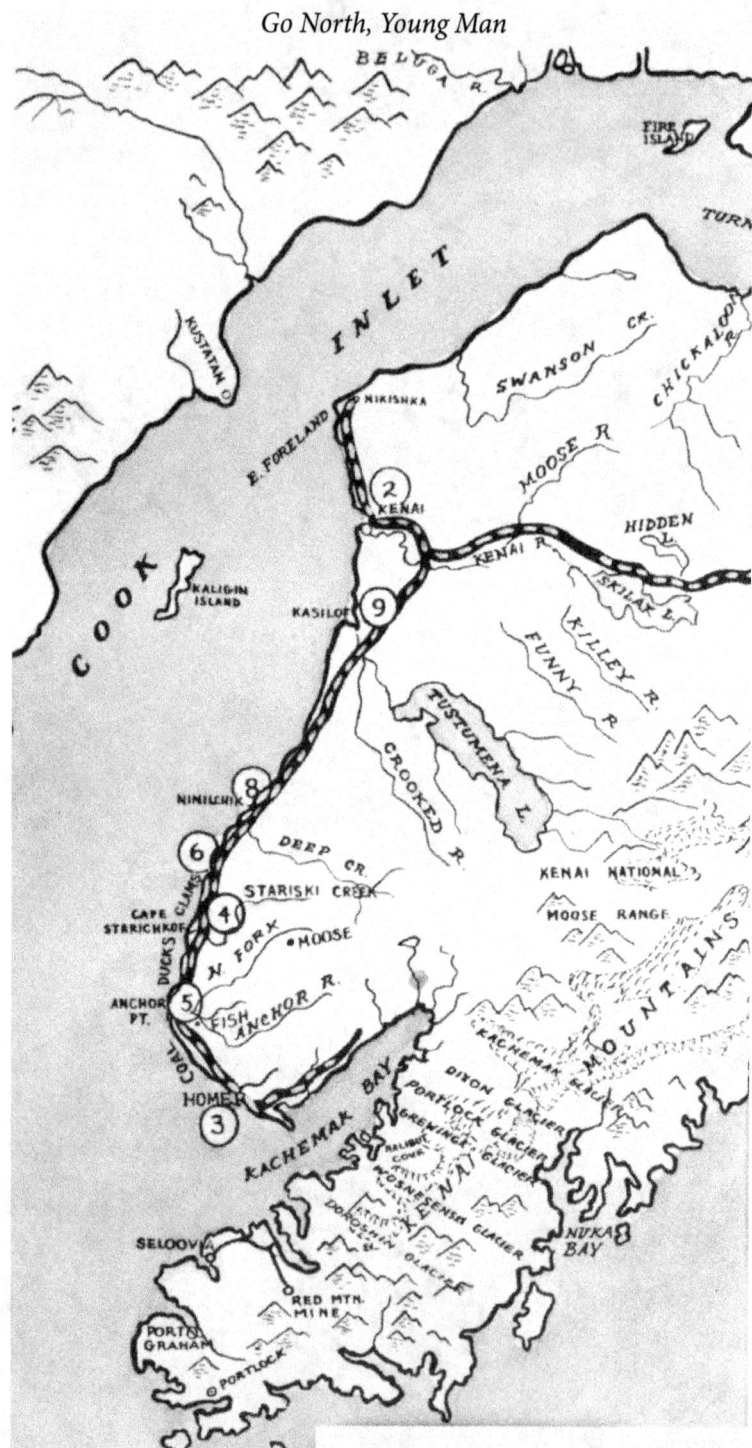

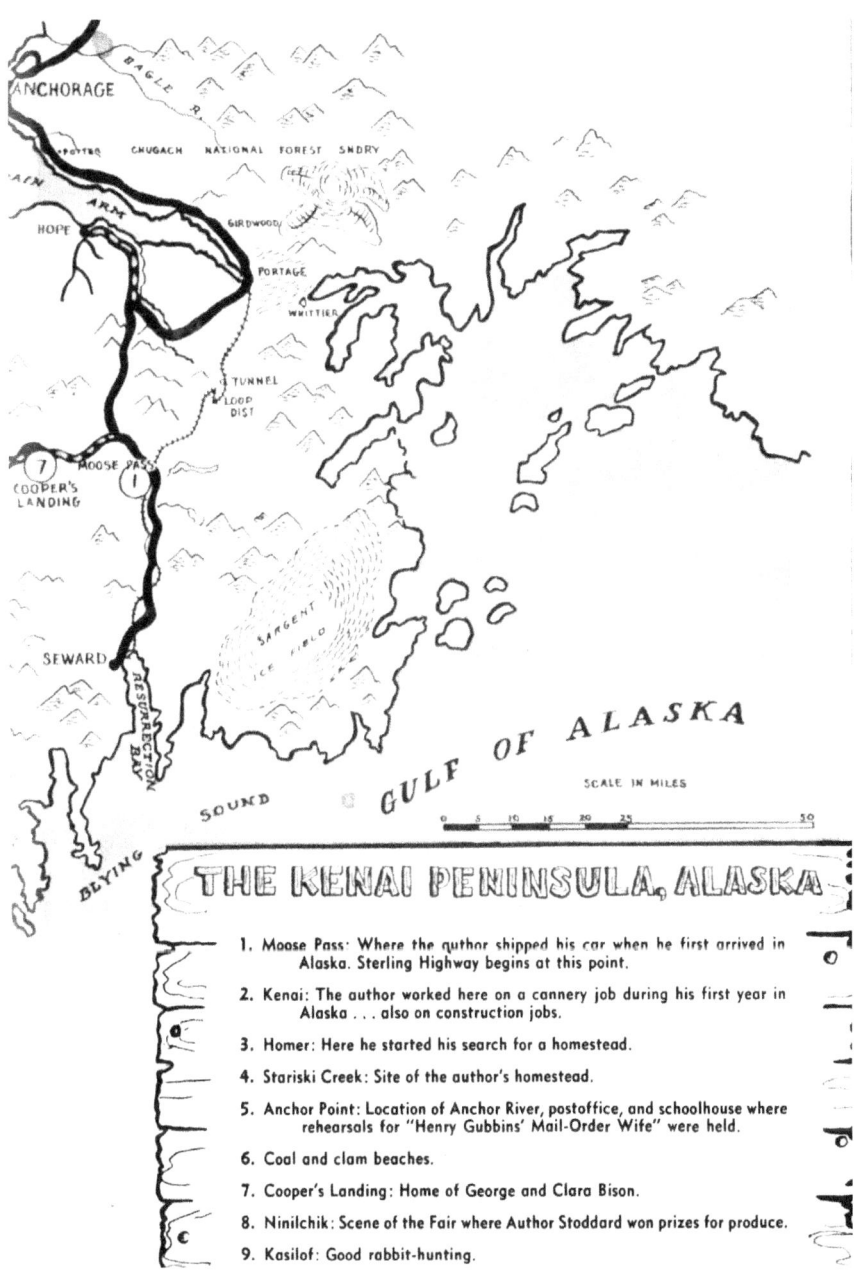

www.ingramcontent.com/pod-product-compliance
Lightning Source LLC
Chambersburg PA
CBHW071959110526
44592CB00012B/1148